In this book, Itai Sened examines the political institution of property and other individual rights. His argument is that the foundation of such rights is to be found in the political and economic institutions which grant and enforce them and not in any set of moral principles of "nature." The book further argues that individual rights are instituted through a political process, and not by any hidden market forces. The origin of rights is placed in a social contract that evolves as a political process in which governments grant and protect property and other individual rights to constituents, in return for economic and political support. Extending neo-institutional theory to the subject, and using a positive game theoretic approach in its analysis, this book is an original contribution to scholarship on the evolution of rights.

THE POLITICAL INSTITUTION OF PRIVATE PROPERTY

THEORIES OF INSTITUTIONAL DESIGN

Series Editor
Robert E. Goodin
Research School of Social Sciences
Australian National University

Advisory Editors
Brian Barry, Russell Hardin, Carole Pateman, Barry Weingast,
Stephen Elkin, Claus Offe, Susan Rose-Ackerman

Social scientists have rediscovered institutions. They have been increasingly concerned with the myriad ways in which social and political institutions shape the patterns of individual interactions which produce social phenomena. They are equally concerned with the ways in which those institutions emerge from such interactions.

This series is devoted to the exploration of the more normative aspects of these issues. What makes one set of institutions better than another? How, if at all, might we move from a less desirable set of institutions to a more desirable set? Alongside the questions of what institutions we would design, if we were designing them afresh, are pragmatic questions of how we can best get from here to there: from our present institutions to new revitalized ones.

Theories of institutional design is insistently multidisciplinary and interdisciplinary, both in the institutions on which it focuses, and in the methodologies used to study them. There are interesting sociological questions to be asked about legal institutions, interesting legal questions to be asked about economic institutions, and interesting social, economic and legal questions to be asked about political institutions. By juxtaposing these approaches in print, this series aims to enrich normative discourse surrounding important issues of designing and redesigning, shaping and reshaping the social, political and economic institutions of contemporary society.

The political institution
of private property

ITAI SENED
Tel Aviv University and
Washington University in St. Louis

CAMBRIDGE
UNIVERSITY PRESS

PUBLISHED BY THE PRESS SYNDICATE OF THE UNIVERSITY OF CAMBRIDGE
The Pitt Building, Trumpington Street, Cambridge CB2 1RP, United Kingdom

CAMBRIDGE UNIVERSITY PRESS
The Edinburgh Building, Cambridge, CB2 2RU, United Kingdom
40 West 20th Street, New York, NY 10011-4211, USA
10 Stamford Road, Oakleigh, Melbourne 3166, Australia

First published 1997

Printed in the United Kingdom at the University Press, Cambridge

Typeset in Minion 10.5/12pt

A catalogue record for this book is available from the British Library

Library of Congress Cataloguing in Publication data

Sened, Itai.
    The political institution of private property / Itai Sened.
        p.   cm.
    Includes bibliographical references.
    ISBN 0 521 57247 9 (hardback)
    1. Right of property.   2. Social contract.   I. Title.
JC605.S46 1997
323.4'6 – dc20   96-36253   CIP

ISBN 0 521 57247 9 hardback

VN

This book is dedicated to the memory of my brother, Yoav Sened (1952–73) and to the memory of William H. Riker (1921–93), my teacher and mentor.

Contents

Figures and tables

Preface and acknowledgments

The essence of social life and, therefore, the principal subject matter of the social sciences, is the content and form of human interactions. I have always thought that human interactions are structured by human beings as opposed to deterministic forces of history and markets. So, for me, the challenge of the social sciences is to unravel the mystery of how the civil society emerges and evolves out of personal decisions and actions of rational individuals. As a student of the Riker school of social choice, I was trained to look for the solution to this puzzle in the analysis of the rational behavior of individual human beings in the context of their relationships with other individuals.

Over the years, it became clear to me that the foundation of the civil society lies in the structures of individual rights that define and promote certain norms of behavior. When I was first drawn into this research by the late William H. Riker, I was struck by how little had actually been written on the subject. Most of what I found in the literature was either overwhelmingly normative in perspective, or simply building on historic or behavioral determinism. Unconvinced by either of these two approaches, my first step was to reject both of them and look for a positive answer that would be based on the rational choice theory I was trained to use.

At that time, within the mainstream of the rational choice research program, the dominant approach to the study of social norms and formal institutions was to regard them as evolving spontaneously out of the social disorder that characterizes, in theory, the "state of nature." Yet, for me, the spontaneous approach to the study of social institutions is unrealistic. The structure of society cannot possibly depend on the good will or the self-imposed norms of self-interested individuals. Contemporary research proves, beyond doubt, that cooperation in large societies is unlikely to survive the stress imposed on it by distributional and other pressures that emanate from the individual agents that are the atoms of which society is made.

Looking for a different answer, I was drawn back to traditional liberalism. Unlike some of its modern offspring, traditional liberalism assigned a crucial role to governments in structuring and maintaining the civil society. Unfortunately, traditional liberalism has failed in its attempt to unravel the mechanism and the logic of the role of the state as the central player that grants and protects individual rights. This book aims to decipher this missing link.

The subject matter of this book is the political institution of property and related individual rights. The fundamental question that I try to answer is: how do individual choices of rational actors yield the political institution of private property?

Property and related individual rights, I argue, emerge as equilibrium outcomes of a political struggle of individuals to improve their well being. This struggle takes place between governments who control social institutions – by their monopoly on the use of force and their role in the legislative process – and other agents who challenge these institutional structures in order to promote their own interests. This book is dedicated to the study of this bargaining process between central governments and individual agents. The ever-evolving outcome of this process is the "social contract" that determines the structure of our civil society by defining and protecting the rights of every agent within it.

I have come as far, thanks to the help and support of so many. First and foremost, I would like to thank the late William H. Riker for his scholarly advice and generous support throughout the last four years of his life. David Weimer and Randall Calvert deserve special thanks for their guidance in the early stages of this project. Thanks must also be extended to David Austen-Smith, Jeffrey Banks, Ted Bluhm, and Larry Bartels who helped with early drafts of various chapters of this book.

I gratefully acknowledge the financial help of Tel Aviv University, the Canadian friends of Tel Aviv University, the US–Israel Educational Foundation, the University of Rochester, and the John M. Olin Foundation. But it is in St. Louis that this book was written, and it could never have been completed without the generous help of the people at Washington University.

While working on this book I benefited from fruitful conversations with colleagues and students. Scott Ainsworth, Mark Fogal, Clifford Griffin, Simon Jackman, Marian Reynolds, Harold Stanley, Annette Steinacker, and Laura Winsky Mattei deserve special thanks. Kathleen Durbeck, Julie Stone,

Mark Fogal, and Laura Winsky Mattei read early drafts and helped with the English. Steve Lewis helped to research the historical illustrations in chapters 4–6.

Among my colleagues at Washington University in St. Louis, special thanks are due to Alexandra and Lee Benham, Douglass C. North, and Norman Schofield, for support and encouragement over the last four years. I am particularly grateful to Jack Knight, who discussed with me every subject that appears in this book. Barry Ames, Robert Durr, Lee Epstein, John Gilmour, John Kautsky, Victor Le Vine, Bill Lowery, Fiona McGillivray, Carol Mershon, Mary Olson, Robert Petersen, Robert Salisbury, Olga Shvetsova, Alastair Smith, Andrew Sobel, and John Sprague deserve special thanks as well.

Among my colleagues in Tel Aviv University, special thanks are due to Avi Ben-Tzvi, Gad Barzilai, Gideon and Becki Doron, Michael Keren, Gil Merom, Shaul Mishal, Dave Nachmias, Yossi Shain, Michal Shamir, and my research assistants: Ravit Hannanel, Shlomo Mizrahi, Dganit Olomoki, Marina Zeltser, and Phaina Courrage. I thank Gabriela Fisman for the index.

Finally, I thank Alex Holzman, Robert Goodin, and Linda Johnson for bringing me to Cambridge University Press. Special thanks are due to Robert Goodin and an anonymous reader for important comments on an earlier version of the manuscript. John Haslam, the editor, Barbara Docherty, the copy-editor, and Jayne Matthews, the Production Controller at Cambridge University Press deserve special thanks for their patience and help in the last stages of the production of the book.

On a personal note, I would like to thank my parents, Yonath and Alexander Sened, my brother Daniel, and my wife Tehila. Tchella, Yoel, Michal, and Dina Schechter; Scott Ainsworth, Galia Amir, Yael Diamant, Gideon Doron, Israel Drori, Natali L. Hansson, Jack Knight, Efrat Leib, Shaul Mishal, Dave Nachmias, Sara Oren, Irit Schori, Bat-Hen Tiery, Laura Winsky Mattei, and Galit Zimran are very special people, who helped me out by being there when I most needed them. My children, Haran, Yanai, and Hagar, are my "raison d'être."

Introduction

The subject matter of this book is the political institution of private property and related individual rights. The term "political institution" refers, here, to two fundamental claims that distinguish my argument on the origin and the evolution of private property from most of the literature on the subject. First, I argue that the origin of private property and related individual rights is to be found in the *political institutions* that grant and enforce them and not in any set of moral principles or "nature." Second, I argue that property rights are *instituted* through a *political* process and not by any hidden, "market" forces.

Property rights result from a long political struggle of individuals to improve their well being. They emerge as outcomes of complex interactions between government officials who control social institutions by their monopoly over the use of force and their unique role in the legislative process, and free agents who challenge these institutional structures to fit them to their own needs.

The general analytical framework that I use is commonly referred to as *Rational Choice Theory*. This means that I adhere to two major premises (Ordeshook, 1986: 1–2):

1. *Methodological individualism:*
   Institutions that protect property and related individual rights, are political outcomes. Like any other political outcome, they emerge from choices made by rational individual agents in society.
2. *Purposeful action:*
   Rational agents have goals and they do whatever they can to achieve these goals, given the physical environment in which they operate and what they expect other agents to do, given the circumstances.

1

The fundamental premise of this book is that institutions that protect property and related individual rights are no different from other social institutions: they emerge as outcomes of complex strategic interactions between different actors in society. The fundamental purpose of this book is to explain how strategic choices by rational actors yield political institutions that define, grant, and protect property, and numerous other, related, individual rights.

It is perfectly appropriate to evaluate the merits of the outcomes of political processes in normative terms. Yet, for too long we have been accustomed to accept, without serious scrutiny, ontological claims about human nature, as well as positive arguments about the origin of human rights, that were assumed or implied by primarily normative traditional theories of rights. A major concern of chapter 1 of the book is to clarify the distinction between a positive theory of the process through which private property and related individual rights emerge and evolve, and the normative evaluation of the likely outcomes of this process.

Often, when attempts are made to question the ontological and positive claims on which most traditional theories of rights are, more or less implicitly, founded, we are told that we should not criticize normative theories for failing to provide positive answers to the question of the origin and evolution of rights. Yet, meanwhile, we have grown accustomed to accept the traditional normative theories of rights, together with so many unwarranted ontological and behavioral claims on which these theories rely.

In this book, I endorse a very different approach. My primary concern is to suggest a reasonable *positive theory* of the origin and evolution of property rights and some other individual rights. My secondary concern is to discuss some normative implications of this positive theory.

A major weakness of the traditional liberal theory of rights is that it was never founded on a satisfactory positive theory of human behavior and political processes. In the second part of the book (chapters 4–6) I explain how traditional liberalism may benefit from an acceptable positive theory of the origin of property rights.

Social systems impose rules that impose restrictions on the conduct of their members. Following Hohfeld (1919), Sumner (1987: 24–30) defines these constraints as directional relations. *First-order relations* require that *duty-bearers* respect the *claims* of *right-holders* over the *content* of a right. The "content" of a right refers to what the right-holder claims to be his or hers – such as property, freedom, etc. – by virtue of being a "right-holder."

Social systems are not static. They include norms and rules that enable certain agents in society to change first-order social relations. These are the *second-order relations* in the Hohfeld–Sumner analytical framework. "Second-order relations" are defined in terms of *power* and *immunity*. An agent has *power* to the extent that he or she has the ability to change first-order relations among agents – e.g., the power of legislative bodies to change the law. An agent has *immunity* if his or her first-order relations cannot be altered. For example, US citizens enjoy immunity as right-holders of the right for "freedom of speech," by the First Amendment to the US constitution. First- and second-order relations determine the position of each individual with respect to all other agents in society.

For the purpose of this book I define an "individual right" as whatever is necessary to give a *right-holder* an *effective* level of control over the *content* of an individual right. A level of control is "effective" to the extent that duty-bearers tend to respect the claims of right-holders over the content of rights conferred by a social system (Sumner, 1987: 54–70).

It is important to distinguish between institutions that protect property and related individual rights, and the rights themselves. Throughout the book I argue that most of the rights enjoyed by individual agents in society depend on political institutions that grant and enforce them. This does not mean that the institutions and the rights are one and the same. Above, I defined individual rights in terms of the control that right-holders obtain over the contents of such rights. I make a positive claim that, in most cases, such control can only be protected by political institutions. I argue that institutions, and the rights they promote, are unlikely to survive unless they are designed and enforced by central enforcement agencies with some monopolistic power over the use of force. In primitive societies such agents could be tribal leaders, magicians, older members or any other authoritative figures in society. In the modern world we live in, the enforcement agencies I have in mind are more likely to be central governments.

Chapters 1 and 2 of this book discuss the history of thought on the origin of private property and related individual rights. They are not intended to be comprehensive surveys, but are included as a critique of existing theories. I discuss both the weak and the more useful elements in the traditional theoretical arguments in order to distinguish the contribution of my own work to this rich body of literature.

Chapter 1 is a critical essay on some traditional theories of the origin of rights. Traditional philosophy is concerned mainly with the normative question of why rights *should* exist. In contrast, this book's focus is on the positive question of why rights *do* exist. I argue that after centuries of debate one cannot escape the conclusion that traditional political philosophy has left us with erroneous and misleading answers to this positive question.

In Chapter 2 I argue that markets are never, and cannot theoretically be, as free of political intervention as some economists would like them to be. Economists, from Marx to neo-classical marshals of the free market, wage a battle against the institution of central governments. The essence of the Marxist argument is that governments are mere tools used by ruthless elites to oppress and abuse the people. Neo-classical marshals of the free market charge that central governments only interfere with some ideal order, induced by "market forces." Therefore, government intervention must lead to suboptimal outcomes.

Well defined, and properly enforced, property rights are a necessary condition for the existence of free markets (Stigler, 1942; Coase, 1960). Property rights cannot exist without central law enforcement (Sened, 1995; Riker and Sened, 1991; Umbeck, 1981; cf. Sugden, 1986; Taylor, 1987). Thus, the neo-classical claim that markets can, and should, operate without any intervention from central governments is misleading. The "hidden hand" needs a very visible hand of law enforcement as an ally, if free markets are to emerge and prosper.

An important weakness of much of the neo-classical literature on the origin of property rights is the failure to distinguish between the *performance* of the economy and the *structure* of the economy (North, 1981). In North's terminology, "performance" refers to the typical concerns of neo-classical, economic theory with maximization of profits, attaining an optimal mix of input factors, and the like. "Structure" refers to "determinants of performance . . . political and economic institutions, technology, demography and ideology of a society" (North, 1981: 1). Neo-classical price theory has gone a long way toward explaining the logic and essence of economic performance. This book follows North's work in studying the logic and essence of the evolution of the *political structures* of the economy.

Neo-classical models of the polity tend to ignore the political structure altogether (Riker, 1988). The common premise in most of these models is that the performance of the economy dictates the political structures that polities impose upon themselves (North, 1990). But the performance of any economy depends on political structures of legal agreements among individual agents in the economy. We must begin to study, *explicitly*, how political structures emerge and how they change, given the performance of the economy under existing social structures, and the expectations that agents have from alternative institutional structures.

From all the historical evidence we have,

> [a]lmost all governments . . . have been founded originally either on usurpation or conquest or both, without any pretense of a fair consent or voluntary subjection of the people. (Hume 1752: 470)

Yet, governments grant rights to their constituents and spend considerable resources to protect these rights (Sened, 1995; Riker and Sened, 1991; Riker, 1990).

Property rights in land, as they exist today in England, to give one example, did not result from any general consent of land owners to create a government that would protect their natural rights. Property rights in land developed in the eleventh and twelfth centuries when the Norman kings started protecting such rights in order to facilitate the collection of taxes (Simpson, 1986).

A central puzzle that this book intends to solve is the apparent contradiction between the fact that governments of all times have acted mainly to further their selfish interests, and the crucial role that these same governments play in protecting the property and other individual rights of their constituents. The key to the solution of this puzzle is to realize the fact that governments' involvement in the grant and enforcement of rights reflects their dependence on the support of their citizens. Most of the benefits that government officials obtain are extracted from the citizens. Governments depend on popular support and tax revenues to remain in power. Their sensitivity to the interests of the common citizen is thus crucial for their own survival and prosperity.

The dominant approach in contemporary theories of institutions relies on game theory to explain how institutions emerge and how they function in terms of equilibria that emerge in games that are used to characterize social environments (Sugden, 1986; Schotter, 1981; Sened, 1991). Institutions are interpreted as rules that agents impose on the way they play the game. Chapter 3 derives from this approach an analytical framework that is used in the remainder of the book to explain the evolution of political institutions that protect property rights.

In chapter 3 I argue that to explain an institution we must describe an environment: a set of agents limited by physical constraints that define the set of actions from which these agents may choose and the utility they derive from different possible outcomes. We must then distinguish decisive subsets of agents, who possess the power to impose their will on all the relevant players. We must then demonstrate the existence of a context, in this environment, in which such decisive agents – be it an individual or a coalition of individuals – are made better off by the imposition of the institution on all the players involved.

Chapters 4–6 use the analytical framework developed in chapter 3 to provide a positive explanation for the origin and evolution of institutions that protect property rights as well as some other basic human rights. My main argument is that institutions that protect property and other individual rights emerge as outcomes in complex games between government officials, who control the institutional apparatus of the polity, and free agents who challenge these institutional structures with new demands. The decisive player in the game I use to explain the emergence of institutions that protect private property and related individual rights, is the government. Government officials commit themselves to protect private property rights in order to induce productivity. Like the kings of England, they realize that in the absence of well defined property rights, economic growth and prosperity are likely to be compromised.

The process by which governments make decisions is a complicated one. But this is not a book about government decision making processes, but about the structure of society. Therefore, I relegate to the background the complexity of the processes by which governments make decisions, in order to focus on a theory of how property rights emerge. I use the term "government officials" to describe politicians, regulators, civil servants, and the like. Because, in the end – by force of sheer power, direct elections, indirect representation, coalition or delegation – government, its delegates or any *decisive coalition* in government, end up making decisions "as if" they were unitary actors. And when they so act, the logic unraveled in this book should prevail.

The novel feature of this book is that it emphasizes the fact that governments must *grant* rights before they can protect them (Sened, 1995; Riker and Sened, 1991). In chapter 4 I provide a precise specification of the conditions under which we should expect government officials to grant and protect property rights.

In chapter 5 I develop a general framework for the study of the process through which agents in society challenge existing institutions and those who control them with new demands for new structures of property rights, and by which governments reach the decision to grant such rights. I show that because governments do not have complete information regarding the preferences of individuals in their constituencies, private citizens have an important role to play in the political process of the evolution of property rights.

The interactions through which governments and individuals sort out their differences regarding the institution of property and other individual rights leave much room for political entrepreneurs to act as intermediate agents. Individual agents who wish to petition governments to obtain new rights face a collective action problem, as each one wants to free ride on the effort of other agents. If other agents obtain the right that a free rider longs for, he or she will enjoy the benefits of having this right just as much, without paying the price of petitioning the government to grant it. A price that, at times, is very high.

Political entrepreneurs help individual agents to alleviate the collective action problem by providing them with crucial information about how the game may be played by other players. But entrepreneurs play a game in which they have two audiences (Ainsworth and Sened, 1993). At the same time that they help organize and mobilize the groups they represent, they provide crucial information to government officials concerning the interests of group members and the size of these groups. The linkage between individual agents and government officials, as it is shaped by political entrepreneurs, is the subject of chapter 6.

Chapter 7 is a case study of a recent decision by the US Department of Transportation to grant individual property rights in air slots (permits to land and take off during well defined periods of time). These rights were established by giving carriers the right to trade air slots. This case provides an empirical illustration of the theory developed in chapters 4–6.

This book offers a positive theory of the origin of individual rights. This new approach is based on a more realistic treatment of the role of politics in the evolution of private property and related individual rights. It allows us to reevaluate some of our old prejudices on the origin and essence of basic human rights. It also allows us to reevaluate old claims on how we should design institutions that grant and protect such rights. We should no longer put our faith in nature or in other abstract origins of rights. We should study governments that control the means to grant and protect property and related human rights.

One logical conclusion of my analysis is that governments must no longer be considered as evil intruders in an ideal Marxist or neo-classical "natural order." Governments are necessary players, on which the very existence of private property and related individual rights depend. If this is the case, we should no longer fight to rid ourselves of this evil agent; instead, we should struggle to make governments more responsive and more sensitive to our changing needs. We must stop hoping for a utopian order without governments, and focus our attention on the design of governments and other institutions, that may be more or less effective in granting and protecting property and other individual rights.

The relevant question is no longer a moral question of *whether* governments are bad or evil. Governments are a necessary part of the structure of social order. They are the only agent that can protect the rights of individuals to their property and other basic necessities. The relevant question becomes the question of *institutional design* and *implementation*. After so many years, it is time to return to the traditional, liberal question of *how to govern*, and let go of the utopian hope for a social order without governments.

Let there be no mistake about it. There is nothing natural, or particularly ethical, about property rights, as such. Property rights emerge because they serve some tangible interests of particular individuals. Such rights cannot emerge or persist unless they serve, directly or indirectly, the interests of the central authorities that pay a remarkable cost to protect and enforce them.

These conclusions lead me to a new interpretation of the concept of the *social contract*. The essence of any social contract should no longer be understood as a delegation of authority by private individuals to a central entity so that this entity becomes the guardian of their "natural" rights. On the contrary, the foundation of any social contract is based on the willingness of government officials to grant individual rights to their constituents in return for political and economic support.

This conclusion leads me to a neo-liberal interpretation of the role that governments and private citizens play in the polity. Governments are not benevolent actors whose authority is delegated by the people. Instead, they should be viewed as rational entrepreneurs who produce law and order in return for political and economic benefits. Private property and other basic individual rights are not deduced from obscure, ethical imperatives. They are granted by rational government officials to their constituents, if those constituents are willing to pay a price for the institution and protection of these rights. Private citizens are not passive entities in a moral order. They play an active role by petitioning the authorities for the creation and protection of institutions that guarantee their claims to the content of desired rights.

The traditional, liberal school of individual rights starts from three premises: the first two are the autonomy of the individual and the necessity of government. The second of these is usually derived from more primitive assumptions about "human nature." It argues that, given human nature, government is necessary for the maintenance of a reasonable level of individual freedom and well being. The central challenge that liberal theorists of all times have tried to answer is how the autonomy of individual agents can be maintained in an orderly society. This question would be of little consequence if it was not for a third essential premise of traditional liberalism that provides the essence and motivation for this tradition: namely, that autonomous individuals are bound to have conflicting interests.

The liberal challenge is best understood as an attempt to reconcile conflicting interests in a sovereign body that rules over an orderly society (Rawls, 1993: 3–4). The sovereign may be an individual, a group or an abstract principle, but its role is always to moderate and resolve the conflict of interests that the liberal tradition assumes to exist in any society of autonomous individuals.

The failure to meet this challenge has led many to abandon liberalism as a viable political philosophy. A central flaw in the traditional liberal theory that led to this failure is its basic misconception of the role of government. Traditional liberalism prescribes a very limited role to government. Government officials are treated as benevolent actors who assume the role of guardians of "natural rights." A central argument in this book is that governments grant and enforce rights not as benevolent actors but as political entrepreneurs who provide this collective good to society in return for tax revenues and political support.

My theory is a liberal theory inasmuch as it is premised on the autonomy of individuals, both substantively and methodologically. Substantively, it assumes that individuals have inalienable preferences that cannot be taken away from them. Methodologically, unlike materialistic and historical determinism, social choice theory uses methodological individualism to explain social outcomes by the actions of individuals with conflicting preferences. The theory advanced in this book thus pays the utmost respect to the autonomy of individuals: it acknowledges the primacy of their preferences and, at the same time, it regards individual actions of rational human beings highly enough to seek in them the only explanation for social phenomena. What matters here are the preferences and the rational expectations of these individuals that allow them to choose individual actions that yield the social outcomes we are trying to understand.

The main feature that distinguishes my theory of the social contract from traditional liberalism is the role it assigns to government officials. Governments cannot possibly limit themselves to the anemic role of benevolent guardians of "natural rights." From a positive point of view, the role that traditional liberalism assigns to governments is unbelievable. From a normative perspective this role is unacceptable. Traditional liberalism failed to meet the challenge it set for itself because, from a positive point of view, it does not allow government to do enough to sustain law and order. Traditional liberal theories failed to understand the role that government must play in structuring and granting property rights before it can start protecting them. From the normative perspective, traditional liberalism expected too much from government officials, hoping that, by some magic touch, they would be different from all other humans and would seek to serve society, rather than acting, like all humans, to further their own selfish interests.

This book shows that self-interested government officials can be expected to serve the public interest. It promotes the idea that instead of ridding ourselves of central governments, for the sake of individual freedom, we must embrace political institutions as a necessary condition for the emergence and maintenance of property and other individual rights.

As a response to the liberal challenge I unravel, in precise terms, the essence of the social contract in neo-liberal terms. Returning to basic assumptions and rejecting any reliance on moral theories in favor of a positive description of this contract, I look for an answer to a centuries-old question: how can autonomous individuals, likely to have conflicting, inalienable, individual preferences, live in a society governed by law and order? The key to the answer is to acknowledge that law and order are public goods provided by central governments in return for economic and political support.

Finally, this book is a contribution to the emerging new research agenda of the *design* of political institutions in general, and political institutions that protect individual rights in particular. By the nature of the subject, studies of institutional design are concerned mainly with normative issues. The questions that are repeatedly studied have to do with economic efficiency and other normative criteria that different institutional designs can or cannot guarantee. This book joins a growing trend in the literature that is more concerned with the positive question of how institutions are actually designed and what determines the *path* of the evolution of institutional designs (Riker, 1995; North, 1990).

1

Classical theories of the origin of rights: the social contract

Introduction

The regulation of property rights in society is a fundamental function of any form of government. Philosophers throughout history have tried to explain why and how members of society accept the duties imposed on them, by themselves or by central governments, and why they should respect the claims of other agents in different domains of their social lives.

In this chapter, I survey possible answers, provided by various philosophers of the classic, liberal, *social contract* theory.[1] The philosophers whose work I discuss in this chapter endorse more or less explicit, descriptive theories of the origin of rights. Hobbes,[2] for example, justified absolute monarchy on the grounds that in a *state of nature* – in the absence of governments and other social institutions – humans would fall into a "war of all against all" and recommended an absolute monarchy to remedy this misery. This is a claim about human behavior under given conditions. All social contract theories are based on such implicit behavioral assumptions (Nozick, 1975: 8–9; Sumner, 1987: 151–62; Taylor 1987: ch. 6).

Some may insist that traditional philosophy is concerned with normative

---

[1] The idea of a social contract first appears in Plato's *The Republic* ((≈ 375 BC) 1968) nos. 358e–359b). However, Plato himself obviously rejects the idea, and no one seems to have taken it seriously again as a descriptive or moral justification for lawful and orderly society until the seventeenth century.

[2] My starting point, Thomas Hobbes, is relatively late in the history of ideas, for a reason: the dominant Greek philosophers, like Plato and Aristotle, were more concerned with the question of social order and had little interest in "individual rights" as we understand the term today. With few exceptions, the prominent medieval philosophers were more concerned with teleological questions than with individual rights that most of them derived, almost automatically, from their teleological theories.

justifications and not with implicit descriptions. Locke, they may argue, claimed that governments are guardians of "natural" rights, because he thought it was an adequate, moral justification for the creation and maintenance of government. But, as I argued in the Introduction, we have grown accustomed to accept Locke's ontological claim that rights are "natural" and his positive argument according to which governments are adequate guardians of these ontological entities.

If rights are natural they do not emerge or evolve. Before I develop a positive theory of the origin of property rights, I must show that such rights are not "natural" in any sense of the word.[3]

Rawls (1971), to give one contemporary example, claims that his principles of justice are self-evident. These principles were shown to be inconsistent with intuitive notions of justice (Dasgupta, 1974; Sen, 1974, 1986), yet Rawls maintains, without a proof, that if people were put behind a "veil of ignorance" they would approve of Rawls' "self-evident" principles. Frohlich et al. (1987a, 1987b) conducted experiments in which students, placed behind a "veil of ignorance," were asked to choose among distributive principles. Rawls' principles received little support. So, Rawls' theory of justice seems to be founded on unwarranted, positive assertions about how humans act under given conditions.

What value do theories that are based on problematic behavioral assertions and flawed ontological assumptions have? With a few exceptions (Sumner, 1987; Taylor, 1987), these theories escaped serious scrutiny. The following five sections are critical essays on five prominent traditional theories of the origin of rights.

The concluding remarks outline an alternative approach to the study of the origin of rights. I argue that social contracts are not based on fundamental principles of justice but evolve as institutional remedies to social dilemmas arising from complex interactions among agents and authorities in society. Instead of founding normative theories on problematic ontological foundations, I propose a positive theory of the origin and evolution of rights, and then study its normative implications. Once we understand how rights emerge and evolve, we may be able to better design institutions that facilitate the emergence and protection of such rights.

John Locke: a natural rights theory of the social contract

Locke's ([1690] 1980) argument that governments do not create property rights but are instituted to serve as their objective guardians is the most celebrated among social contract theories that rely on the premise of

---

[3] For an exposition of this argument, usually attributed to Jeremy Bentham, against the very concept of "natural" rights, see Sumner (1987: 111–26).

the primacy of natural rights. According to Locke, a natural sense of reason dictates to humans what is right and what is wrong. Locke argued that humans would have lived according to this idea of justice, except that when scarcity arises, they become biased, and favor their selfish interests at the expense of the welfare of others. Since society is constrained by the scarcity of resources, governments are established to guarantee unbiased judgments in the daily process of human interactions concerning property rights which regulate the use, trade, and ownership of those scarce resources (Locke [1690] 1980, ch. II and nos. 87, 88). Variations on this theme have informed three centuries of arguments in favor of a very limited role for government in the management of law and order in society.

There are two major flaws in Locke's argument. The first concerns the very concept of "natural rights" as such. The second is related to the notion that governments could serve as objective guardians of such "natural" rights.

By definition, theories of natural rights are founded on the premise that, historically and logically, rights exist prior to the creation of government. Yet, individual rights in general and property rights in particular exist only if, and to the extent that, duty-bearers respect them. In most cases law enforcement is a necessary condition for this respect (cf. Sugden, 1986; Taylor, 1987). As Rousseau eloquently stated it ([1757] 1987: 151–2):

> This is the reason why the right of the first occupant, so weak in the state of nature, is able to command the respect of every man living in the civil state.

Locke himself notes that ([1690] 1980, no. 1144, italics in the original) that:

> [Laws] need a *perpetual execution*, . . . therefore it is necessary there should be a *power always in being*, which should see to the *execution* of the laws that are made [by the legislature].

If property rights are so natural, why do we need so much *power* to enforce them, and if so much power is needed to enforce them, in what sense are they natural? From a positive perspective the very notion of "natural rights" is a contradiction in terms (Bentham, 1954, vol. 1: 334). Hobbes ([1651] 1968: 188, 190) states this point most bluntly:

> The notions of Right and Wrong, Justice and Injustice have there [in the natural state] no place. Where there is no common Power, there is no Law: where no Law, no Injustice. Force and fraud are in warre the two Cardinal vertues. Justice and Injustice are none of the faculties neither of the Body, nor mind . . . It followeth, that in such conditions, every man has a Right to every thing; even to one anothers body.

Without a mechanism or authority to decide on what is right or wrong, it is impossible to assign any meaning to the word "right." Who is to decide what is "right" or "wrong"? Who is to provide a list of natural rights, and according to what standards? Centuries of research and animated political debate on these questions have failed to yield any clear answer.

The heated political debate over abortion issues is an excellent example. When all is said and done, who has the ultimate right? The mother to choose, or the fetus to live? Is there a "natural" answer to this question? Obviously not (Waldron, 1992: 410). Answers to such questions have always been, and apparently will for ever be, political.

Locke, like many traditional proponents of the theory of natural rights, resorts to divine authority to assign a meaning to the notion of "natural" rights, but by modern standards of analytical research, to hold that it is "self evident, that all men . . . are endowed by their Creator with certain unalienable Rights," is meaningless (Smith, 1989; Hart, 1979; Sen, 1986). Thus, the first premise on which Locke's political theory is based, that individual rights are natural, in any sense of the word, is simply untenable:

> The modern analysis of rights made an enormous leap forward when it was realized that talk about natural rights . . . is not a way of giving . . . answers, but a way of promising to give them. (Waldron, 1992: 400–1)

The second fundamental premise in Locke's political theory, namely that representative governments can serve as "objective" guardians of our "natural" rights, is just as problematic as the first. Even if rights were inherent in humans as life itself – and they are not – one still has to show why we should expect more or less representative governments to serve as impartial guardians of these rights. Contemporary research on this subject has shown the generic vulnerability of representative legislatures to different forms of manipulation (Riker, 1982; Ordeshook, 1986). There is evidence that politicians and political theorists have been aware of this vulnerability since, at least, the times of the ancient Roman Empire (Rousseau, [1757] 1987: 55–6, 204; Riker, 1986).

Thus, the Lockean theory of natural rights implies, or assumes, problematic positive assertions based on problematic ontological assumptions. It is, therefore, not surprising that it turns out to be an inadequate normative foundation for the institutional designs of modern, western democracies, for which it is so often used as a justification.[4]

Most important for our purposes here, the Lockean argument leaves open the question of why governments protect individual rights in general and property rights in particular. Property and other legal rights, almost invariably, depend on law enforcement. Therefore, when we try to explain

---

[4] For an interesting explanation of how the theory of "natural" rights has survived this straightforward criticism, see Sen (1986: 47–51, 70–8).

the origin and evolution of such rights in the civil or political society we must provide a convincing argument as to why legislative bodies embody these rights in the legal system, and why they allocate resources to executive bodies to protect these rights through law enforcement.

Thomas Hobbes: a positive theory of the social contract

Hobbes ([1651] 1968) developed a social contract theory that is immune to the criticism of the natural rights theory discussed in the previous section.[5] To achieve this goal he changed the very essence of the concept of "natural" rights. For Hobbes, humans have a *natural* right of self-preservation only insofar as they have a natural inclination to preserve themselves (Hobbes, [1651] 1968: 189; Bluhm, 1984: 59–60). From this natural inclination and an assumption about the rationality of humans, Hobbes derived his justification for the necessity of governments and the basic rights that these governments must protect (Hobbes, [1651] 1968: 188–91).

Because humans are inclined to preserve themselves, and since they know that they are basically equal in their capacity to inflict injury on one another, they see in any other human being a potential threat.[6] So, in the "state of nature" – i.e. in the absence of governments and other social institutions – we expect humans to do everything they can to eliminate one another in a "war of all against all."

Hobbes' central argument is that humans, as rational beings, recognize the threat of such a gloomy future. This rational expectation leads them to form a social contract in which they trust the responsibility for their defense to the hands of whomsoever they crown as their absolute sovereign. From this point on, not the individual but the sovereign is the guardian of the fundamental human right (or inclination) to life.

A central flaw in this argument is that it *assumes* a benevolent sovereign who protects the rights of his or her subjects, instead of explaining the motivation of a sovereign to do so. To force duty-bearers to respect claims of right-holders requires different means of law enforcement, particularly if we believe the Hobbesian portrait of human nature. Enforcement agencies with a monopoly over the use of force, however can, and often do, deprive

---

[5] Hobbes' *Leviathan* was published in 1651, almost four decades before Locke's *Second Treatis on Government* ([1690] 1980). I am not interested in the historic order of events, but rather in the logical foundations of theories of the origin of rights.

[6] In most modern versions of social contract theories, scarcity is the force that motivates the use of violence (e.g. Umbeck, 1981). For Hobbes, the motivation to use violence has three causes: the search for material gain, the quest for personal safety, and the pursuit of reputation by other individuals in the state of nature (Hobbes, [1651] 1968: 185; Bluhm, 1984; 62–5).

citizens of individual rights just as well as they protect such rights. To explain the evolution of legal systems that protect the rights of individual citizens, we must explain not how governments come into being but why, given their monopoly over the use of force, they would protect private property or any other individual rights.

The Hobbesian social contract theory suffers from yet another weakness that characterizes social contract theories to this day (e.g. Umbeck, 1981; Buchanan and Tullock, 1962): it is not enough to show that individual agents recognize the advantage of having a government that enforces basic rights. One must explain why and how, if at all, strategic, rational agents would erect, maintain, or obey such a government.

Contemporary game theory uses games as theoretic abstractions of complex social interactions. The game theoretic model most commonly used to describe and analyze what Hobbes called the "state of nature" is usually referred to as the *prisoners' dilemma* game (Taylor, 1987).[7]

For the purpose of the argument developed in subsequent chapters it is important to understand this simple abstract model of the state of nature. Consider the two-person version of the game summarized in table 1.1. Each player can choose between two strategies: to respect or not to respect the rights of the other player. The numbers in the cells indicate the utility each player gets from any possible combination of strategies chosen, simultaneously, by the two players. The first number in every cell indicates the utility that player 1 gets. The second number indicates the utility that player 2 gets. For example, if both players chose to respect each other's rights, each would receive a utility of 1, while if both chose not to respect each other's rights, neither of them would get any utility – by Hobbes' description of the state of nature, they would both probably be dead.

A commonly used solution concept in contemporary game theory is known as the *Nash equilibrium*. The use of this equilibrium concept to predict the outcome of a social interaction is based on a simple intuition of John Nash (1951, 1953). A combination of strategic choices constitutes a Nash equilibrium if no player can alter his or her strategic choice of behavior, given the strategic choice(s) of the other player(s), and get a higher payoff. We expect Nash equilibria to be stable outcomes in the games and in the human interactions of which these games serve as abstractions, because if no player can obtain higher payoffs by unilaterally changing his or her strategic choices, then no player has an incentive to change his or her

---

[7] The *n*-person prisoners' dilemma is not the only possible nor, at times, the most accurate, abstract representation of the problem of the provision of public goods (Taylor, 1987, ch. 2). Nevertheless, the *n*-person prisoners' dilemma is a widely used game theoretic representation of this problem (Hardin, 1982). Taylor (1987) developed a parallel argument to the one I develop here, and provided interesting insights on how the discrepancies in Hobbes' theory could be reconciled.

Table 1.1. *Two-person prisoners' dilemma*

Players		Player 2	
	Strategies	Cooperate (*C*)	Defect (*D*)
Player 1	Cooperate (*C*)	1,1	$-1,2$
	Defect (*D*)	2,-1	0,0

behavior, as long as the other players stick to their strategic choices (for more precise definitions, see the appendix to chapter 2, p. 53).

It is easy to show that in the prisoners' dilemma the only equilibrium outcome is for both players to defect. Thus, our prediction is that both players will fail to respect each other's rights. In chapter 4 I present a formal *n*-person version of the game. Note that if players could somehow commit themselves to cooperate, they would be better off.

Hobbes argued that rational agents should realize the advantages that each player would get if all agents respected each other's rights and opted for a social contract in which they conceded their natural right (inclination) for self-defense, and trusted their security to whomsoever they agreed to regard as their absolute sovereign. This behavior, however, as I just explained, is not an equilibrium behavior. Hence, we do not expect it to be the outcome of the human state of nature as described by Hobbes.

Once again, Hobbes may have meant to advance only an abstract, normative argument. But he has brought so many of us to accept the ontological assumptions he makes about human nature, and the positive argument he implies about the origin of government. The game theoretic model presented here shows the basic weaknesses of the positive social contract theory implied by Hobbes: the fact that humans are rational, and the fact that they recognize the misery in which they live in the absence of a social contract, does not necessarily entail that they will do anything to work their way out of this misery and into one or another form of a social contract.

The civil wars in Lebanon, Bosnia and the African continent, as well as the gang wars in the urban centers of the USA are sad contemporary reminders of this simple fact. These devastating wars last because, just as the game above illustrates, the head of each war gang believes that, eventually, the other gangs will respect his or her "right" to extract different benefits through the use of violence. The unfortunate outcome is the Hobbesian "war of all against all" which leads to social and individual devastation.

In other words, given his ontological assumptions about human nature, Hobbes was correct in predicting the "war of all against all," and wrong in hoping that humans would realize their misery in this state of nature and opt for any form of a social contract.

Unfortunately, not only do rational players fail to leave the violent Hobbesian state of nature for a *civil* social contract, but modern history is rich with examples in which rational players left more or less "civil" states of affairs in favor of ferocious "wars of all against all." The former Yugoslavia is a sad contemporary example, and what used to be the Soviet Union risks producing yet many more such examples. For the purpose of my argument in the remainder of this book, it is important to realize the devastating consequences that the collapse of these "social contracts" into ferocious civil wars had on the structures of property rights. Whatever property rights existed in the Bosnia of the early 1990s, the Lebanon of the 1970s, or the urban centers in the USA, devastated by gang wars in the 1980s and 1990s, they had little, if any, useful meaning.

A central claim of this book is that Hobbes was correct to argue that only strong, stable structures of governments, by enforcing law and order, can help society avoid the war of all against all that awaits any group of rational players in the absence of such structures. Yet, it is important to recognize that Hobbes was wrong to argue that such structures are bound to emerge, spontaneously, in any group of rational agents, just as he was wrong to argue that the survival of these structures depends on the benevolence of those to whom society trust the power to govern, and the fear of rational agents from the collapse of the social contract back into a state of nature.

One must distinguish between a theory of the origin of rights and a theory of the origin of governments. How governments emerge from a state of "natural anarchy" is a puzzle I do not pursue here. I recognize, however that, in the world we know, most property rights are enforced by governments. Therefore, any theory of the origin of property rights must explain why, and under what conditions, agents in society can rely on central governments to enforce such rights. Neither Hobbes nor other social contract theorists have addressed this question. They either assume a benevolent government or simply avoid the issue.

David Hume: the role of conventions in the social contract

Hume's political theory[8] relies on the following statement of the social problem:

> . . . possessions . . . we have acquir'd by our industry and good fortune . . . are exposed to the violence of others and may be transfer'd without suffering

---

[8] Hume never developed a comprehensive political theory as Hobbes did in the *Leviathan*. Nevertheless, centuries of research enable us to appreciate Hume's contribution to this debate. A remarkable discussion of this contribution is found in Taylor (1987).

any loss or alteration; while at the same time there is not sufficient quantity of them to supply every one's desires and necessities. As the improvement, therefore, of these goods is the chief advantage of society, so the instability of their possession, along with their scarcity, is the chief impediment (1888: 487–9)

Thus, for Hume, much as for Locke before him, the chief concern of any form of civil, social life is the regulation of property rights. Yet, like Hobbes, Hume explicitly rejects the premise of natural rights and claims explicitly that "rights are not deriv'd from nature but from *artifice*" (1888; 489–9, italics in the original):

... when men ... have observ'd that the principal disturbance in society arises from those goods ... their looseness and easy transition ... they must seek for a remedy, ... This can be done after no other manner than by a convention enter'd into by all the members of the society to bestow stability on the possession of those ... goods ... This convention ... [induces] all the members of the society ... to regulate their conduct by certain rules. I observe that it will be for my interest to leave another in the possession of his goods, *provided* he will act in the same manner with regard to me. He is sensible of a like interest in the regulation of his conduct. When this common sense of interest is mutually express'd and is known to both it produces a suitable resolution and behaviour ... [This convention] acquires force by ... our repeated experience of the inconveniences of transgressing it.

Hume's logical analysis preceded by two centuries similar contemporary game theoretic arguments (Axelrod, 1980a, 1980b, 1981, 1984; Taylor, 1987; Calvert, 1989): if agents face a social dilemma repeatedly, then under some conditions there exist equilibrium outcomes in which rational human beings can be expected to "cooperate" in each repetition of the game (see chapter 3 for a discussion of this point). This cooperation can induce human beings to respect each other's property rights.

Hume had more faith in human nature than Hobbes. He emphasized the tendency humans have to respect each other's rights in repeated social interactions. He certainly regarded this tendency as an important aspect of social life, but he did not think that this "possibility of cooperation" (Taylor, 1987) could guarantee the peaceful coexistence of agents in society, as many modern students of property rights seem to believe (Sugden, 1986; Taylor, 1987).

The reason for Hume's skepticism is his acknowledgment of another basic aspect of human nature: *selfishness* (1888: 486). For Hume, selfishness and the scarcity of basic commodities define the problem that agents face in the natural state. The way Hume describes how this problem is resolved is closer to Hobbes' argument than generally thought. Hume hardly deviates from Hobbes' premises concerning human behavior. His crucial contribu-

tion lies in his analysis of the consequences of these assumptions. Hume agrees with Hobbes that the laws of justice are established by the artifice of humans (1888: 484), but while Hobbes believed that only an absolute sovereign could be their author, Hume gave this role to 'conventional wisdom' (1888: 491):

> . . . we can [not] have any idea of property, without fully comprehending the nature of justice, and shewing its origin in the artifice and contrivance of man. The origin of justice explains that of property. The same artifice gives rise to both . . . our first and most natural sentiment of morals is founded on the nature of our passions . . . the convention for the distinction of property and for the stability of possession, is of all circumstances the most necessary to the establishment of human society, . . . after the agreement for the fixing and observing of this rule, there remains little . . . to be done towards settling a perfect harmony and concord.

For Hume, the origins of justice and property rights are pragmatic conventions that acquire "force by . . . our repeated experience of the inconveniences of transgressing" them. This is a reasonable theory of the origin of social order in general and property rights in particular, but Hume understood that voluntary cooperation and respect for mutual property rights in large societies are bound to fail. They fail not because humans are stupid or evil, but because there are so many equilibrium outcomes in repeated games, including outcomes in which agents do not cooperate (e.g. Fudenberg and Maskin, 1986). The repeated game argument explains why we may see cooperation among social agents, but it does not imply that such agents *tend* to cooperate (Bianco and Bates, 1990: 137). Without the technical tools of contemporary game theory, Hume was aware of the multitude of equilibria and the consequent fragility and instability of social equilibria in such circumstances (1888: 487–90):

> This is the reason why men so often act in contradiction to their known interest; and . . . prefer any trivial advantage, that is present, to the maintenance of order in society . . . The consequences of every breach of equity seem to lie very remote and are not able to counterbalance any immediate advantage, that may be reap'd from it . . . and as all men are . . . subject to the same weakness . . . the violations of equity must become . . . frequent in society, and the commerce of men . . . render'd . . . dangerous and uncertain.

Hume derives the necessity of government in society from two consequences of this argument. First, large societies cannot rely on the remote possibility of cooperation. Each agent, eager to "free himself of the trouble and expense . . . wou'd lay the whole burden on others" (1888: 538).

Second, individual agents cannot be relied upon to overcome the natural tendency to prefer present values to remote rewards (1888: 537):[9]

> Here then is the origin of civil government and society. Men are not able radically to cure, either in themselves or others, that narrowness of soul, which makes them prefer the present to the remote. They cannot change their natures. All they can do is to change the situation, and render the observance of justice the immediate interest of some particular persons, and its violation their more remote. These persons, then, are not only induc'd to observe those rules in their own conduct, but also to constrain others to a like regularity . . .

Thus, like Hobbes and Locke before him, Hume fell short of solving the puzzle of why should we trust governments with the role of protecting property rights. Hume himself argued that (1752: 470): "Almost all governments . . . have been founded originally either on usurpation or conquest or both, without any pretense of a fair consent or voluntary subjection of the people." Yet, when he comes to the conclusion of his argument, here, he argues that (1888: 487–9):

> . . . render the observance of the laws of justice our nearest interest, . . . being impractical with respect to all mankind, it can only take place with respect to a few, whom we thus immediately interest in the execution of justice. These are the persons, whom we call civil magistrates, kings and their ministers, our governors and rulers, who . . . being satisfied with their present condition . . . have an immediate interest in every execution of justice, which is so necessary to the upholding of society.

Benevolence is not an explanation for the existence of reliable law enforcement. We must have an explanation for why civil magistrates assume the role Hume wants them to assume. To conclude the argument by assuming that magistrates are immune to the weaknesses that characterize other human beings simply contradicts Hume's own assertion that no humans can be trusted to overcome these weaknesses.

Hume came as close as anyone to resolving the puzzle of the origin of property rights and social order. Property rights are not natural. Pragmatic considerations, conventional wisdom, and the mutual dependence of individuals in society are the building blocks of this human artifice. Yet, weaknesses of human nature require that governments be the guardians of this conventional wisdom and enforce its imperatives. We still need to find

---

[9] Eager to prove Hume's argument invalid, Taylor (1987: 159) quotes and "refutes" only half of Hume's argument. Hume's argument about the necessity of governments is much more convincing than Taylor's dismissal of this and other arguments concerning the role of central governments in the establishment of law and order in society (1987: 164–79).

how this social contract emerges, and why, and under what conditions can we trust governments to be its faithful guardians.

Humanity would have saved itself much trouble had it pursued the road mapped out by Hume for the resolution of this puzzle. Unfortunately, it has not. In the next two sections I examine this unfortunate twist of history.

Jean-Jacques Rousseau: the end of the liberal social contract tradition

The historical proximity of Rousseau's writing to the events of the French revolution brought many to regard Rousseau as a chief inspiration for the constitution of the French Republic. In spite of this undeniable fact, Rousseau's impact on the liberal, social contract school was to drive it into a logical impasse that would last for two centuries. There are many reasons for the decline of the liberal, social contract philosophical tradition of thought in the nineteenth century but, from a philosophical standpoint, Rousseau's criticism of this school and his remedies for its theoretical shortcomings mark the end of the classical, liberal, social contract school of thought.

Rousseau's critique of the liberal, social contract theory can be reduced to three main arguments (Cranston, 1954, ch. 3). First, he argued that this theory failed to adequately describe the pre-social *natural state*. Most social contract theorists premise their argument by the claim that life in the natural state is, by some important standards, inferior to life in the *civil* state. In *Emile* and The *Discourse on the Origin and Foundation of Inequality Among Men* ([1754] 1981b), Rousseau describes the human condition in the state of nature as one of genuine freedom, in which primitive humans care for their own basic needs, with much skill and grace and little violence. Rousseau did not think that the state of nature was characterized by violence. He blamed Hobbes for attributing features of the modern civil society to the state of nature. For Hobbes, the chief reason for war was natural aggressiveness. For Rousseau, war results from the

> unequal division of possessions in the context of scarcity, coupled with the corruption of human passions which was the work of culture rather than of nature. (Cranston, 1954: 76)

For our purposes this line of criticism is crucial. While for Hobbes, Locke, and Hume, violence results from the absence of well defined property rights, for Rousseau it is precisely this civil definition of property rights that enhances violence in society.

Rousseau's second line of criticism of the liberal, social contract tradition has to do with his view of the *civil* state. Rousseau described the constitutions of his time in somber colors. He described the state of nature in very bright colors. This created a difficulty that is absent in the literature I have surveyed so far. Rousseau had to explain why humans ever left the state of nature for any form of civil life.[10]

Rousseau's answer originated in his *Discourse on the Origin and Foundation of Inequality Among Men* and was further elaborated in his *Essay on the Origin of Languages* (Rousseau, 1966). According to Rousseau, humans did not choose to pass from the state of nature to their civil state, but were driven into social life through a series of natural catastrophes that forced them to unite in order to win their war, not against each other as Hobbes suggested, but against nature. In this war, the weak had either to unite or submit themselves to the governance of the strong to protect themselves against the punishment of nature.

This is how family and other social structures evolved. In the state of nature, ties between male and females were weak and not binding. Women could provide themselves and their children with all their needs without the help of men, making them perfectly independent. But in the face of recurrent natural catastrophes, women blessed with children could not defend themselves in the harsh conditions imposed by nature. Thus, women learned to depend on men to help them fight nature's harshness, while they cared for the infants. This is the first stage in the evolution of the hierarchical inequality that characterizes modern society. Natural catastrophes "coupled with the corruption of human passions," caused the gradual evolution of modern society, characterized, for Rousseau, by the abuse of the poor and the weak by the strong and the rich (Cranston, 1954: 71–7).

This accidental process can rarely bring about the establishment of ideal social orders. Yet, this can be corrected by conscientious human agents (Cranston, 1954: 62):

> Rousseau adopted Hobbes' idea that men had lost their original freedom when they entered civil society, but he took from Machiavelli a further idea: that men could recover freedom – or find a new kind of freedom – in a well ordered republic. The development of this second idea is to be found in . . . *The Social Contract.*

Rousseau's third criticism was his objection to the assumption of the existence of natural rights. Human beings, according to Rousseau, did not have natural rights but natural freedom. For him, the main characteristic of

---

[10] In his *Discourse on the Origin and Foundation of Inequality Among Men* ([1754] 1981b) Rousseau went so far as to argue that most existing social contracts were based on the ability of the rich to abuse the poor through the imposition of these contracts. Marx usually denied Rousseau's influence, but it is hard to deny this influence if one reads the *Discourse.*

the natural state was *freedom* and most social contracts place *unbearable* constraints on freedom.

Rousseau saw his task and vocation in finding a form of a social contract in which a civil substitute for the original freedom would be found. Most students of Rousseau agree that Rousseau's argument is fraught with contradictions and inconsistencies (Bluhm, 1984; Peled, 1980). This rich research notwithstanding, my intention here is only to explain the role of Rousseau's work in the collapse of the liberal, social contract school of thought.

Rousseau's ultimate goal was to find a civil substitute for the natural freedom, forever lost in the course of history. To legitimate any form of a social contract he had to find a way to grant members of society the freedom of which most existing social orders deprived them. Rousseau's argument is summarized in Cranston (1954: 83–4):

> [Rousseau] believed it was possible to combine liberty and law, by instituting a regime which would enable men to rule themselves. Such an arrangement would entail, as Hobbes' system did, a covenant being made between individuals to surrender their . . . rights to a sovereign: but that sovereign should be none other than the people themselves, united in one legislative corps . . . Rousseau's response to the challenge of Hobbes is . . . simple. Clearly men can be at the same time ruled and free if they rule themselves. . . Rousseau was going a good deal further than liberal theorists. For Rousseau there is no investment or transfer of sovereignty: sovereignty not only originates in the people, it stays there.

Cranston's argument, as stated above, reflects a commonly accepted interpretation of Rousseau. But Rousseau did not go a good deal further, but moved a great deal further away from the liberal school of the social contract theory. In so doing, he robbed the liberal theoretical framework of its meaning.

The liberal, social contract school, to which I have dedicated most of this chapter, is based on three premises. The first two are the autonomy of individuals and the necessity of government. The second of these, which is often derived from more fundamental assumptions concerning human nature, is that given human nature, government is necessary if we are to maintain a decent level of individual freedom and well being. The real liberal challenge is to find how the autonomy of individuals can be maintained in an orderly society ruled by a central government. This challenge would be of little consequence if it was not for the third premise of classical liberalism, that autonomous individuals are bound to have competing interests. The liberal challenge is best understood as an attempt to reconcile opposing interests of autonomous agents within a sovereign orderly society ruled by a central government, whose role is to moderate and resolve the conflict of interest that the liberal tradition assumes to exist in any society of autonomous individuals. As Rawls pointed out (1993: 3–4):

> The political culture of a democratic society is always marked by a diversity of opposing and irreconcilable religious, philosophical, and moral doctrines. Some of these are perfectly reasonable doctrines political liberalism sees as the inevitable long-run result of the powers of human reason at work within the background of enduring free institutions.

Rousseau did not respond to Hobbes' challenge. He simply avoided it. For him, the only way sovereignty can be maintained by the people, "united in one legislative corps," is if they agree on the essential features of their lives. To do so, they must remain attentive only to the *general will*, which is one, and keep themselves from listening to the divisive force of the *will of all*, which embodies the selfish interests of each individual in society.

But if men were to agree on the basic features of their lives by paying careful attention to some "general will," the liberal question loses its meaning. Rousseau simply rejects all of the three basic, liberal assumptions, and this rejection had a huge influence on the future of political thought in the next two centuries. Rousseau's answer to the liberal question sacrifices the very autonomy of individuals in society that the liberal tradition was set to defend. What kind of liberty can Rousseau's freedom, based on a total submission to the general will, offer? Here, one can hardly escape Talmon's conclusion that Rousseau's writings have a central place among *The Origins of Totalitarian Democracy* (1955).

There is much debate in the literature as to the origin and essence of the "general will." This debate is irrelevant to our purposes, since as long as individuals buy their freedom only through total submission to the general will, the origin of this master, and the form it takes, is of little interest.[11]

Rousseau introduced to modern political theory a concept of freedom that is very different from the notion of individual autonomy defended by traditional liberalism. Traditional liberalism associates freedom with individual rights in general and property rights in particular. Rousseau puts little emphasis on individual rights in general and has almost a hostile attitude towards property rights. He associates freedom with something that is probably more poetic but much less tangible.

Rousseau also rejects the second premise of traditional liberalism, the premise of the necessity of government. His solution in *The Social Contract* is one of a direct democracy. The people govern, not the government. As I

---

[11] It should be stressed that this argument does not point to yet another contradiction in Rousseau's work. Rousseau would not have seen any contradiction involved here, since he regarded the "general will" as the very idea – in the Aristotelian sense of the word – of "individual freedom."

quoted Cranston (1954: 84) above: "For Rousseau there is no investment or transfer of sovereignty: sovereignty not only originates in the people, it stays there."

But Rousseau's departure from the liberal tradition originates in his rejection of the third underlying liberal assumption. The primacy of the general will over the will of all summarizes the whole issue. Rousseau actually believed in some objective ontological entity he called the "general will," which represents the 'will of the people' better than any government. Thus, governing can be done by the people for the people and without a government. And the autonomy of individuals? This autonomy manifests itself in the "will of all," a divisive force, and Rousseau spares no words to describe its evil nature.

A central premise of this book, which is also a central premise of traditional liberalism, is that political institutions are necessary for the maintenance of private property and other individual rights. Rousseau represents one of the most remarkable departures from this view, a departure that is echoed in the rejection of government, and other political institutions in general, by so many different modern schools of thought.

Rousseau also marks the beginning of a great divide between the continental and the English and American political philosophy. The liberal social contract school of thought was characterized by the attempt to reconcile the autonomy of the individual in society with the need for social law and order. After Rousseau, continental philosophers, such as Kant, Hegel, and Marx, shared a fascination for guiding principles of social life, being less concerned with the role and place of the autonomy of individuals. While continental philosophy neglected the autonomy of the individual in favor of grand principles, English and American philosophers focused their attention on the autonomy of individuals, but neglected to place this autonomy within a comprehensive theory of government. To quote Rawls (1993: 4–5):

> the course of democratic thought over the past two centuries . . . [is marked by] a conflict . . . between the tradition associated with Locke, which gives greater weight to what Constant called "the liberties of the modern," freedom of thought . . . basic rights of the person and of property [rights], and the rule of law, and the tradition associated with Rousseau, which gives greater weight to what Constant called the "liberties of the ancient," the equal political liberties and the values of public life.

Mill: autonomy of individuals as a constraint on social contracts

English utilitarianism seems to have offered an adequate response to the tendency of continental philosophers to neglect the individual as an autonomous entity in favor of general principles of government. The utilitarian principle, first suggested by Bentham and further elaborated in J. S. Mill's *Utilitarianism* ([1861] 1979), seems to have returned the focus of attention to the individual inasmuch as it requires that

> we should always perform that act, of those available, which will bring the most happiness, or least unhappiness, to the greatest number of people. (Sher, 1979: vii)

One problem of this principle is that it requires a yardstick that would allow us to compare utilities across individuals. In his attempt to defend this principle Mill has pointed to, and may have realized, this weakness ([1861] 1979: 8):

> It is quite compatible with the principle of utility to recognize the fact that some kinds of pleasure are more desirable and more valuable than others . . . If I am asked what I mean by difference of quality in pleasures, . . . there is but one possible answer. Of two pleasures, if there be one to which all who have experience of both give a decided preference, . . . that is the more desirable pleasure.

Yet, can we compare the utility each individual gets from each possible pleasure? The answer is "no," for two reasons: first, we cannot compare the pleasure different individuals get from different activities. Different people extract different, non-commensurable pleasures from different activities. Second, to give priority to one pleasure over another is a flagrant intrusion into the autonomy of the individual.

Mill's position and his genuine struggle to teach the "ignorants" to enjoy the pleasures of the "educated" is not compatible with genuine liberalism. It requires agents in society to submit themselves to a test of quality and a rule for measuring it against quantity, designed

> by those who, in their opportunities of experience, to which must be added their habits of self consciousness and self observation, are best furnished with means of comparison. ([1861] 1979: 11–12)

This is just a variation on Rousseau's argument that individuals must totally submit themselves to the "general will," except that Mill reduces it to "the taste of the tasteful." An autonomous individual should not be required to submit himself or herself to any of these. Thus, the utilitarian principle is closer in spirit to the continental concern with abstract principles of government than to the liberal concern with the autonomy of individuals.

Isaiah Berlin placed Mill's liberalism in a category by itself, arguing that Mill strove to defend the liberty of individuals against the oppression of the state. Berlin, in his essay *Two Concepts of Liberty* (1958), refers mainly to Mill's essay *On Liberty*. There, Mill promotes a very different view, endorsing the following *principle of demarcation* (Rapoport, 1978: xv–xvi):

> A person ought to be subject to social coercion only to prevent the violation
> of a distinct and assignable obligation to . . . other . . . persons.

This principle is incompatible with the utilitarian principle that Mill
espoused elsewhere.

Modern liberals have long understood that there is nothing liberal in the
utilitarian principle and have adopted instead, in one way or another, the
principle of demarcation that, as Berlin correctly points out, is unique in as
much as it states not what governments ought to do but, instead, what
governments must avoid doing. Government must avoid, as much as
possible, any intervention in the autonomous life of the individual. *On
Liberty* is dedicated to a remarkable defense of this principle. Mill himself
never addressed the obvious inconsistency between the interventionist
principle of his *Utilitarianism* and the principle of demarcation of *On
Liberty*, but to judge from his *Autobiography*, he regarded *On Liberty* as the
more important essay of the two (Rapoport, 1978: xx–xxi).

American liberalism is closer in spirit to the principle of demarcation
than to any other known principle of government. It is, thus, quite
remarkable that so little attention has been given in this literature to the fact
that the principle of demarcation is not a principle of government, but a
principle of defense of the autonomy of individuals. Once again, while
continental philosophy neglected the autonomy of the individual in favor
of different principles of government, American liberal philosophy – from
Thoreau's *Civil Disobedience* (1849) to Dewey's liberal individualism
(Dewey, 1962) – elaborated the principle of demarcation and its commitment to the autonomy of the individual and neglected to deal with
principles of government.[12]

Most western democracies are committed to more or less liberal
intuitions about the importance of individual rights as well as the
importance of sound principles of government. But, to date, there exists no
sound, comprehensive liberal theory of democracy. One reason for this
absence is that the genuine liberal challenge – the attempt to reconcile the
conflict of interests of autonomous individuals with the rule of a sovereign
body over a lawful social order – was neglected towards the end of the
eighteenth century.

Most citizens of western democracies believe in one or another set of
liberal intuitions. Most western democracies allegedly implement these
intuitions but lack a comprehensive theory of government within which to

---

[12] Generalizations about rich philosophical traditions, such as the American or the
continental philosophical traditions are, by nature, inaccurate. French existentialism is
obsessed with the place of the individual in society, while Nozick, Tullock, and
Buchanan are only three examples, among many, of American philosophers who spent
much time and effort trying to work out sound theoretical principles of government.

incorporate them. Much of the blame is to be found in the fact that, after Rousseau, philosophers like Kant, Hegel, and Marx shared a fascination for guiding principles of social life, leaving aside any serious consideration of the essence of the autonomy of individuals. Meanwhile, philosophers like Mill, Thoreau, and Dewey made genuine efforts to define and defend the autonomy of individuals in society, but failed to incorporate this defense in a sound theory of government. As Rawls concluded (1993: 4):

> The course of democratic thought over the past two centuries or so, makes plain that there is at present no agreement on the way the basic institutions of a constitutional democracy should be arranged if they are to satisfy the fair terms of cooperation between citizens.

Mill's contribution to the debate on property and other individual rights is to introduce the autonomy of individuals as a constraint on what government *should not do*, in their role as guardians of law and order. But Mill, and generations of liberals after him, failed to advance a comprehensive liberal theory of government that would meet this constraint. Hence the urgency to develop a research agenda of institutional design that would fill this void. This book is meant as a contribution to this growing research agenda (Eggertsson, 1990).

Concluding remarks: a positive origin to property and individual rights

Governments and citizens operate within social contracts that specify the law of the land, the rights protected by this law, and the punishment that those who violate the law are to expect. This contract also commits governments to protect the claims of right-holders and to punish reluctant duty-bearers.

Traditional (Hobbes, [1651] 1968) and modern (Umbeck, 1981) social contract theorists, however, paid little if any attention to the study of how such contracts emerge and evolve. This is the subject of this book: to provide a positive theory of the emergence and evolution of social contracts through which governments protect the property and other individual rights of their citizens.

I want to argue that all social contracts have a simple positive and logical foundation: government officials repeatedly write and rewrite these contracts to advance their own interests. They do not protect property and other individual rights because they have a "natural" vocation or duty to do so, or because the "people," in whatever sense of the word, have delegated this role to them. They protect property and other individual rights because protecting such rights helps them obtain the political and economic support that is necessary for the maintenance of their governments.

The people of the American colonies did not gather one day to write a Constitution.[13] Fifty-five persons gathered one day to write the Constitution. The exact motivations of the authors of the Constitution are unimportant here.[14] What is important is that the inclusion of a Bill of Rights in the Constitution was by no means a top priority for the Constitution's authors. The idea was introduced very late and was *rejected* by a vote of 10 to 0 (with Massachusetts absent) after a brief debate (*The Records of the Federal Convention* of 1787, vol. 2: 582–9). The Bill of Rights was added to the Constitution to make it attractive enough to the *opponents* of the Constitution. In an effort to gain the support of a majority in the Massachusetts' state convention, the Federalists promised that the first Congress would amend the Constitution to include a Bill of Rights. This tactic was repeated in other conventions including those of Virginia and New York (Aldrich et. al., 1986: 40, 61). Based on this promise, the first Congress amended the Constitution to include the Bill.

This American example illustrates an important point: to claim that governments pursue their own interests does not imply that they are insensitive to the interests of their constituencies. Modern legislators can secure the stream of benefits to which their public office entitles them only if they can secure their reelection. To secure their reelection, they usually have to be sensitive to the interests of their constituencies. In general, pursuing their own interests, governments often serve the interests of their citizens as well. The Federalists gave in to pressure from the colonies to include the Bill of Rights and obtained, in return, support for the Constitution.[15]

Governments obtain their monopoly over power in so many ways. Yet, once they obtain this monopoly, they constantly write and rewrite the social contract, in order to maintain it, by gaining support for new policies, reelection, and more direct benefits. With the enactment of every law, the government commits itself to enforce this law at whatever cost required.

Every government, democratic or totalitarian, depends on popular support. The latter type of government obtains the support of a small minority and uses this minority to oppress the rest of the subjects, the

---

[13] I owe much of the content of the following two paragraphs to a series of conversations with the late William H. Riker.

[14] For a remarkable account of this issue, see Riker (1995).

[15] It is of some interest to notice that the Bill of Rights that was finally included in the Constitution included only three of the nine basic rights that the Federalists in Massachusetts promised the Anti-Federalists they would include in the final Bill – the first, the sixth, and probably the eighth (cf. *The Documentary History of the Ratification of the Constitution*, vol. XVI: 67–9; Aldrich et al.: A9–A10). This is not surprising. An examination of the basic rights that were proposed by the different conventions demonstrates the parochial and local interests involved. The final Bill of Rights included only those "basic rights" which were important to enough delegates and did not alienate too many others.

former distributes rights more equally. But any government must grant rights to obtain the support it needs to remain in power. Governments are not benevolent actors who get their authority, by delegation, from the people. They are rational entrepreneurs who produce law and order in return for political and economic benefits. Property and other individual rights are not deduced from ethical imperatives; they are granted by governments to their constituents if those constituents are willing to pay a price for their institution and protection. Individual citizens are not passive entities in "moral" orders. They are active agents in a human world who bargain with their governments over the creation of institutions that would grant them, and protect *for* them, the rights they desire.

Social contracts evolve through repeated interactions between government officials that control the use of coercive force and individual agents that challenge this control. The former constantly write and rewrite the contract to serve their most selfish needs, while the latter constantly petition government to change it to serve their interests. This continuous interaction between government officials and more or less active citizens yields a social contract that defines the legal position of each individual in society and the extent to which governments are committed to protect and enforce property and other individual rights that are specified by this social contract.

There is nothing natural, or particularly ethical in property rights as such. Property rights emerge because they serve tangible interests of particular individuals. Such rights cannot emerge or persist unless they serve, directly or indirectly, the interests of central authorities that pay a remarkable cost to protect and enforce them.

This leads me to a new interpretation of the concept of the social contract. The essence of a social contract is not a delegation of authority by individuals to a central entity so that this entity becomes the guardian of their "natural" rights. Social contracts evolve when governments grant rights to their constituents, in return for political and economic support. Social contracts are bargained agreements between citizens and governments over the rights that governments are expected to protect for the welfare of their citizens, in return for the political and economic support given by the citizens to their governments.

This book looks for the origin of property rights in such bargained agreements. For too many years, the theoretical study of the emergence and evolution of property rights was made within somewhat abstract, often too normative, theoretical frameworks. In this book I try to break away from this tradition and provide a more specific account of how property rights emerge and evolve, in the bargaining process between governments and citizens, that structures the social contract by which they all abide.

While this is only a first step, it is made with the conviction that institutions that grant and protect property rights are designed by human beings, not by nature, and not by market forces, nor can they be derived from any set of moral axioms. It is therefore somewhat urgent that we begin to study how exactly such institutions are designed, so that, maybe, in some foreseeable future, we will know how to design them better.

2

Neo-classical theories of the origin of property rights: non-strategic individuals in a world without politics

Introduction

The interest of economists in the origin of property rights was renewed following the publication of Coase's Theorem (1960). Coase demonstrated that if property rights are well defined then, in the absence of transaction costs, the efficiency of production and resource allocations for production are not affected by the initial distribution of property rights. This Theorem directed the attention of economists to the study of the origin of property rights.

This chapter surveys some of the literature that resulted from this renewed interest in the origin of property rights. I point to three flaws in this literature. First, economic models tend to ignore political aspects of market interactions (Riker, 1990; Riker and Sened, 1991). Economists acknowledge that a structure of well defined property rights is a necessary condition for the prosperity of free markets (Stigler, 1942: 22). Yet, they

> relegate the role of governments to the background in order to concentrate on the price mechanism as the main mechanism of coordination among rational actors in the marketplace

and systematically overlook the role of law enforcement, or the mechanism of "coordination through authority" (Demsetz, 1982: 6–9).

Second, most neo-classical models fail to recognize the distinction between the *performance* and the *structure* of an economy (North, 1981). They usually assume, or imply, that the performance of the economy determines its structure, and that market forces eventually lead to the implementation of efficient political structures. I argue that there are no theoretical or empirical grounds to support these common claims.

33

Finally, neo-classical theories of the origin of property rights systemati-cally overlook the strategic aspects of interactions among agents. Using cooperative game theory as their main analytical tool, these theories focus on predicting outcomes of complex social interactions without carefully analyzing the strategic behavior of the agents involved.

As in chapter 1, this chapter is not intended to be a comprehensive survey of the neo-classical literature on the origin of property rights (for an excellent survey, see Eggertsson, 1990). I discuss this literature in order to highlight its strengths and weaknesses and provide the necessary back-ground for my argument in the subsequent chapters.

Demsetz's neo-classical theory of the origin of property rights

One of the most influential neo-classical theory of the emergence of property rights is due to Harold Demsetz (1964, 1967, 1969, 1972).[1] Demsetz's argument begins with the observation that some goods have no market price, either because the good is not scarce enough to be valuable, or because the costs of enforcement activities aimed at creating exclusive property rights, by excluding all but right-holders from using the good, are too high. That is, the marginal benefits from trading the goods are not high enough to offset the cost of enforcing property rights over these goods (Anderson and Hill, 1975).

Technological and other economic developments affect the values of goods. A significant increase in the demand for a good, or a technological innovation that significantly reduces the cost of producing the good, may make it worthwhile to protect exclusive property rights of producers and buyers. The cost of protecting such rights becomes less than the marginal value of the right to producers and buyers. Once a good becomes so valuable, property rights emerge in order to protect owners, sellers, buyers, and producers of the good.[2]

In an interesting sense, Demsetz's theory is a variation on the traditional theory of natural rights, inasmuch as Demsetz's argument rests on the claim that as soon as a good becomes valuable, property rights "naturally" emerge to protect the value of this good. In a sense, this is the ultimate theory of natural rights: traditional proponents of natural rights theories, like Locke, delegated to the government the role of the guardian of rights. So, they acknowledged that a comprehensive theory of rights must include a theory

---

[1] The most comprehensive example of this approach is probably found in Barzel (1989). See also Eggertsson (1990, part IV).

[2] A formal model of Demsetz's argument is found in Anderson and Hill (1975). For a brief discussion of this and related models see Eggertsson (1990: 247–62).

of government. Demsetz's argument does not assign any role for governments in the evolution and maintenance of property rights.

Unlike traditional natural rights theories, however, Demsetz's theory does not rely on normative arguments. Instead, Demsetz adheres to the Hobbesian position that rights are natural inasmuch as humans have a natural inclination to try to protect them. It is surprising that Demsetz failed to recognize the consequences of his argument. If humans have a natural inclination to protect, for *themselves*, property rights over valuable goods, conflict between individual interests is bound to arise. A theory of the evolution of property rights must explain not only how this conflict arises, but how it is resolved, because prior to such resolution property rights are not established in any meaningful sense.

The crucial weakness of Demsetz's argument is that it does not provide a theory of the emergence of property rights. His theory only explains why property rights become valuable (Buchanan, 1975: 22–3). Demsetz (1967: 350) points at two conditions that render property rights valuable: *scarcity* and the need to *internalize externalities*. Demsetz relies on the most common premises of neo-classical economic theory. If a certain good is not scarce, it has no market value and any property rights that protect the trade of this good in the market are worthless. Externalities are costs or benefits associated with the production or consumption of goods that affect agents in the market without their consent. Air and water pollution are examples of negative externalities that result from different production processes. "Second hand smoking" is commonly used as an example of a negative externality associated with consumption. Externalities bring consumers to buy too much, or too little, of the good produced. For example, men and women buy too many cigarettes because they ignore the costs associated with the damage cigarettes cause to their health. Meanwhile, other agents in the environment of the market pay the cost of negative externalities without enjoying any benefits from the good produced. An example is the cost of the health hazards associated with "second hand smoking," paid by bystanders when others smoke in their presence. Secure and enforceable property rights can eliminate the economic inefficiencies that result from the presence of externalities associated with the production or consumption of different goods (Weimer and Vining, 1989: 56).

Demsetz fails to distinguish between the *performance* of the economy and the political *structure* that allows it to perform. He overlooks the distinction between the content of property rights and the structure that protects property rights. The former can be properly exchanged in the market only if the latter are well defined. As Umbeck (1981) notes, protection of property rights is not an economic good like cattle and corn. Stable property rights require enforcement agencies with a monopoly in the production of extreme means of violence which allows them to (threaten to) use force when duty-bearers show disrespect for right-holders' claims over the content of the right (Umbeck, 1981: 9). Until we explain the role of these agencies – which, in western democracies, are usually identified with central governments – in the evolution of rights, we cannot pretend to have a theory of the origin of rights. The omission of central governments from the analysis is crucial because, as North (1981: 20) emphasized, the state seems to be, at the same time, "essential for economic growth" and "the source of man-made decline."

Many fail to understand the devastating implications of North's criticism for Demsetz's theory of rights. North's analysis, in his *Structure and Change in Economic History* (1981) and subsequent works on the role of the state in the evolution of political structures that define and protect property rights, shows that scarcity and the need to internalize externalities, or reduce transaction costs, is neither necessary nor sufficient for the emergence of property rights (North, 1990; Riker and Sened, 1991). If Demsetz's conditions were sufficient for the emergence of property rights, we would expect more uniformity across societies in the evolution of institutions that protect property rights. If these conditions were necessary it is hard to explain how man-made rules led to decline of economies throughout history (North 1981: 20).

Demsetz's work established the importance of scarcity and the incentive to internalize externalities in the process that leads to the emergence of property rights. But as a theory of the evolution of property rights it is not satisfactory, because it does not account for the role of central governments and other political institutions in this process (Furubotn and Pejovich, 1972; Eggertsson, 1990; North, 1990; Riker and Sened, 1991). In the following section I discuss two attempts to incorporate central enforcement agencies into neo-classical theories of the origin and evolution of property rights (for a complementary survey see Eggertsson, 1990: 247–9, 317–58).

Neo-classical theories of the social contract and the state

One attempt to incorporate the role of enforcement agencies in a neo-classical model of property rights is Umbeck's *Theory of Property Rights* (1981). The starting point of Umbeck's argument is a production function with two input factors: *productive work* and *violence*. In the absence of property rights, violence is used as a means to appropriate property. According to standard economic theory, individuals would use a mix of violence and productive labor to maximize their benefits. Assuming equal skills and technology across individuals, all the members of any primitive society would use the same amount of violence. A stable equilibrium will occur when no one stands to gain any extra property by using violence.[3] Yet, if we allow for free entry, all economic benefits will dissipate in equilibrium. If entry is costless, the influx of new entrants will stop only when there are no economic gains left to be made.

Umbeck uses this model to develop a theory of the emergence of property rights: when individuals observe the dissipation of their economic gains, they realize the advantages of a contract that acknowledges the rights of members, and establish a central enforcement agency that serves as a *barrier of entry* by increasing the amount of violence that new entrants must use to obtain access. Enforcement agencies take advantage of economies of scale in the production of force in order to scare away new entrants and allow members of society to concentrate on productive work (Umbeck, 1981: 22–8).

Umbeck confuses the emergence of governments with the emergence of rights. Umbeck really provides us with a theory of the emergence of law enforcing governments in response to external threats.[4] He tells us little about why such governments respect the rights of their individual subjects. Umbeck's confusion is illustrated in his own comment (1981: 136, n. 26):

> Demsetz is the only modern economist to address the question of how private property emerges . . . other writers have chosen to explain the emergence of . . . the "state" . . . because they view the "state" as the agency that establishes private property . . . I have been unable to identify . . . in the literature any distinguishing feature of the state that would allow me to separate state and nonstate . . . the closest I can come to identifying the state would be an institution that is created by specific contractual stipulations for the purpose of enforcing existing agreements between individuals. The state is formed out of the original contract to act as a "third party" in all disputes arising over the enforcement of individual rights. This is nothing more than a restatement of . . . the social contract theory presented by Hobbes and Rousseau.

The distinguishing feature of the state, that allows us to "separate state and nonstate" is the monopoly the state guards for itself to use coercive force to enforce the law, including property rights, as it sees fit (Weber, 1958). What Umbeck and other social contract theorists overlook is that once the state's enforcement agency is installed, there is usually nothing to stop it from using its monopoly over the use of force against those that have

---

[3] This would be true even if we relaxed the assumption of equal skills, only that the resulting division of property will be unequal as well.

[4] In this respect it is interesting to compare Umbeck's argument to Riker's theory of the origin of federalism as he develops it in his *Federalism: Origin, Operation, Significance* (1964) and more recently, Olson's theory of "Dictatorship, Democracy, and Development" (1993).

installed it.[5] To explain the evolution of rights we must explain why such enforcement agencies continue to enforce property rights by threatening to use violence against offenders, instead of using their force to take away the very property they were installed to protect (Olson, 1993).

Umbeck (1981: 24–5) specifies two necessary conditions for the emergence of social contracts: economies of scale in the production of violence and an advantage to a first holder of a property. Both conditions have little to do with the evolution of rights and everything to do with the ability of the state's law enforcement agencies to maintain their monopoly over the use of coercive force in protecting such rights.

For our purposes, Umbeck's contribution lies in his observation that rights can only be secured if some agents have a monopoly over the use of coercive force in the enforcement of law and order (Olson, 1993). This monopoly depends on the existence of economies of scale in the relevant range of technologies of law enforcement. Economies of scale and the advantages governments have over contenders, inasmuch as they often assume the role of "the first holder," prevent competing groups from entering the market of protecting rights.[6] Umbeck (1981) correctly points out that without an agency with a monopoly over the use of force, the benefits from establishing property rights would dissipate. The competition among enforcement agencies would erode all such potential benefits.

Specifying conditions under which an agency can maintain some level of monopoly over the use of coercive force, however, does not constitute a theory of the evolution of property rights. A theory of the origin of property rights must specify the conditions under which such agencies would use their monopoly to grant and protect private property and related individual rights in the polity. If Umbeck's argument was aimed at explaining the emergence of property rights only in "stateless societies," then the question arises whether Umbeck's theory could generalize to many cases of "stateless societies"? There is no doubt that some basic institutions, such as social

---

[5] This may not have been the case during the gold rush in California in the middle of the nineteenth century. Umbeck's description of this environment suggests that the means of violent enforcement remained in the hands of the gold miners. I agree with Umbeck's thesis that "property rights are established and maintained through the use or threat of violence" (1981: 101). Yet, I believe that Umbeck's empirical work is more relevant to the study of federalism (e.g. Riker, 1964) or international relations, where agreements among equal players are studied (observed), than to the study of property rights and law enforcement where, usually, only a very limited group of players has any access to the means of production of extreme forms of violence.

[6] Note that if one argues that the production of violence is a natural monopoly – i.e. that returns to scale are increasing (marginal costs are decreasing) in the relevant range, the second condition would be unnecessary or redundant. Since the appearance of the national state as the main producer of violent means of law enforcement, one could argue that the production of warfare and other extreme means of violence is a natural monopoly.

norms and conventions, emerge spontaneously as equilibria in complex social games. History provides many examples of property rights institutions emerging spontaneously to resolve local disputes over scarce resources (Olson, 1993: 567–8; Eggertsson, 1990: 247–316). Yet, the following quote from Bates' *Essays on the Political Economy of Rural Africa* (1983: 20) neatly summarizes the state of existing empirical evidence for the emergence of property rights' institutions in stateless societies:

> recent scholarship has argued that too much emphasis has been placed upon decentralized systems. On the one hand, their occurrence appears to be relatively infrequent; on the other, even in so far as decentralized societies do exist, they can arguably be regarded as transitory – as societies which once were centralized or which are in the early stages of a movement toward more centralized forms.

Relying on this and numerous other studies, Eggertsson concludes that "the institutional equilibrium of stateless societies has, in most cases eventually given way, and the state in its various forms has emerged" (1990: 305).

There are good reasons to expect that this should be the case. As Knight (1992) argues, informal institutions are constantly put under distributional pressures. Informal institutions, without central enforcement agencies, are unlikely to stand up to such pressures. Eventually, such institutions lead to instability, collapse of law and order or, more likely, powerful agents taking control of the institutional structure that protects private property and related individual rights (Olson, 1993).

North (1993) added an interesting argument for why developed societies must rely on formal institutions of property rights. He argues that the task of coordinating the economic activities of numerous economic agents in developed economies, characterized by remarkable interdependence among very specialized participants, can only be orchestrated by central governments. North reasons that only centralized governments can provide the necessary structure of property rights and special incentives to guarantee economic growth in societies that rely so heavily on precise information and sophisticated technological innovations.

Buchanan and Tullock's *The Calculus of Consent* (1962) offers another version of the neo-classical social contract theory. The central premise in this and related works is that rational individuals, when confronted with choices regarding the regulation of social interactions, act to minimize the expected costs, or to maximize the expected utility from social interactions (Buchanan and Tullock, 1962: 49–62).

Buchanan and Tullock distinguish among three types of costs. Let c_i denote the cost of making activity i subject to collective decision making; b_i denotes the cost of individual contracting and a_i denotes the cost of leaving activity i to the voluntary, uncoordinated, decisions of individuals in society. If $a_i < b_i \leq c_i$, or $a_i < c_i \leq b_i$, individuals would leave the activity subject to voluntary decisions; if $b_i < a_i \leq c_i$, or $b_i < c_i \leq a_i$, they prefer individual contracting, or relying on the market mechanism, but if $c_i < a_i \leq b_i$, or $c_i < b_i \leq a_i$, they prefer to sign a "social contract," or, as the authors call it, choose "at the time of the ultimate constitutional decision" (1962: 57) to leave that activity subject to collective decision making mechanisms.

Like most of the models surveyed above, this approach fails to consider the strategic behavior of individuals when they are confronted with decisions that involve other agents as well. Yet, Buchanan and Tullock use sufficiently rigorous, logical arguments to allow a more precise critique.

In a more recent publication, Buchanan (1975) uses the prisoners' dilemma to illustrate the underlying argument. The general characterization of the prisoners' dilemma as a two-person game in normal form is given in table 2.1.

Table 2.2 is a numerical example of the two-person game in normal form summarized in table 2.1 (it duplicates table 1.1 from chapter 1). Recall that each player can choose between two strategies: cooperate (C) and respect the right of the other player; or defect (D) from cooperation. The numbers in the cells indicate the utility each player gets from any possible combination of strategies chosen, simultaneously, by the two players.

I have shown in chapter 1 that, regardless of what the other player does, each player is better off defecting than cooperating. Our prediction is, thus, that both players would defect, failing to respect each other's rights. I explained in chapter 1 the Nash equilibrium solution concept, behind the prediction that both players will defect (Nash, 1950b). A Nash equilibrium is a vector of strategies that satisfies the property that no player can get a higher utility, given the strategies chosen by all the other players, by unilaterally altering his or her strategic choice (for precise formal definitions see the appendix to this chapter, p. 53). Recall that the only Nash equilibrium in table 2.2 is one in which both players defect.

Buchanan (1975: 27) uses the prisoners' dilemma as a model for the analysis of the emergence of property rights. The prisoners' dilemma is often used to characterize such social interactions (Axelrod, 1980a, 1981, 1984; Schotter, 1981; Hardin, 1982) for reasons that will become apparent as I develop my argument in this and subsequent chapters. I agree with Buchanan's choice of the game to characterize the problem, but disagree with his choice of solution concept to predict the outcome of this game.

Recall that if we adhere to a non-cooperative game theoretical framework, then the two most striking characteristics of the prisoners' dilemma game are:

Table 2.1. *Two-person prisoners' dilemma*

Players		Player 2	
	Strategies	Cooperate (C)	Defect (D)
Player 1	Cooperate (C)	R,R	S,T
	Defect (D)	T,S	P,P

Where $T > R > P > S$ and $R > (T+S)/2$.

Table 2.2. *Two-person prisoners' dilemma*

Players		Player 2	
	Strategies	Cooperate (C)	Defect (D)
Player 1	Cooperate (C)	$1,1$	$-1,2$
	Defect (D)	$2,-1$	$0,0$

1. It has a unique (dominant strategy) Nash equilibrium: this means that we have a unique prediction according to which the outcome of the game will be one in which both players defect and fail to respect the rights of each other.
2. This equilibrium is *Pareto inferior*,[7] i.e., players prefer the outcome (C,C) to the outcome they end up with (D,D), which is what the "dilemma" is all about.

Buchanan uses the cooperative solution concept of the *core*. The *core* of the game described in table 2.2 is the one in which both players cooperate, (C,C).

This example demonstrates the difference between the cooperative and non-cooperative game theoretic approaches to the study of institutions in general, and to the study of the emergence and evolution of property rights in particular. As we demonstrated above, the prisoners' dilemma has a *unique Pareto inferior Nash equilibrium and a unique Pareto optimal core.* Roth (1979: 20, n. 1) draws a clear distinction between the two analytical frameworks (I explain these concepts in detail in the appendix to this chapter, pp. 50–3):

---

[7] An outcome *o* is Pareto optimal if there is no outcome *o'* so that all players weakly prefer *o'* to *o*, and at least one player strictly prefers *o'* to *o*. It is Pareto inferior if it is not Pareto optimal.

> A non-cooperative game . . . consists of a set of players $N = \{1,\ldots,n\}$, a collection of strategy sets, $\sigma_1,\ldots,\sigma_n$ and a payoff function $\Pi: \sigma_1 X, \ldots, X\sigma_n \Rightarrow R^n$. The interpretation is that each player chooses an element of his strategy set, and the resulting n-tuple of strategy choices determines the outcome of the game . . . a game is considered non-cooperative if players must make their choices independently, without being able to conclude a prior binding agreement, while a game is [considered to be] cooperative if the players can conclude a [prior] binding agreement as to what outcome should be chosen. Consequently, cooperative games . . . [are] not described in strategic form, which emphasizes the individual choices of the players, but . . . by the set of outcomes which each coalition of players may potentially agree on.

Thus, the cooperative game theoretic approach is ill-suited to explain the emergence of institutions because it presupposes the existence of an enforcement mechanism, which is in and of itself an institution. Without pre-existing enforcement mechanisms, it is hard to see why players involved in a prisoners' dilemma game would stick to the optimal strategy combination of (C,C), as Buchanan argued. If individuals maximize utility, each individual player should defect, as our earlier analysis makes clear. This is why Taylor (1987: 15) asserts so strongly that: "The prisoners' dilemma is defined to be *non-cooperative*. If it were not, there would be no 'dilemma.'"

A second disadvantage of using cooperative game theory as an analytical framework for the study of the origin and evolution of institutions is that it does not help us understand the strategic interactions among players, because the strategic behavior of individual players is never explicitly analyzed.

Economists tend to underestimate the consequences of their choice between these two analytical frameworks. Eggertsson (1990: 287) noted recently that

> the conflicting conclusions of political scientists, anthropologists and economists regarding the institutions of primitive society sometimes remind the impartial reader of the story of the five blind men and the elephant.

This conflict is due, in part, to the choice of analytical frameworks. Cooperative game theory, as a central tool of neo-classical economics, assumes the pre-existence of mechanisms that ensure that agreements among individuals are binding. But this is precisely the role of property rights' institutions. Cooperative game theory is, therefore, ill-suited to explain the origin of such institutions. We can rely on cooperative game theory when we analyze systems with existing property rights' institutions, and with enough sellers and buyers to render the strategic behavior of sellers and buyers inconsequential. But in a study of the origin of institutions in general, and the behavior of law enforcement agencies in crafting and enforcing institutions that protect property rights in particular, we cannot ignore the strategic behavior of the individuals that control and manipulate them.

One can almost draw the dividing line of specialization that separates modern political science from neo-classical economics along the line that distinguishes between cooperative and non-cooperative game theory. As expected, the growing field of political economy tends to vacillate between the two analytical frameworks. The former is better suited to analyze more or less competitive markets where the forces of the market are more important than the strategic behavior of individual agents. The latter is better suited for the study of imperfect political markets, where the strategic behavior of a single player may make all the difference in the world (e.g. Riker, 1995).

To conclude, while Umbeck offers an interesting theory of the emergence of governments, he advances us very little towards a theory of the evolution of property rights. While Buchanan suggests a powerful model for the study of the origin of property rights, there are strong grounds to claim that he chose the wrong analytical framework to analyze the implications of this model. Both authors overlook the strategic behavior of rational players in this type of social situation.[8] To overlook the strategic aspect of interactions between free agents seems to be inconsistent with the assumptions of methodological individualism and rational behavior of utility maximizing individuals, to which both authors are committed (Feddersen et al., 1990).

One important conclusion from this discussion is that a radical change in methodology is required in order to clarify the essence of the political institution of private property and related individual rights. In chapter 3 I explore such a new tool, building on contemporary theory of institutions as it has developed in the last two decades (Sened, 1991).

North's theory of institutions and institutional change

Probably the most influential paradigm on the topic of the origin and evolution of property rights is the *transaction costs' paradigm*. Transaction costs are "the costs associated with the transfer, capture, and protection of rights" (Barzel, 1989: 2). The transaction costs' paradigm is based on the premise that property rights emerge and evolve in response to changes in

---

[8] Nozick (1975) makes a similar attempt to rely on a cooperative solution concept and the notion of economies of scale to explain the emergence of the 'minimal state' as a 'protective association' that is basically a coalition of individuals that provides protection of property rights to its members. Schotter (1981: 45–51) makes an interesting attempt to translate Nozick's argument into the formal language of cooperative game theory.

relative costs of transfer, capture and protection of property rights. Barzel (1989: 31), for example, argues that

> [w]hen transacting is costly, . . ., all contract forms are costly; and in that case sharing may be chosen . . . [not only] for its effect on risk but also because of some properties of transaction costs.

Barzel (1989) offers many such transaction costs hypotheses to explain different types of organizations associated with different structures of property rights in society.

One of the most influential and articulate spokespersons of this paradigm is Douglass North. Much of North's recent work is dedicated to the study of ways in which political institutions, limits of human knowledge, enforcement mechanisms, conflicting interests, and major economic entrepreneurs, may stand in the way of economic growth in general, and efficient property rights' institutions in particular. In *Institutions, Institutional Change and Economic Performance* (1990: 7), he explains how his theory emerged and distinguishes himself from the transaction costs' paradigm:

> In North and Thomas (1973) we made institutions the determinant of economic performance and relative price changes the source of institutional change. But we had an essentially efficient explanation; changes in relative prices create incentives to construct more efficient institutions . . . In *Structure and Change in Economic History* (North, 1981) I abandoned the efficiency view of institutions. Rulers devised property rights in their own interests and transaction costs resulted in typically inefficient property rights prevailing. As a result it was possible to account for the widespread existence of property rights throughout history and in the present that did not produce economic growth . . . It was possible to explain the existence of inefficient institutions, but why wouldn't competitive pressures lead to their elimination? Wouldn't the political entrepreneurs in stagnant economies quickly emulate the policies of more successful ones? . . . The answer hinges on the difference between institutions and organizations and the interaction between them that shapes the direction of institutional change. Institutions, together with the standard constraints of economic theory, determine the opportunities in society. Organizations are created to take advantage of those opportunities, and as the organizations evolve they alter the institutions. The resultant path of institutional change is shaped by (1) the lock-in that comes from the symbiotic relationship between institutions and the organizations that have evolved as a consequence of the incentive structure provided by these institutions and (2) the feedback process by which human beings perceive and react to changes in the opportunity set.

Talking more specifically about property rights, North argues (1990: 51):

as a first approximation we can say that property rights will be developed over resources and assets as a simple cost-benefit calculus of the cost of devising and enforcing such rights, as compared to the alternative under the status quo. Changes in relative prices or relative scarcities of any kind lead to the creation of property rights when it becomes worthwhile to incur the costs of devising such rights.

A major criticism of the transaction costs' argument is that it could lead to the unwarranted conclusion that property rights are simply a function of the relative costs and benefits of transfer, capture, and protection of property rights. The awareness of this problem distinguishes North's work from the mainstream transaction costs' literature (e.g. Barzel, 1989; Williamson, 1975, 1985; cf. North, 1990: 54, n. 1; Knight, 1992: 32–3). Eggertsson (1990: 248) notes that: "In fact, the [transaction costs'] approach suggests a macro version of Coase's law" (italics in the original):

> *The economic growth and development of a country are basically unaffected by the type of government it has, if the cost of transacting in both the political and economic spheres is zero. However, when transaction costs are positive, the distribution of political power within a country and institutional structure of its rule-making institutions are critical factors in economic development.*

This statement raises two risks: first, there is a risk of trivializing the analysis of the political game involved. Second, there is a temptation to expect efficient property rights' institutions in environments that seem to meet the condition of low transaction costs. In his work, North is sensitive to these dangers (1990: 52):

> In North (1981), I revised the 1973 argument to account for the obvious persistence of inefficient property rights. These inefficiencies existed because rulers would not antagonize powerful constituents by enacting efficient rules that were opposed to their interests or because the costs of monitoring, metering, and collecting taxes might very well lead to a situation in which less efficient property rights yielded more tax revenue than efficient property rights.

North acknowledges the non-trivial nature of how politics determines the structure of the institutional build up that protects property rights and uses it to explain the persistence of inefficient property rights in environments where transaction costs seem to play a lesser role.

The most comprehensive critique of North's argument, to date, is found in Knight's *Institutions and Social Conflict* (1992). Knight's criticism of North's and other transaction costs' theories of institutional evolution in general is that they put too much weight on the claim that "[i]nstitutions exist to reduce the uncertainties involved in human interactions" (North 1990: 25). Knight argues that political and economic institutions emerge out of a bargaining process among asymmetrically powerful agents, with conflicting political and economic interests. Institutions have far reaching distributional consequences that have little to do with reducing transaction costs or different types of uncertainties (Knight 1992: 33):

> Here we arrive at the crux of the problem for explanations based on minimizing transaction costs or, for that matter, on maximizing social efficiency more generally. The possibility of a conflict between individual and collective interests is, contrary to North and the other transaction costs theorists, much more widespread than are instances of state involvement . . . The theoretical problem is what becomes of social efficiency when actors have conflicting interests.

The transaction costs' analytical framework suggests that efficient institutions will eventually supersede less efficient ones. Knight argues that social agents may prefer inefficient institutions if such institutions ensure higher payoffs to some of the agents involved (1992: 33–34).

Recent research clearly shows that if we allow individual preferences to play a role in institutional choice, and most modern constitutions do, then all we can hope for are short-term, inefficient, institutional arrangements that soon fall victim to the inherent instability of human preferences over institutional outcomes (Riker, 1980; see the discussion in chapter 3).

One reason to qualify this bleak prediction is that institutional structures induce stability (Shepsle and Weingast, 1981; Shepsle, 1986), and are often much harder to change than Riker believed (North, 1993). But it is still necessary to demonstrate that institutional structures that induce stability reduce transaction costs. In one sense they do so, inasmuch as they reduce uncertainties regarding social outcomes. But at what cost? Are transaction costs' theorists willing to argue that here, too, the simple cost-benefit calculus will determine the final result, making political actors prefer stability inducing institutions only if the net benefit from stability is greater than the cost of such institutions? North suggests that this is not the case (1990: 6):

> The major role of institutions in society is to reduce uncertainty by establishing a stable (but not necessarily efficient) structure to human interaction.

How, then, is the conflict between efficiency and stability resolved? What is the main force behind institutional change? Is it risk aversion that makes social agents prefer stable institutions? Is it efficiency that motivates them, or distributional considerations (Knight, 1992: 126–51)? Transaction costs' theorists seem to implicitly assume that institutions that reduce instability automatically reduce transaction costs, thereby inducing efficiency.

An interesting counter-example to the implicit assumption that stability inducing institutions enhance efficiency is the US insurance industry in general, and the institutional structure of the health care sector, in particular. The health care system in the USA is dominated by strong insurance companies and some powerful interest groups, including the American Medical Association. This domination is due to inelastic demand curves – our well known willingness to pay any price necessary to reduce any uncertainty about our health – and the lack of public information about medicine (Phelps, 1992). The institutional structure of the health care sector exemplifies a set of institutions that emerged to reduce uncertainty and provide important information to consumers. It is well known that this stable institutional structure oversees one of the most inefficient health care systems in the western world (Hollingworth and Hanneman, 1990: 147).[9]

Transaction costs' theories of the origin and evolution of rights overlook a crucial piece of the puzzle: the game of politics. There are two separate issues here, one is simple and well known: "a theory of property rights, cannot be truly complete without a theory of the state" (Furubotn and Pejovich, 1972: 1140). North advanced the transaction costs' theory to recognize the importance of political structures but, so far, has fallen short of complementing it with a theory of the state.

The second issue goes back to methodology and the line that separates economics from political science, to which I referred above. The following citation will help clarify the problem (North, 1990: 52):

> The efficiency of the political market is the key to this issue. If political transaction costs are low and the political actors have accurate models to guide them, then efficient property rights will result. But the high transaction costs of political markets and subjective perceptions of the actors more often have resulted in property rights that do not induce economic growth.

As Knight (1992) argues, more often than not the political game is not about reduction of transaction costs or the identification of the "accurate" models of property rights that may induce economic growth. The political game is played between unequal players, who worry more about distributional consequences and conflicting interests than they worry about social or any other kind of efficiency. This complex bargaining process may or may not result in an efficient institutional structure of property rights, but we will not know the answer to this question until we analyze it explicitly using the appropriate analytical tools.

North has brought neo-classical economic theory as close to a general theory of institutions and institutional change as anyone. Still, I argue that North leaves us with one missing element: the game of politics. I dedicate

[9] For a colorful, popular account of this inefficiency, see Bogdanich (1991). For a scientifically comprehensive survey of the issue, see Phelps (1992). A comprehensive study of Britain, France, Sweden, and the USA is found in Hollingsworth et al. (1990).

the remainder of this book to the study of this one missing piece in North's puzzle. I specify the game of politics in as clear terms as I possibly can, and then solve it, in the hope of answering some central questions pertaining to the emergence and the evolution of institutional structures that protect property rights, which remained unanswered by the neo-classical transaction costs' theories.

I agree with North (1990: 7) that political

> institutions, together with the standard constraints of economic theory, determine the opportunities in society. [Economic] organizations are created to take advantage of those opportunities, and as the organizations evolve they alter the institutions.

The remainder of this book clarifies how this process works with respect to property and other individual rights, because this part of the puzzle is still largely misunderstood.

Concluding remarks: towards a political theory of property rights

The failure of neo-classical theories to develop adequate explanations from the emergence and evolution of property rights comes, primarily, from its tendency to overlook the distinction between structure and performance (North, 1981), and the tendency to disregard the former and overemphasize the role of the latter in the attempt to explain the emergence and persistence of property rights. A second weakness that characterizes the neo-classical literature on the origin of property rights is the failure to model explicitly the role of players with advantageous access to power and authority. As Demsetz (1982: 6–9) notes:

> . . . the neo-classical inquiry into decentralization retained the price system for study, setting aside considerations of the underlying system of law, [and] government . . . The legal system and the government were relegated to the distant background by . . . [assuming] that resources were "privately owned" . . . The model adds much to our understanding of coordination through price, nothing to our understanding of coordination through authority.

Neo-classical economists are not alone in their attempts to explain coordination among players without structures of authority. Buchanan (1986: 36–7) notices that:

> A major deficiency in the political–legal–social philosophy of the nineteenth and twentieth centuries has been the failure to . . . model the behavior of those persons who are empowered or authorized to act on behalf of the state or government. This failure has been far more pervasive than any like failure

to model what we may call "private man." The latter has often [been] modeled as *homo economicus* for the legitimate purpose of assisting in dialogues on law and reform. By contrast, "public man" has rarely been modeled at all, save implicitly as "saint."

Unlike previous works, this book is dedicated to the study of coordination through authority. It is an attempt to model "public men and women" – i.e. government officials – as utility maximizing individuals like all other agents in society. It is based on a premise that the existence of some form of government is necessary for any meaningful individual rights to emerge (Olson, 1993). Agents in society have beliefs about the conditions under which utility maximizing government officials will grant and protect private property and related individual rights. This allows them to calculate their strategic behavior and obtain the protection of such rights. A theory of property rights must describe the strategic behavior of individual agents of society *vis-à-vis* the institutions that characterize the polity in which they live. It must also allow us to predict under what conditions we would expect alterations in the institutional make up of society that protects private property and related individual rights.

From here on, my goal is to answer two separate questions: first, what type of institutional structures should we expect a government with a monopoly on the use of coercive force to implement in order to protect private property and related individual rights? Second, given these expectations from existing institutional arrangements, how would we expect individuals in society to behave? In the conclusion to this book I argue that my neo-liberal theory of the political institution of property rights, developed in chapters 4–6, is a sound, positive substitute for previous, normative attempts to develop a liberal theory of that sort. I believe that this success is due to my insistence on the crucial role of political institutions in promoting and securing individual rights. The challenge to which I respond was formulated by North (1990: 59):

> I conclude this analysis of enforcement by pointing out where it is taking us. Third-party enforcement means the development of the state as a coercive force able to monitor property rights and enforce contracts effectively, but no one at this stage in our knowledge knows how to create such an entity. Indeed, with a strictly wealth-maximizing behavioral assumption it is hard even to create such a model abstractly. Put simply, if the state has coercive force, then those who run the state will use that force in their own interest at the expense of the rest of the society.[10]

[10] The reader may find a previous debate on this same issue of great interest by comparing Ostrom (1971), Riker (1976), and North (1990: 59–60).

This book is dedicated to the construction of such an abstract model. When such a model is carefully constructed, it can explain why a state uses its coercive force to grant and protect private property and related individual rights rather than to rob its citizens of their assets.

Contemporary economic theory may have been chasing lofty goals. Political institutions that protect property rights, like other social institutions, are *not* constructed to satisfy some abstract normative requirements. They are constructed with real goals in mind. Agents anticipate future events and develop institutions to cope with such events. Such institutions are not "fair" in some abstract Kantian or Rawlsian sense. They are beneficial in the sense that they improve, *ex ante*, expected payoffs from anticipated events. To understand the origin of private property rights and other social institutions, we must point to the problems they were created to solve and to the strategic agents that designed them and not to abstract so-called "market forces" that have, at best, an indirect role to play in the origin and the design of political institutions that grant and protect private property and related individual rights.

In chapter 3 I build on contemporary political theory of institutions to specify a general, analytical framework for the study of political institutions. In chapter 4 I use this framework to specify a simple, formal model of the state. This game theoretic model allows me to study the essence of the relations between central governments and other agents in the polity. In subsequent chapters I extend this model to explore different types of interactions between individual agents in society and the state, as well as the role of economic and political entrepreneurs in these types of interactions.

The design of institutions has become a central interest of contemporary social sciences. Without a positive theory of the evolution of property rights, we are unlikely to be helpful in answering questions concerning the institutional design of social institutions that grant and protect such rights. For too long we have neglected the study of these *political* mechanisms, in favor of over simplified abstract models that bore little, if any, resemblance to the actual political structures that protect our most cherished possessions and rights. The purpose of this book is to start to remedy this situation by providing a more realistic theory of the state as a new baseline for the study of the institutional design of institutions that protect private property and related individual rights.

Appendix: cooperative and non-cooperative game theory

Social scientists have been using two main game theoretical frameworks to analyze political situations: cooperative and non-cooperative game theory. This appendix clarifies the concepts on which these theoretical frameworks are based.

The cooperative approach

The central concept in the cooperative game theoretic analytical approach is the concept of the *core*. To understand this concept let $u(o) = (u_1(o), \ldots, u_n(o))$ be a payoff n-tuple associated with outcome o. Let $u_i(o)$ be the payoff that player i receives from outcome o. Recall that N is the set of all the agents who participate in the game, and let C be a subset of N, often referred to as a *coalition*.

DEFINITION 2.1: A *characteristic function* of the coalition C, $v(C)$, is a collection of utility vectors, such that if C can guarantee to any i of its members at least $u_i(o)$ then $u(o)$ is in $v(C)$.

A *game in characteristic function* form is denoted by: $\Gamma = (v, N, U)$ where N is the set of players, v is the *characteristic function* (or correspondence) that assigns to every subset of players a vector of payoffs (or a set of vectors of payoffs) that this subset of players (or "coalition") can secure for its members, and U is the set of all feasible payoff n-tuples given the set of feasible outcomes O. Let $v(i)$ denote the payoff any player i can guarantee himself, or herself, by acting as a "coalition of one." Using these notations we can define the solution concept of the *core* (Ordeshook, 1986: 340–1):

DEFINITION 2.2: $u(o)$ dominates $u(o')$ with respect to C if $u(o)$ is in $v(C)$ (i.e. C can secure $u(o)$ to its members) and for any member i of C $u_i(o) > u_i(o')$. $u(o)$ dominates $u(o')$ if there exists a coalition C, such that $u(o)$ dominates $u(o')$ with respect to C.

DEFINITION 2.3: *The core of a game in characteristic-function form is the set of undominated payoff vectors in U.*

The core serves as a main underlying solution concept in the cooperative approach to a complex multi-person bargaining problem. The idea behind using the core as a basic solution concept is straightforward: we predict that if a core exists, it will be the outcome of the game, or the bargaining problem that was modeled by the game, precisely because it is "undominated" – i.e. no winning coalition can offer an outcome with higher payoffs to all its members than the core payoff distribution.

The major drawback of the cooperative game theoretic approach and the *core* solution concept is that they presuppose that players can reach agreements through costless communication and, even more troubling, they assume the existence of mechanisms that can successfully enforce these agreements (Binmore and Dasgupta, 1987: 5). This may be a perfectly good assumption to make in analyzing well regulated activities such as majority rule decisions in parliaments, or market interactions, when property rights are well defined. We know, however, that many political bargaining contexts do not have such obvious enforcement mechanisms. A central challenge in the analysis of the emergence of institutions that protect property rights is precisely that in this context one cannot assume the pre-existence of such enforcement mechanisms.

The second disadvantage of the cooperative game theoretic approach is that it does not help us understand the strategic interactions among players, because the strategic behavior of individual players is never explicitly analyzed.

The non-cooperative approach

The non-cooperative approach is supposed to provide remedies to both of these shortcomings of the cooperative approach. In the non-cooperative game theoretic approach, a game, Γ, is defined by three elements $\Gamma = \{N, \sigma, \Pi\}$. $N = \{1, \ldots, n\}$ is the set of players. σ is the strategy space, or all possible combination of strategic choices of the n players involved in the interaction studied. Each player, $i \in N$, has to choose a strategy σ_i, from his or her strategy set, σ_i, with $\sigma_i \in \sigma_i$.[11] σ is a Cartesian product, $\sigma = \sigma_1 X \ldots X \sigma_n$, that describes the set of all possible combinations of individual strategic choices by all the n players involved in the game. Finally, Π is a payoff function $\Pi: \sigma \Rightarrow R^n$ that assigns to each such combination (or vector) of strategic choices by all the individuals involved in the game a payoff vector that specifies the exact payoff that each player gets out of the outcome that results if this combination of strategic choices is chosen by the individual players in the game.

The idea behind the non-cooperative approach is that each player chooses a strategy out of his or her strategy set, so as to guarantee that the resulting n-tuple of strategy choices, that determines the outcome of the game, will yield the highest payoff s/he can hope for, given the set of players N, the strategy space σ, the payoff function, Π, and what s/he expects the strategic choices of other players to be. Unlike the cooperative approach, players must make their choices here independently, without being able to conclude prior binding agreements.

The commonly used solution concept in this approach was formalized by Nash (1950), and is known as the Nash equilibrium. To understand this solution concept, define a (pure) strategy as a rule specifying a single action that a player may choose out of the set of feasible actions at any possible instance in the game in which he or she may be called upon to

---

[11] We restrict our discussion to pure strategies. "Pure" strategies are distinguished from "mixed" strategies. Mixed strategies involve the use of different "pure" strategies by the same player at the same move, using some probabilistic procedure to choose which strategy is actually played at that move. At this stage, there is no need to fully understand this distinction.

act. We denote a strategy of a player i by σ_i and the set of feasible strategies for i by σ_i. σ is the Cartesian product of the strategy sets, known also as the strategy space, where $\sigma \in \sigma$ and $\sigma = (\sigma_1, \ldots, \sigma_n)$ is a strategy vector that specifies a particular strategy for every agent. Finally, let $\sigma_{-i} = (\sigma_1, \ldots, \sigma_{i-1}, \ldots, \sigma_{i+1}, \ldots, \sigma_n)$ denote the strategic choice of all agents except player i.

DEFINITION 2.4: The strategy vector σ^* is a Nash equilibrium if and only iff every player $i \in N$, $u_i(\sigma^*) \geq u_i(\sigma^*_{-i}, \sigma_i)$, for every $\sigma_i \in \sigma_i$.

That is, a Nash equilibrium strategy vector, σ^*, is a vector of strategies that specifies a strategy σ_i^* for each player $i \in N$. The payoff, $u_i(\sigma^*)$, that each player gets from the outcome that results from this combination of strategic choices is determined by the payoff function $\Pi: \sigma \Rightarrow R^n$. To be a Nash equilibrium strategy vector σ^* must have the property that, given the strategies of all the other players, σ^*_{-i}, no player can be made better off, i.e. get more than $u_i(\sigma^*)$, by unilaterally playing a different strategy, $\sigma_i \in \sigma_i$, $\sigma_i \neq \sigma_i^*$, than the strategy, σ_i^*, he chose to play in equilibrium.

The use of the Nash equilibrium solution concept, as a predictive concept, relies on a simple intuition. A combination of strategic choices constitutes a Nash equilibrium if and only if no player wants to alter his or her strategic choice of behavior, given the strategic choices of all the other players. We expect such combinations of strategic choices to be stable outcomes of the bargaining process precisely because no individual player in the political interaction has an incentive to change his or her behavior, as long as the other players stick to their strategies. Since this is true for all the players, we expect all players to stick to their choices.

The advantage of the non-cooperative approach is the detailed analysis that it allows us of the strategic choices of social agents. The main objection to this approach is that, more often than not, scientists must make arbitrary decisions on how to structure the game in terms of the strategy space and payoff function. One way to deal with this objection is to judge each model to see how true the formal model seems to be to the context it pretends to model. Non-cooperative models in political science must be judged not only on whether or not they provide us with the correct prediction, but also on the extent to which they model the environment of the problem studied in a way that mirrors accurately the different aspects of that problem.

3

A game theoretic approach: contemporary theory of institutions[1]

Introduction

A theory of institutions, often referred to as *new institutionalism*, is emerging from the combined efforts of students of the spatial theory of electoral competition (Shepsle, 1979, 1986), management of common-pool resources (Ostrom, 1990), the evolution of institutions (North, 1990; Knight, 1992; Knight and Sened, 1995), and contemporary game theory (Schotter, 1981; Sugden, 1986; Calvert, 1989, 1995; Sened, 1991).

In this chapter I explore the *negative* and *positive heuristics* of this new research program:[2] How should we define an institution? What are the puzzles that motivate this research (Kuhn, 1970)? What do practitioners in the field regard as interesting questions, and what do they accept as adequate answers?

What constitutes an adequate explanation for the origin of any institution? I need an answer to this general question before I endorse any

[1] I thank Jack Knight, Randall L. Calvert, and William H. Riker for lengthy discussions on the subject, and Elinor Ostrom for numerous useful comments on an earlier draft of this chapter that appeared in the *Journal of Theoretical Politics* (Sened, 1991).

[2] I use these terms in the sense that Lakatos uses them (1986: 47):

> [every research] programme consists of methodological rules: some tell us what paths of research to avoid (*negative heuristic*), and others what paths to pursue (*positive heuristic*)

to which he adds in a footnote (n. 1):

> One may point out that the *negative* and the *positive heuristic* gives a rough (implicit) definition of the "conceptual framework" (and consequently of the language).

explanation for the origin of institutions that protect property rights or any other individual rights. Otherwise, any explanation I may put forward will be ad hoc. The main argument of this chapter is that to explain the origin of an institution one must identify a decisive group of agents, able to impose its will on all of the relevant players, and a situation that this group of individuals anticipates, in which it expects to be better off with the institution than it would be without it.

The first section outlines some definitions and states a set of requirements that any attempt to explain the structure of any institution must satisfy. The second section uses these definitions to draw a sharp distinction between norms and conventions, on the one hand, and formal institutions, on the other. The next two sections discuss formal explanations for different institutions in two interrelated subfields of contemporary social sciences – spatial theory of electoral competition, and non-cooperative game theory. The fifth section compares and contrasts the two competing views – the spontaneous and the intentional approaches – to explanations of the origin and the evolution of institutions. I conclude with an outline of a positive approach to a deductive theory of institutions.

Some definitional comments

Little agreement exists on how the term "institution" should be defined (see Ostrom, 1986, for a comprehensive review). The following definition, suggested by Schotter (1981: 11), is often cited in the literature:

> A regularity R . . . in a recurrent situation G is an institution if [and only if] it is true . . . and common knowledge [to all agents] in N that (1) everyone conforms to R; (2) everyone expects everyone to conform to R; and (3) either everyone prefers to conform to R on the condition that [all] other [agents] do, in which case uniform conformity to R is a coordination equilibrium; or (4) if anyone ever deviates from R it is known that some or all of the others will also deviate and the payoffs associated with the recurrent play of G using these deviating strategies are worse for all agents than the payoff associated with R.[3]

There are several difficulties with this definition. First, it must not be common knowledge that all members of society conform to the rules. A weakened version of the second requirement in Schotter's definition above would read that it is sufficient that everyone "expects most agents to conform to R." Most of us respect each other's property rights even though there are thieves among us. In addition, it is not necessary that *all* agents realize lower payoffs than those associated with R, in any case of deviation.

---

[3] This definition is based on an earlier work by Lewis (1969: 42).

Suffice it that deviators realize lower payoffs than those associated with R.

More troubling is the similarity of this definition to the notion of equilibrium. This is a common difficulty in the study of institutions. As Homans (1950: 269) notes, two meanings of the word "institution" are often confused: "institution" as a certain kind of activity or regularity of behavior and "institution" as an organizational or legal structure. Here, we want to clarify the distinction between these two separate meanings of the term.

Game theorists associate social events with *games* (Riker and Ordeshook, 1973: 119; Gardner and Ostrom, 1991). A *game* is a set of rules that specifies the strategies available to each relevant player and the payoffs associated with each strategy vector. In his definition, Schotter captures the intuition that every institution must be the result of equilibrium behavior by all the participants involved (Calvert, 1995). However, not every recurring pattern of behavior is an institution. We must distinguish between *institutions* and *behavioral regularities*. "Behavioral regularities" reflect the features of the events, including generic features of human behavior. "Institutions" are rules that humans devise to reshape or constrain behavior. They devise these constraints because they anticipate the regularities that they expect with and without the rules and, *ex ante*, they expect to obtain higher payoffs from the regulated event. Thus, while every stable institution must be an equilibrium outcome, not every equilibrium behavior is an institution. The following definitions are meant to sharpen the intuitions advanced above (for detailed explanations of the formal definitions, see the appendix to chapter 2, pp. 50–3).

DEFINITION 3.1: *A game* $\Gamma = \{N,\sigma,\Pi\}$, is an abstract representation of a social event *E*:

1. $N = \{1,\ldots,n\}$ is the set of relevant players.
2. Each player, $i \in N$, has a set of strategies from which he or she can choose a particular strategy: $\sigma_i \in \sigma_i$. The Cartesian product of these choice sets $\sigma = \sigma_1 X \ldots X\sigma_n$, is called the *strategy space*. $\sigma = (\sigma_1,\sigma_2,\ldots,\sigma_n) \in \sigma$, is a strategy *n*-tuple (vector), or a particular combination of strategic choices.
3. A payoff function $\Pi: \sigma \Rightarrow R^n$, assigns a payoff $u_i(\sigma)$ to every agent, $i \in N$, given any vector $\sigma = (\sigma_1,\ldots,\sigma_n)$, of strategic choices of all the agents involved in the game.

DEFINITION 3.2: The strategy vector σ^* is a Nash equilibrium iff for every player $i \in N$, $u_i(\sigma^*) \geqslant u_i(\sigma^*_{-i},\sigma_i)$, for every $\sigma_i \in \sigma_i$.

In words: a strategy vector is a Nash equilibrium if no player "would have obtained a larger payoff had [he or] she adopted an alternative strategy, given the strategies [chosen by] the other players" (Friedman, 1986: 3; see formal discussion in the appendix to chapter 2, pp. 50–3). Since agents are assumed to be utility maximizers, we expect them to use only equilibrium strategies. Thus, for every social event, E, represented as an abstract game, Γ, we can use the set of Nash equilibria strategy vectors, that we will denote as $NE(\Gamma)$, to predict the set of outcomes of E. Thus, we represent social events as abstract games and then find the set of Nash equilibria of these games and use these sets as the "predictive" sets, i.e. the sets of outcomes that we would expect to be the results of the social events under study.

Let L be a set of rules. Let $(\Gamma \mid L) = \{(N \mid L),(\sigma \mid L),(\Pi \mid L)\}$ denote the event E, represented by Γ, augmented by a set of rules L. By that we mean that the game $(\Gamma \mid L)$ is an abstract representation of the event E, represented by the abstract game, Γ, after a set of "man-made rules," L, has been imposed. The set of rules, L, imposed whenever the social event reoccurs, may change the game in one or more of three different, but related, ways. First, it may limit or expand the set of relevant players N – e.g. the rules concerning who is allowed to participate in the election may have been changed to include minorities, or younger voters. Second, L may alter the strategy space σ. Agents may get, by the set of rules L, permission to do things they were not allowed to do before, or L may limit what individual agents can do in future occurrences of the event. For example, a town may decide to elect a sheriff to be in charge of law enforcement, or it may decide that such a sheriff is not needed and eliminate the position and the expenses involved. Finally, the set of "man-made rules," L, can alter the payoffs' structure of some or all the agents in the event under study. For example, $(\Pi \mid L)$ may include fines to law offenders, or special incentives for cooperative agents.

DEFINITION 3.3: *An institution L* is a set of "man-made rules" relevant to some (possible) social event E, represented by Γ.

The reference to "man-made rules" is clarified by Ostrom (1986: 5–6):

Rules . . . are distinct from physical and behavioral laws . . . game theorists consider . . . [man-made rules] as well as physical and behavioral laws to be "the rules of the game." If a theorist wants only to analyze a given game or situation, no advantage is gained by distinguishing between rules, . . . physical or behavioral laws, . . . [If we study how] outcomes of a [given] situation [may change], however, it is essential to distinguish rules from behavioral or physical laws. Rules are the means by which we . . . change the structure of incentives in situations . . . Theoretically, rules can be changed while physical and behavioral laws cannot.

Physical laws in this framework are exogenously fixed constraints which are beyond the control of the agents involved. Behavioral laws are derivatives of "human nature" described, in this framework, by the assumption of methodological individualism, discussed in the Introduction. This assumption is often reduced to the statement that all agents in the game are utility maximizers (Riker and Sened, 1991). "Man-made rules" are rules by which utility maximizing agents change the structure of the interaction in which they are involved.

DEFINITION 3.4: An essential institution is a set of "man-made rules" L, such that

$$NE(\Gamma) \neq NE(\Gamma \mid L).$$

That is, the set of equilibria of $(\Gamma \mid L)$ is not identical to the set of equilibria of Γ. I use the term "institutions" to denote only "essential institutions" as defined in definition 3.4 above.[4] Taylor (1987: 21–2) makes the following, related, useful distinction (italics in the original):

> There are . . . two sorts of solutions to collective action problems, . . . "internal" solutions and "external" solutions. *Internal* solutions neither involve nor presuppose changes in the game, that is, in the possibilities open to the individuals, . . . *External* solutions . . . work by changing the game, that is changing people's possibilities, attitudes or beliefs. The changes do not necessarily originate outside the group of individuals who have the collective action problem.

I identify institutions with what Taylor calls "external solutions." Internal solutions are just equilibria. They depend solely on physical and behavioral laws and not on "man-made" rules.

Of particular interest, for my purposes, are "external" solutions that "do not . . . originate outside the group of individuals who have the collective action problem." A distinctive feature of human beings is that they can anticipate future events and prepare themselves for such events. One way humans cope with recurrent events is by discovering the internal solutions – i.e. learning the "equilibrium behavior" in such events. For example, people learn about free riding and take it into account in their actions. A more sophisticated way, for humans, to cope with recurrent events is by devising "external" or institutional solutions that help them achieve more desirable outcomes. For example, enforcement agencies change the incentive structure so that free riding is no longer an attractive strategy for the players involved. Property rights are enforced by law so that every

---

[4] Nash equilibrium is not the only solution concept used by game theorists to predict outcomes of social events; I use this concept rather than others because it is so intuitive and generally accepted. Most of what I say below can be easily restated, using any conventional solution concept instead of Nash equilibrium.

consumer must pay the cost of production and eliminate the phenomenon of free riding as such.

If it is not an equilibrium behavior to construct an institution then this institution will never emerge, and if it is not an equilibrium behavior to respect the rules that constitute an institution, this institution will not survive. Thus, "external" solutions to the game Γ are "internal" solutions in a more complex game, that I will denote as Γ^X. The complex game Γ^X is a game where agents must first decide whether, whenever they confront the event E, they wish to play Γ or $(\Gamma \mid L)$, and then play the game they decided to play when the event E actually occurs.

To explain the institution L we must show that when playing the game Γ^X, a decisive coalition among the set of relevant agents will choose to play $(\Gamma \mid L)$ rather than Γ. To do so, we must specify the payoff function and strategy space for Γ^X, and show that, in Γ^X, in equilibrium, agents prefer playing $(\Gamma \mid L)$, with the set of man-made rules, L, rather than Γ. Let O be the set of all possible outcomes of event E and let $U = \{u_1, \ldots, u_n\}: O \Rightarrow R^n$ be a smooth utility function representing the preference profile of all agents in E over O.

DEFINITION 3.5: Let $\mathbb{D}\Gamma$ be the set of decisive coalitions for the game Γ. Define the set of decisive coalitions for the game Γ as:

$$\mathbb{D}\Gamma = \{C \subseteq N: \forall x, y \in XyP_i x \forall i \in C \Rightarrow y\Gamma x\}.$$

In words: a decisive coalition in a game Γ is a set of relevant players in Γ, such that if all the members of the coalition prefer one outcome over the other, this outcome is imposed on all the participants in the game. Social scientists try to explain why agents construct and support the institutions they impose on themselves. This means that we have to be able to demonstrate that for every existing institution L, a decisive coalition prefers $(\Gamma \mid L)$, to Γ when playing Γ^X. Ultimately we may want to specify a set $\mathscr{L} = (L_1, \ldots, L_k)$, of all possible institutional designs that could be imposed whenever the event E occurs, and then explain the institution $L^* \in \mathscr{L}$ as the equilibrium institution given $\mathscr{L}$. But institutional designs are a function of human ingenuity and the set $\mathscr{L}$ may be hard, if not impossible, to specify.

It is important to emphasize that the existence of a decisive coalition does not necessarily presuppose pre-existing "man-made rules" in Γ. Γ could be an "institution free" "natural state" game. The coalition may be decisive because of the skills and powers of its members that allow them to impose their will on other agents. As Hobbes suggests in his discussion "Of the Natural Condition of Mankind" ([1651] 1968: 183):

> Nature hath made men so equal, in the faculties of body and mind; as that
> though there be found one man sometimes manifestly stronger in body, or

of quicker mind then another . . . the weakest has strength enough to kill the strongest, either by secret machination or by confederacy with others.

Norms, institutions, and constitutions

The purpose of this section is to clarify the distinction between norms and institutions that has been obscured in the literature on the subject. Explaining norms is, and should be, a categorically different exercise than explaining institutions, even though the same methodology can and should be used to explain both types of social phenomena (Crawford and Ostrom, 1995).

Sugden defines a "convention" as "any stable equilibrium in a game that has two or more stable equilibria" (1986: 32). Norms and conventions are "internal solutions." What distinguishes an institution from a norm is that the emergence of the former entails the introduction of "man-made rules" that change the incentive structure of the game (Ostrom, 1986: 6; Taylor, 1987: 21–2) and, if the institution is of any consequence (see definition 3.4 above), the set of equilibria of the game.

Consider the prisoners' dilemma game. It is well known that if agents face a prisoners' dilemma problem an infinite number of times, and if they discount future payoffs by "little enough," they may reach an infinite set of possible equilibria (Axelrod, 1984; Taylor, 1987; Calvert, 1989). Any one of these equilibria can emerge as a social norm, including "Pareto optimal" and "Pareto inferior" equilibria. If all the agents are content with the social norm that emerges, they are unlikely to look for "external" institutional solutions. If, however, the norm that emerges is unsatisfactory to some or all of the players involved, agents could try to establish "external" institutional solutions that make some of them or all of them better off (Ostrom, 1990: 34).

"External" institutional solutions often depend on third parties that play the role of law enforcement agencies (Schelling, 1984), but external coercion is not a necessary, nor a sufficient condition for Pareto improving external institutional solutions. In her extensive survey of different solutions to the dilemma of the management of common-pool resources, Ostrom (1990) demonstrates, using formal models and empirical evidence, that external institutional solutions can be, and often are, self-enforcing.

This distinction between norms and institutions is meant to clarify, not diminish the role of norms in the evolution of institutions. As Knight (1992) points out, norms provide rational agents with crucial information about how they are expected to act. By providing an additional structure they help such rational agents make strategic decisions (Ostrom, 1990: 35–7). Institutions often emerge not in response to the set of all possible equilibria in a given social situation, but as a response to those equilibria that have become the conventional norm of behavior.

From a positive standpoint, to explain a norm we only have to show why a pattern of behavior is an equilibrium behavior in a given social context. To explain an institution we must show why a decisive set of agents chose a set of rules that changed the incentive structure of the event, and how they were able to enforce these rules on those, including themselves, who played a role in the relevant social event.

Kiser and Ostrom (1982: 207–15) distinguish between institutions at the "collective choice level" and institutions at the "constitutional choice level" (cf. Ostrom, 1990: 50–3). "Collective choice" institutions determine, maintain or alter the set of acceptable strategies and the ways and means to deal with deviators of all kinds. "Constitutional" institutions determine, maintain or alter institutional arrangements at the "collective choice level." I made a similar distinction in the Introduction between first-order and second-order social relations (pp. 2–3). The former determine the relations among different individuals in society and the latter determine how these relations can be altered.

Knight (1992) argues that norms provide important information to those who construct institutions at the "collective action level," helping them form expectations about patterns of behavior that these institutions are constructed to induce, given any set of norms that is commonly observed in society. Institutions at the "constitutional level" are constructed to deal with anticipated behavior, given the "collective choice" level of institutional structure. Yet, at both levels one logic should be used in trying to provide positive explanations for the emergence and evolution of institutions: To show that it is equilibrium behavior for a set of agents to support "L" as an institution, we must specify the payoff function and strategy space for a game Γ^X and show that at least one equilibrium outcome of Γ^X is one in which the agents end up playing $(\Gamma \mid L)$. Γ^X may be regarded as a "constitutional level" game, the outcome of which may be any institution $L^* \in \mathcal{L}$ of the set of all possible institutional designs $\mathcal{L} = (L_1, \ldots, L_k)$, at the "collective action level."

No institution constrains the behavior of individuals so as to fully determine what they will end up doing. Any "collective action" institutional design, $L^* \in \mathcal{L}$, that emerges as an equilibrium outcome of the "constitutional level" institutional game, Γ^X, may bring about the emergence of different conventional norms as equilibrium behavior given $L^* \in \mathcal{L}$. Such norms often become catalysts for institutional change, as they highlight the weaknesses and possible improvements of existing institutional structures.

In chapter 4 I explain the emergence of property rights' institutions, which are "collective action" institutions, by showing that governments have an incentive to enforce such institutions inasmuch as they increase tax revenues and political support. By their monopolistic control of the use of force and their special role in the legislative process, governments are treated as decisive agents in this game. In chapter 4 I prove that in order to make their threat to enforce institutional structure of property rights credible, governments must make their laws public knowledge. The "right to know your rights" is probably a "constitutional institution" in this context. It turns out that without institutions that guide governments to publish their laws at the constitutional level of the institutional structure, the enforcement of property rights by central governments will not be an equilibrium behavior, and thus institutions that protect property rights are unlikely to emerge.

It is well known that arbitrary governments that do not publish the legal codes according to which they operate are not the best guardians of property rights. North and Weingast (1989) provide a wonderful example in their account of the events surrounding the Glorious Revolution (1688) in England. They show how:

> England's institutional commitment to secure [property and other civil] rights was [made] far stronger [by] limiting the Crown's legislative and judicial powers, . . . [which] limited the Crown's ability to alter rules *ex post* without parliamentary consent [and] by creating a balance between Parliament and the monarchy – rather than eliminating the latter as occurred after the Civil war – parliamentary interests greatly enhanced the predictability of governmental decisions.

In the following two sections I illustrate and elaborate on the ideas developed in this section by reviewing several recent works that use various variants of the theoretical approach developed above to explain different social institutions.

Spatial theory of electoral competition: disequilibrium of tastes

The spatial theory of electoral competition represents ideal policy positions of agents and alternative policy positions as points in space R^m. Every vital political issue is represented as one of the m dimensions of this space. The utility $u_i(x)$ that agent i derives from a policy position $x \in R^m$, is assumed to be a function of the Euclidean distance between x and ρ_i, i.e. $u_i(x) = \phi_i(\| x - \rho_i \|)$, where ρ_i represents the most preferred point, or ideal point, for i in R^m. We assume that each agent seeks to realize policy points as close as possible to his or her ideal point. This is the theoretical basis of the spatial theory of electoral competition (Austen-Smith, 1983). A central solution concept in this paradigm is the "core" or "simple majority equilibrium." Its definition is based on the notion that the set of decisive coalitions $\mathscr{D}\Gamma$, in a majority rule game Γ, is any set of players that includes more than half of the relevant players (Austen-Smith, 1983: 441).

DEFINITION 3.6: $x^* \in R^m$ is a *simple majority equilibrium*[5] if, for any other feasible alternative $y \in R^m$, at least half of the agents prefer x^* to y.

When the core is non-empty, i.e. if there is an outcome that satisfies definition 3.6, we expect the outcome of an interaction among rational agents using majority rule to be the core. This is so because, by definition, there is no position that a majority of the relevant agents prefers to the core position and, therefore, no position can defeat the core position in a simple majority rule game.

The "spatial theory of electoral competition" was introduced to political science by Black's seminal work on *The Theory of Committees and Elections* (1958). What made Black's work exemplary (in Kuhn's, 1970, sense of the word), is that it familiarized political scientists with the *Median Voter Theorem*: in uni-dimensional political settings, using plurality rule, if voters have single peaked preferences, and voters and candidates have complete information about voters' preferences and candidates' positions, then candidates will endorse the ideal point of the median voter as their platform (Black, 1958; Feddersen *et al.*, 1990; Shepsle, 1990).[6] This result provides a rationale to use plurality rule as a political institution inasmuch as it shows that in uni-dimensional political contests, plurality rule promotes central positions that have the advantage of being "as close as possible to as many voters as possible."

The next scientific step was to see if this elegant result would hold under the more realistic assumption of multi-dimensional political environments. McKelvey and Schofield show that in policy spaces with two dimensions or more, *simple majority equilibria* rarely exist and, if an

---

[5] Two related concepts (Austen-Smith, 1983) are: (1) $o^* \in O$ is a *simple plurality equilibrium*, if for any other alternative $o \in O$, the set of individual agents who strictly prefer o^* to o, is at least as large as the set of agents who prefer o to o^*. (2) $o^* \in O$ is a *simple majority core* if for any feasible $o \in O$, the set of agents who prefer o to o^* is no greater than $n/2$. For our purposes, the distinction among the three is not crucial. For further discussion on the distinction among the three solution concepts and its consequences, see Austen-Smith (1983); McKelvey and Wendell (1976).

[6] To be perfectly accurate this result is actually due in part to Hotelling (1929). On the role of exemplary past achievements in the development of science, see Kuhn (1970: 174–5, 187–91). Without a doubt the median voter theorem is a good example of such an "exemplar." It should be noted that while the theory is due to Duncan Black (1958), it was brought to the attention of many political scientists by Downs' *An Economic Theory of Democracy* (1957).

equilibrium does not exist, then agendas can lead to almost any outcome (McKelvey, 1979; Schofield, 1984a; McKelvey and Schofield, 1987).

These results imply that the use of majority rule in multi-dimensional political settings may often lead to "intransitive social choices." Using majority rule and binary comparisons to order the preferences of society over a set of alternatives is likely to yield cases in which society ends up with cyclical preferences. In simple words, the use of majority rule as a social choice mechanism is likely to cause inherently unstable social choices (Riker, 1980). So, the use of majority rule to make social choice in a "multi-dimensional" political environment is problematic. The inherent instability induced by majority rule as a social choice mechanism is often cited as the underlying rationale behind the choice of "super majority rules" as alternative institutional designs.

Schofield (1984a, 1984b) shows that super majority mechanisms, that require more than a simple majority to change the status quo, are less likely to yield intransitive, cyclical, social choices. The authors of the US Constitution chose a particularly robust institutional design to guarantee the stability of constitutional provisions and amendments. There are actually four different ways to amend the Constitution: in the first stage, the amendment must either be passed by a two-thirds majority of both houses of Congress, or by a special constitutional convention. In the second stage, the amendment must either be approved by three-quarters of the state legislatures or be ratified by special ratifying conventions in three-quarters of the states (Aldrich *et al.*, 1986: 51; in fact, except for the Twenty-First Amendment, only the Congress–state legislatures' route has ever been used). Many legal systems include similar institutional designs to protect the most important basic laws or constitutional provisions of the land.

The writers of the Constitution chose this special mechanism to defend the Constitution from the instability that characterizes more flexible choice mechanisms, such as the simple majority rule discussed above. One could think of the writers of the Constitution as choosing a constitutional institution, L, among a set of many possible institutional designs $\mathscr{L} = (L_1, \ldots, L_k)$ with the distinct quality that it is less likely than simple majority rule to yield cyclical social preferences, which could cause an inherent social instability.

Shepsle (1979) was the first to emphasize, in this context, the role of institutional structures in inducing stable outcomes (Shepsle, 1986: 51–5):

> . . . [the] relationship between social choices and individual values is a mediated one. Standing between the individual qua bundle of tastes and . . . available social choices are institutions . . . – frameworks of rules, pro-cedures, and arrangements – [that] prescribe and constrain the set of

choosing agents, the manner in which their preferences may be revealed, the alternatives over which preferences may be expressed, the order in which such expressions occur, and generally the way in which business is conducted.

Shepsle (1979) went on to formalize the notion of *structure induced equilibria* (SIE), and to show that, in general, institutional arrangements tend to induce equilibria where, without these arrangements, no equilibrium exists.[7]

If institutions make a difference, however, then rational agents should realize that, and whenever institutions stand in their way in achieving whatever policy point they wish to achieve – and can achieve in the absence of the institutional structure – they will seek to change or nullify the institution. This concern was first raised by Riker (1980: 444–5) in his discussion of Shepsle's concept of SIE:[8]

> insofar as a constitutional system supplies an outcome that is not the same as outcomes that might have been obtained from simple majority rule in the system without [institutions] . . . losers are likely to change the [institutions] . . . in the hope of winning on another day . . . institutions are no more than rules and rules are themselves the product of social decisions. Consequently, . . . losers on a series of decisions under a particular set of rules will attempt (often successfully) to change institutions and hence . . . the decisions produced under them . . . Thus, the only difference between values and institutions is that the revelation of institutional equilibria is probably a longer process than the revelation of [the] disequilibrium of taste . . . If institutions are congealed tastes and if tastes lack equilibria, then [so] do institutions, except for short-run events.

Riker's argument, however, is inconclusive. A broad body of research has since established that institutions often "restrict" the damage that rational agents anticipate, given the "disequilibrium of taste" and benefit some or all of the agents concerned in some broad sense of *ex ante* expectations. When this is the case, institutions may be more stable than Riker anticipated (Sened, 1991).

The argument is that each *essential institution* is chosen from a set of possible institutional designs $\mathcal{L} = (L_1, \ldots, L_k)$, at some underlying game Γ^X at the "constitutional choice level," because the chosen institution, L^*, is regarded as best, given $\mathcal{L}$, by a decisive coalition that is able to impose its will on the rest of the relevant agents. Such a coalition may form in a legislative body, be a ruling government, or an individual that enjoys "dictatorial powers."

---

[7] The main results are found in Shepsle (1979), or in Ordeshook (1986, ch. 6). Further discussion is found in Shepsle (1986).

[8] For an interesting response to Riker see Shepsle (1986).

A remarkable example was provided by Riker himself, who demonstrated quite convincingly, that

> Madison provided the agenda and the outline of the ultimate [US] constitution [in order to remedy] the tendency of states to make bad laws and the inability of the national government to control state excesses. (1995: 135)

Riker argues that if it was not for the respect that other participants in the constitutional convention had for Madison and "his" so-called "Virginia Plan," the convention would have, very likely, resulted in an ineffective and unstable institutional structure (1995: 143–4). Whatever the case may be, it is a matter of fact that the US Constitution has survived much stress in the last two centuries and induced remarkable stability in the legislative process in the US federal and state governments.

I argued above that to explain an institution one must identify an event in the anticipation of which a decisive coalition of players, who prefer the set of equilibria of $(\Gamma \mid L)$ to the set of equilibria of Γ, impose the institution L so that they play $(\Gamma \mid L)$ rather than Γ if E occurs. Madison and other delegates to the constitutional convention played the "constitutional choice level" game Γ^X, where they made decisions about procedural rules that they then had to follow in the "collective choice level" legislative decision making. As Riker pointed out, the US Constitution was promoted and imposed by a decisive coalition, dominated by Madison, within the 55 delegates that came to the convention. Madison's Virgina Plan, that left such a decisive imprint on the the US Constitution, was written by Madison to accomplish goals that were first and foremost Madison's own goals.

Riker (1995) suggested several explanations for the fact that the framers of the US Constitution escaped cycling in the issue space while framing the Constitution, and later while trying to secure its ratification (Riker, 1995: 259–63). Whatever the case may be, it is clear that the Constitution, as it was finally ratified, has had two major, long-lasting consequences that were part of what Madison and his coalition of delegates to the constitutional convention intended the US Constitution to achieve in the first place. First, it is clear that the US Constitution provided an institutional setup for a relatively stable legislative process. Second, and more to the point of this book, the institutional design of the US Constitution and the resulting structure of US political institutions, is an important variable in explaining the evolution of stable private property rights' institutions and a stable and remarkable economic growth of the US economy in the nineteenth century that was promoted by these institutions (Weingast, 1995).

In a separate analytical effort Schofield (1986) establishes necessary and sufficient conditions for a "structurally stable core" (SSC) to be non-empty. Schofield shows that if instead of a legislature made up of individual players, governments in multi-party, proportional rule systems depend on the support of political parties, SSCs are often non-empty in two-dimensional spaces. So, Schofield shows that the institutional structure of a "multi-party proportional rule electoral system" can induce equilibria where, without this institutional mechanism, *simple majority equilibria* would not exist.

The discussion above provides a partial answer to Riker's (1980) concern that "If institutions are congealed tastes and if tastes lack equilibria, then [so] do institutions, except for short-run events." The reason why we may expect institutions to be more stable than tastes is that institutions do not necessarily favor one party at the expense of another. Institutions constrain the set of achievable outcomes in ways that, in the long run, favor large majorities of the agents involved.

Coordination games and prisoners' dilemma games

In *The Emergence of Norms* (1979), Ullmann-Margalit distinguishes among three types of problems from which she expects social institutions to emerge: problems of coordination, problems of prisoners' dilemma, and problems of "norms of partiality." Schotter (1981: 26) shows that the third category is merely a subclass of coordination games. The remaining two categories are by no means exhaustive, but together with the "generic disequilibrium of tastes" discussed in the previous section, they seem to be the most important types of problems that could give rise to social institutions.

The distinctive feature of the prisoners' dilemma problem is that it has a unique, Pareto inferior equilibrium outcome. Players would be better off if some mechanism forced them to play strategies that yielded the Pareto superior outcome. However, if agents face a prisoners' dilemma an indefinite number of times and if players discount future payoffs by "little enough," there exist equilibria in the repeated "supergame" in which agents play repeatedly strategies that yield Pareto optimal outcomes in each repetition of the game (Axelrod, 1984; Taylor, 1987; Calvert, 1989, 1995).

These results, however, must be interpreted very cautiously from the substantive and the technical points of view. Substantively, one must not confuse cooperation with institutions. If players facing a repeated prisoners' dilemma game were to cooperate, they would not need institutions (Taylor, 1987: 158, 194 n. 10). Institutions arise because, in many cases, players fail to choose such "optimal strategies." They fail to do so not because they are stupid or particularly naughty, but because there are many other equilibrium strategy vectors, and players cannot tell *ex ante*, without *a priori* communication, which equilibrium strategy vector they will end up with.

From the technical point of view, the objection is that "cooperative" equilibrium strategy vectors are not the only equilibria that exist in the repeated prisoners' dilemma supergames. The "Folk Theorem" (e.g. Fudenberg and Maskin, 1986) proves that almost every feasible payoff vector can be supported by some Nash equilibrium in the repeated prisoners' dilemma supergame.

THE FOLK THEOREM:[9] Given some restrictive conditions,[10] in infinitely repeated games, with finite action sets at each repetition, any pattern of actions observed in a finite number of repetitions, is the outcome of some *subgame perfect*[11] Nash equilibrium.

This result is more devastating than many are willing to admit. It shows that while the repeated game argument explains why we may see cooperation among players who anticipate facing the same prisoners' dilemma an infinite number of times,[12] it does not imply that agents will *tend* to cooperate in such circumstances (Bianco and Bates, 1990: 137; Banks and Sundaram, 1990; Kalai and Neme, 1989).

This discouraging conclusion, however, can be interpreted in a positive way: since the correct conclusion is that repeating the game yields a multitude of equilibria, repeating the game *does* make a difference. In the one-shot prisoners' dilemma game there is a unique equilibrium in which all players defect. In the repeated version of the game there is a multitude of equilibria. Instead of arbitrarily emphasizing one set of equilibria over others, we should study how players may react to this multitude of possible

---

[9] So called because no one knows who should get credit for it.

[10] These conditions are (Rasmusen, 1989: 92):

1. The rate of time preference is sufficiently small.
2. The probability that the game ends at any repetition is sufficiently small.
3. The set of payoff combinations that strictly Pareto dominates the least payoff any player can guarantee to himself (the minimax payoff) in the mixed extension of the one-shot game is n-dimensional.

None of these conditions is particularly demanding or unrealistic. For further discussion see Rasmusen (1989: 92–4). For the technically advanced reader, see Fudenberg and Maskin (1986).

[11] *Subgame perfection* is a widely used refinement of the Nash equilibrium solution concept. For a brief discussion see Myerson (1978). Every subgame perfect equilibrium is a Nash equilibrium but the converse is, obviously, not true: not every Nash equilibrium is subgame perfect. I define and discuss the subgame perfection solution concept in chapter 4.

[12] On strategies that support cooperation in the repeated prisoners' dilemma game see Axelrod (1981, 1984). For a brief explanation see Ordeshook (1986: 442–8). For a more technical but accessible survey see Bianco (1988).

equilibria in the repeated "supergame." This observation leads us to shift our attention from prisoners' dilemma games to coordination games.

The definition of an equilibrium strategy vector implies that, given the strategy of all the other players, no player can be better off by playing any strategy other than his or her equilibrium strategy. Thus, any game with more than one equilibrium presents a coordination problem to the players (Banks and Calvert, 1992). Theorists analyzing games with multiple equilibria usually assume "that players can coordinate their strategy choices on any desired equilibrium," they then

> proceed by "refining" Nash's notion of equilibrium to ensure that if it is already common knowledge that a particular equilibrium is expected . . . it is actually in each player's interest to play his equilibrium strategy. (Crawford and Haller, 1989)

The analysis of coordination games is motivated by the observation that coordination may present a problem in and of itself. The social dilemma that coordination games highlights is that in games with multiple equilibria, such as the infinitely repeated prisoners' dilemma, agents must coordinate the equilibrium strategies they play, but without a communication stage prior to the game, and even with such a stage it is not a trivial task to reach coordination.

Players who anticipate facing coordination problems may wish to resort to some mechanism that, *ex ante*, lets each get the most out of any realization of the coordination problem (Schotter, 1981: 23; Banks and Calvert, 1992). Banks and Calvert (1992) study one such coordination game described by table 3.1.

This game has three Nash equilibria: two pure-strategy equilibria where player 1 prefers $\sigma = (\sigma_{11},\sigma_{22})$ and player 2 prefers $\sigma = (\sigma_{21},\sigma_{12})$, and one mixed-strategy symmetric equilibrium with each player playing σ_{i1} with probability $t/(t+1)$ (e.g. if $t = 1$, each player plays each of the two strategies available to him, with probability $1/2$). Suppose that players know that they are likely to face such a game but do not know what the value of t may be for each one of them. Thus, the game they anticipate is the game described in table 3.2 that I will denote as Γ_c.

Ex ante, agents do not know the value of t_i. Once the game starts, each learns the value of his or her type (t_i) but not the type of the other player. Once players learn their types, they decide simultaneously – without knowing the decision of the other player – which strategy to play and proceed to play the game accordingly. Banks and Calvert ask whether there exists some mechanism that can increase the players' *ex ante* expected payoffs and at the same time be *incentive compatible*.

Table 3.1. *A simple coordination game*

Players		Player 2	
	Strategies	σ_{21}	σ_{22}
Player 1	σ_{11}	0	1
		0	t
	σ_{12}	t	0
		1	0

$t \geq 1$

Table 3.2. *A coordination game with incomplete information*

Players		Player 2	
	Strategies	σ_{21}	σ_{22}
Player 1	σ_{11}	0	1
		0	t_1
	σ_{12}	t_2	0
		1	0

DEFINITION 3.7 (Banks and Calvert, 1992): A *direct mechanism* is a communication process having the following simple form. First the players privately report their types to a single outside actor, the "mediator": they may lie. Second, the mediator uses a rule known to the players – the *mechanism* – to derive from their reports a recommended decision for playing Γ_c; he communicates his recommendation to each player privately.

DEFINITION 3.8 (Banks and Calvert, 1992): A direct mechanism μ is *incentive compatible* if honest reporting of types and obedience to the mediator's recommendation by both players constitutes a Bayesian equilibrium.[13]

Banks and Calvert (1992) show that, in the case of complete information, a "cheap talk" communication mechanism can help players achieve efficiency in equilibrium. A communication mechanism allows players to communicate before they start the game. "Cheap talk" refers to the fact that players can send non-binding, non-verifiable messages – i.e. they can lie and there is no cost attached to lying (Farrell, 1987).

---

[13] A clear discussion of the Bayesian equilibrium as a solution concept is found in Banks (1991).

In the case of incomplete information, unmediated communication is insufficient to achieve the efficiency that the mediated communication allows players to achieve in the case of complete information. Banks and Calvert prove that, in such circumstances, players anticipating the event modeled by Γ_c may, in equilibrium, accept two types of institutional arrangements. One is a complicated "signaling language," the other is an arbitration process involving a mediator. Both institutions improve the players' *ex ante* payoffs from an anticipated event. The former is a self-enforcing institution. The latter requires the intervention of a third party, but this third party does not use coercion to obtain obedience and truthful revelation of preferences from players.

In this way, Banks and Calvert provide a positive answer to the questions: why do institutions emerge, and why do they persist? They emerge because agents anticipate coordination problems. Agents erect institutions that help them improve their *ex ante* expected payoffs from such events. These institutions persist because it is in the best interest of all players involved to be obedient and truthful, rather than disobedient and untruthful, to such a mediating institution. They also provide a partial answer to Riker's objection that institutions are only rules that impose outcomes and that if instability characterizes tastes over outcomes, it will characterize tastes about institutions as well. Riker's objection notwithstanding, institutions like the one described by Banks and Calvert emerge in an environment of instability, enhanced by a multitude of equilibria and coordination problems. They are unlikely to be challenged by the players since, *ex ante*, they work to the benefit of every one of them.

On the spontaneous emergence of institutions

Theories of spontaneous emergence of social institutions from Hayek (1967) to Sugden (1986), differ in scope, methods, and logic, but share the notion that institutions emerge as equilibria in social games without much intentional planning. Calvert (1995: 80) argues that:

> The institutions-as-equilibria approach . . . says nothing directly about the emergence of institutions, [assuming] . . . that the players arrive unanimously at identical equilibrium expectations through *a priori* reasoning.

How rational agents reach this unintentional coordination is never very clear. At least with respect to institutions that protect private property rights, which is the subject matter of this book, Hayek (1967) seems to put his faith in the "invisible hand" and market competitive forces, while Sugden (1986) seems to suggest that the physical characteristics of each situation lead players to choose the equilibrium that best fits these *a priori* conditions. Both expect such social equilibria to evolve into the "spontaneous social order" that they believe to emerge as an unintended consequence of individual actions (Knight, 1992: 11). Calvert (1995: 80) provides the most eloquent account of this theme:

> The spontaneous emergence of an institution is fundamentally a problem of coordination . . . different institutions . . . are possible . . . The problem of the players is to arrive together at one such equilibrium. Still, the institutions in this chapter are not all that complex, and over an extended period of play it is reasonable to expect that similar institutions could arise by trial and error with a minimum purposeful planning.

This is a reasonable account as long as small communities and relatively simple informal institutions, such as norms and conventions, are concerned (Calvert, 1995). It cannot explain the formidable institutional structures that characterize modern polities (Olson, 1993). As Hume pointed out, informal norms and conventions are necessary but rarely sufficient to maintain social order. They are necessary because they provide informational background that allows the intentional planning of complex formal institutions (Knight, 1992).

An organized social order, however, requires formal institutions, sustained by agents who enforce law and order. In this context, the emergence of institutions is the result of the intentional design of agents who control existing institutions and means of enforcement, which is the subject of chapter 4, and agents who challenge those institutions hoping to change them for their own benefit, which is the subject of chapter 5. Chapter 6 explains how political entrepreneurs alleviate the coordination problem, to which Calvert alludes in the quotation above, by directing agents to specific equilibria, and away from other equilibria in which the collective action problem may remain unresolved (Ainsworth and Sened, 1993).

One can summarize the literature on the subject in a two by two matrix:

	Spontaneous emergence	Intentional emergence
Formal institutions	B	D
Informal institutions	A	C

Given my argument so far, explanations of Type A promote spontaneous, informal institutions. Such accounts include the most remarkable works on the subject from Hayek (1967) to Schotter (1981), Axelrod (1981), Sugden (1986), Calvert (1989, 1995) and, most recently, Knight (1992). Calvert (1995) and Sugden (1986) argue that formal institutions could evolve out of a spontaneous process of the emergence of informal institutions, examples of Type B explanations. Several interesting accounts of the institutional emergence of Type C deal with the role of leadership in different social settings (Calvert, 1987, 1989; Bianco and Bates, 1990).

Ostrom (1990) and North (1990) use a combination of all four types in their work. The remainder of this book follows a lead by Riker (1988, 1995; Riker and Sened, 1991) in an attempt to develop a theory of intentional formation of formal institutions of type *D*, designed by governments and other agents in society to protect private property and the related individual rights of private citizens.

Concluding remarks: towards a deductive theory of institutions

Any institution is a puzzle inasmuch as it results from a series of decisions by which a group of individuals determines how to conduct and regulate the interactions among members of the group. Given what we know about the generic disequilibrium of tastes or, interchangeably, of the multitude of equilibria in repeated games and other coordination problems, the existence of any stable institution comes as some surprise.

I defined an institution to be a set of man-made rules imposed by participants in a social event upon themselves and other participants in the event. An adequate deductive explanation for an institution begins with an abstract description of this anticipated event: the set of players, the actions they can undertake and the outcome, or payoff vector, associated with any vector of actions undertaken by the participants. To *explain* an institution we must show that, anticipating such an event a decisive group of agents impose on themselves, and others, the rules that constitute the institution we wish to explain, because they prefer the expected set of outcomes when the institution under study is imposed over the set of outcomes expected when no such institution is in place.

There is one aspect of the evolution of institutions on which I have, so far, said very little. Consider the following claim (Riker, 1980: 445):

> Outcomes are the consequence not only of institutions and tastes, but also of the political skill and artistry of those who manipulate agenda, formulate and reformulate questions, generate "false" issues, etc., in order to exploit the disequilibrium of tastes for their own advantage.

Institutional changes involve subtle *ex ante* computations of payoffs over prolonged periods of time. Such institutional changes also involve "the opening of a Pandora's box of disequilibrium" (Fink, 1987: 15) because institutions *induce* equilibria (Shepsle, 1979, 1986) whether they represent genuine "congealed tastes," or the "heresthetical"[14] ingenuity of their creators (Riker, 1980, 1986: 21–2).

---

[14] The notion of "heresthetic" was introduced to the field by Riker (1986: ix) and has since become a key concept in any discussion on political maneuvering. Riker defines the word as follows:

> heresthetic is [the] art [of] . . . managing and manipulating and maneuvering to get the decisions [one] wants [to get].

North (1993) advances a similar argument. He notes that institutional structures result from – and depend on – complex networks of economic and social organizations as well as complex belief systems and informal norms of behavior:

> Since it is the norms that provide "legitimacy" to the set of rules, . . . Both institutions and belief systems must change for successful reform since it is the mental models of the actors that will shape choices. (1993: 21–2)

North goes on to argue that in the absence of "norms of behavior that will support and legitimize new rules . . . polities will tend to be unstable" (1993: 22).

One can use these arguments to explain the "excess stability" of institutional structure, as well as stagnation and conservatism with respect to institutional changes. Existing institutions and those who control them and benefit from them induce, implicitly or explicitly – through well financed campaigns, for instance – belief structures that support existing institutions. Existing systems of beliefs may serve, or be used, to constrain and counter pressures for institutional change.

An interesting example is the massive advertising campaign launched by the health insurance companies in the USA in 1993, following the plea of the Clinton administration for a radical change in the institutional structure that regulates health care provision. This campaign was financed by benefits, made by those who control the industry under existing institutional structures. The campaign was very successful in eroding the public support for the administration's plan for institutional changes. It used simple tactics to make voters believe they were better off under the existing institutional structure than they would be under the new institutional structure designed by the Clinton administration. This campaign was instrumental in the failure of the administration's drive for institutional change.

It is easy to think of this phenomenon in terms of the problem of multiple equilibria we discussed earlier. In an important sense, every equilibrium is not just an equilibrium of actions but, more importantly, an equilibrium of beliefs. In any game with multiple equilibria, a particular equilibrium can be sustained only if all the relevant agents *believe* that each one of them will do what each one of them ends up doing in equilibrium. If social agents are convinced that they are playing a particular equilibrium combination of strategies, it may be very difficult to convince them to choose a new strategy even if they are aware that if all players changed their behavior in some way they might all be better off.

Structures of beliefs about the world, or deeply imbedded ideologies, could deter players from changing norms of behavior or institutional structures, even when these changes seem beneficial to all players involved.

Human history is richer with examples of how mutual suspicion prevents players from improving their conditions than with examples of how mutual confidence makes individuals cooperate to reach mutually beneficial institutional changes.

Finally, one trivial point is too often forgotten: institutions give tactical and strategic advantages to those who control them, advantages that any attempt to change them must surmount.

To recapitulate my central argument in this chapter: to explain any institution one must show that the institution somehow solves a problem for a decisive coalition of players, and under what conditions it is in the best interest of this decisive coalition to solve the problem by imposing the institution. One must specify the set of actions from which each agent can choose and then demonstrate that, in equilibrium, agents choose strategies that result in the emergence of the institution or the institutional change under study.

I undertake this task in the next three chapters. I start in chapter 4 by showing why and under what conditions it is in the best interest of government officials to grant private property rights and related individual rights to their constituents, and in the best interest of individuals to obey the laws that protect such rights. In chapter 5 I develop a more general model that shows how individual agents, other than government officials, can cause institutional changes. Chapter 6 introduces political entrepreneurs into this theory of the political evolution of individual rights. Political entrepreneurs often alleviate the collective action problem that stops citizens from challenging political institutional structures of rights. Political entrepreneurs also provide both members of interest groups and government officials with information about the benefits each side should expect from petitioning for – or changing – the political structures that shape and protect private property and related individual rights (Ainsworth and Sened, 1993).

4

A neo-liberal theory of the state: the role of government in the evolution of property rights

Introduction

From the standpoint of the game theoretic analytical framework, the evolution of property rights is often explained in terms of behavioral regularities, or equilibrium outcomes of recurrent, conflictual interactions concerning the allocation of scarce resources (Schotter, 1981; Sugden, 1986; Taylor, 1987). Sugden, for example, defines a *convention* (1986: 132) as: "any stable equilibrium in a game that has two or more stable equilibria." He then argues that legal codes

> merely formalize . . . conventions of behavior that have evolved out of essentially anarchic situations; . . . [and] reflect codes of behavior that most individuals impose on themselves. (Sugden, 1986: 5)

According to this argument, formal property rights evolve out of a spontaneous process of the emergence of informal norms of respect of property rights among more or less identical social agents.

In this chapter I begin to develop a different game theoretic model of the evolution of property rights' institutions. This model rests on the premise that property rights are designed, granted, and protected by law enforcing governments. Governments should, therefore, be included in any comprehensive model of the evolution of property or any other human rights. The main purpose of this book is to explain the emergence of important institutions that define and protect property rights in an environment that includes a law enforcing government.

In chapter 3, I argued that in order to explain any institution one must point to a decisive coalition, able to impose its will on all the relevant players, and an event that this decisive coalition anticipates and in which it is made, *ex ante*, better off by creating the institution. The remainder of this book provides a series of such explanations for the emergence and evolution of private property and related individual rights. The "decisive player" in my model is a government, with a monopoly on law enforcement. The underlying event that serves as a starting point for my argument is an n-person prisoners' dilemma. The argument is straightforward: governments anticipate inefficient production in environments without property rights, which I model as n-person prisoners' dilemma. Governments expect the grant of property rights to induce more efficiency and productivity to the economy. They grant property rights to citizens in the hope of making tangible benefits from the excess productivity, through increased tax revenues (Levi, 1988) or enhanced political support (Riker and Sened, 1991).

In this chapter I specify the conditions under which governments will grant and enforce property rights assuming an environment with complete information. In chapter 5 I generalize the argument by relaxing this assumption. In chapter 6 I develop the model further by incorporating into the model "political entrepreneurs," who serve as mediators between ordinary citizens and central governments in the political bargaining process through which property rights emerge and evolve. Chapter 7 is a case study of the grant of private property rights in air slots. It illustrates how property rights emerge when government officials attempt to improve the efficiency of production by granting property rights in an environment that suffers from inefficient allocation of resources that is due, mainly, to the absence of well defined property rights.

The first section summarizes earlier work by Riker and Sened (1991) in which we laid the foundations for the theory of the origin of property rights that I develop further in the second section. The third section restates the argument in precise game theoretic terms. The fourth section discusses the role of the norm of making law public in this context. In the fifth section I provide a graphical account of the argument and discuss some related issues. The sixth section returns to Coase's problem of social cost. The seventh section provides a short discussion of the effects of political competition on the efficiency of institutional structures of property rights in democratic regimes. The eighth section provides an historic illustration of the means by which governments create credible property rights, through the story of the Northwest Ordinance. In the concluding remarks I discuss the relation of all of this to the issue of institutional design and set the stage for the chapters that follow.

A political theory of the origin of property rights

In our earlier work (Riker and Sened, 1991), we identified three types of actors involved in the evolution of property rights' institutions: governments, (potential) right-holders, and (potential) duty-bearers. We then developed a model of the emergence of private property rights, based on two main postulates:

ASSUMPTION 1: Social agents maximize their utilities.

ASSUMPTION 2: Governments have a monopoly over the use of coercive force.

Assumption 1 subsumes the usual axioms of rationality and applies to governments, right-holders, and duty-bearers. Government officials maximize toward diverse goals: possession of resources, tax income, implementation of policies, benefits of being in office and the like (Levi, 1988). Their maximization problem is not trivial; they must win office, pursue diverse goals, and remain in office. Granting rights is one means politicians use to achieve these goals.

Assumption 2 follows the argument of chapters 1–3 of this book, according to which it is unrealistic to try and explain institutional structures on which individual rights in general, and property rights in particular, depend, ignoring the role that central governments play in granting, shaping, and maintaining these structures. The fundamental feature, common to all central governments, that allows them to play a central role in the evolution of property rights, is the monopoly governments have on the use of force. A central puzzle this chapter is meant to solve is why governments with such power would use it to constrain certain agents in society, *including themselves*, in erecting, changing, and maintaining institutions that protect the property rights of their constituents.

In our earlier work we argued that assumptions 1 and 2 imply four necessary conditions that are, together, sufficient for the emergence of individual rights in society. These were (Riker and Sened, 1991):

I. The content of the right is valuable

All the benefits that governments obtain by granting and, then, enforcing individual rights, come from whatever price the right-holders are willing to pay for gaining or maintaining a claim over the valuable content of the right, a price they regularly pay in taxes and different forms of political support. If the content of a right has no value (potential) right-holders will not pay anything to obtain or maintain the right and governments will never benefit from granting it. The expected benefit to governments from *costly* enforcement of such rights is *negative*. Thus, governments will never enforce rights that have worthless content.

II. Right-holders desire to possess the right

Note that condition (I) does not automatically imply condition (II). The content of a right may be valuable, but the cost of maintaining a claim over it may make (potential) right-holders expect negative payoffs. Furthermore, the expected benefits for each agent depend on the strategic behavior of governments, other (potential) right-holders, and (potential) duty-bearers, as well as subjective tastes. A very valuable property right may be judged by potential right-holders as illegitimate or of particularly bad taste.

III. Rule makers desire to enforce the right

Assumption 2 implies that governments can change the legal position of individuals *by force*. Only central governments can erect the efficacious mechanism necessary for the enforcement of the legal system on (potential) duty-bearers. By assumption 1 a government will enforce and protect property rights only if they expect to obtain some marginal benefits from so doing.

IV. Some duty-bearers respect the right

The value of the right is a function of the extent to which, or how many, duty-bearers respect the right. Assumption 1 implies that (potential) duty-bearers will respect a right only if the expected costs offset the expected benefits of disrespect.

By setting this model we introduced the notion that the emergence of rights is an event in which identifiable actors have identifiable motives and sets of feasible actions: rule makers grant rights, giving right-holders some control over valuable content by imposing on duty-bearers the duty to respect right-holders' claims.

We should expect rule makers to grant rights when the cost of forcing duty-bearers to respect the rights of right-holders is smaller than the benefit they expect to gain from the enriched right-holders who pay taxes and the net value of political support they hope to obtain from the new right-holders *less* the political opposition of duty-bearers. The net value of political support is a function of the added marginal probability of maintaining the monopoly of using force that rule makers associate with the marginal political support and tax revenues they gain from granting new property rights, multiplied by the benefit of staying in power for the foreseeable future.

The model we proposed (Riker and Sened, 1991), however, lacked clarity and precision. It was not clear in what sense, exactly, these four conditions were necessary, and what made them sufficient. More importantly, the logic of the process through which governments may benefit by structuring institutions that protect private property rights of individual agents in society was never precisely specified. The following section begins to clarify these issues.

Public goods, property rights and the role of government

Under what circumstances should we expect the conditions specified in the previous section to be met? For the sake of concrete reference I start with an analysis of the emergence of property rights in the context of the frequently invoked social dilemma of the provision of public goods (Samuelson, 1954, 1955; Olson, 1965). The distinction between public and private goods rests on two features:

1. *Rivalry*: what is consumed by one agent cannot be consumed by others.
2. *Excludability*: some agents have exclusive control over the good.

Public goods are non-excludable and non-rivalrous while private goods are excludable and rivalrous.[1] Providers of public goods cannot exclude anyone from using them. Therefore, it is much harder to make users pay producers for the use of those goods. For this reason, public goods are usually overconsumed, undersupplied, or both (Weimer and Vining, 1989: 40–4).

The problem of the provision of public goods can be solved through the creation of well defined property rights. In the *natural state*, all goods are public goods because no one can exclude anyone from consuming the scarce resources in the public domain, except by resorting to force. A *civil society* establishes property rights over some goods that are then called "private goods." No good is inherently non-excludable, or non-rivalrous (or both). Goods remain *public* as long as property rights over them have not been established.

Tomatoes are a classical example of private goods. But if one could not stop others from picking tomatoes in his or her own back yard, tomatoes would be a public good. We consider tomatoes to be private goods only because some structure of property rights protects the ownership of those who grow them. These property rights are precisely what allows us to

---

[1] A third distinctive feature of public goods is the absence of *free disposal*. If a public good is provided, agents may not have the freedom not to consume the good. The common example is national defense. For our purposes, however, this additional characteristic is of little theoretical interest.

exclude others from using the good. Air is a classic example of a *non-excludable* and *non-rivalrous* public good. But when air pollution became a big enough problem, property rights were established in pollutants (Hahn and Hester, 1989). When congestion in the air became a problem, property rights were established in air slots (Riker and Sened, 1991; Sened and Riker, 1996; ch. 7 of this book). From the moment such property rights were established, air pollutants and air slots became rivalrous and excludable and are now being traded in the market like any other private good (Hahn and Hester, 1989; Sened and Riker, 1996).[2]

Thus, the question of "how do property rights emerge?" can be restated as: "how do 'public goods' become 'private goods'?" The central argument in this book is that public goods become private goods when governments decide to protect the property rights of right-holders over these goods.[3]

Historical evidence clearly shows that property rights rarely emerge as conventional equilibria in repeated games (as in Sugden, 1986). Rather, almost always, they were imposed by governments (local in the middle ages and more centralized thereafter) in order to enhance support and revenues (Simpson, [1962] 1986; North, 1981; Levi, 1988; Riker and Sened, 1991; Sened and Riker, 1996; Olson, 1993).

In most cases, property rights emerge when authorities take the initiative to, first, grant the rights and, then, enforce them. In this way authoritative governments make (potential) right-holders better off and gain additional revenues and popular support (North, 1981; Levi, 1988). In the next section I state this argument in a more formal language, for the sake of precision.

Why do governments grant property rights?

The *n*-person prisoners' dilemma is commonly used as a game theoretic conceptualization of the problem of public goods (Hardin, 1982; Schofield, 1985; Taylor, 1987). I use this game to demonstrate how the problem of

---

[2] While the emergence of property rights is usually associated with solving the problem of non-excludability, it can, and often does, solve the problem of rivalry as well. A favorite example that economists use for non-rivalrous goods is air. Riker and Sened (1991, cf. Sened and Riker, 1996) report how air became a rivalrous good when a government decided to enforce property rights in air slots. Hahn and Hester (1989) provide other examples where the creation of property rights turned classical "non-rivalrous goods" into "rivalrous goods."

[3] I am not the first to note that governments can "free" their citizens from the *n*-person prisoners' dilemma or "help" provide public goods (Olson, 1965; Frohlich *et al.*, 1971). This argument dates back at least to Hobbes (Taylor, 1987, ch. 6). A more recent attempt, albeit in a very different model and setting is Bianco and Bates (1990). Three more recent examples of discussions of the subject are: North (1981), Levi (1988) and Olson (1993).

public goods provides governments with an incentive to grant and enforce property rights.[4]

Consider the classic n-person prisoners' dilemma.[5] Suppose each agent pays some cost c_i to *bear the duty* and respect the right of another agent. For simplicity let $c_i = 1$. Every duty-bearer who respects the right of a right-holder, increases the value of the right for this right-holder by some marginal benefit. Again, for simplicity let the marginal benefit that i gets if any other agent, $j \in N$, who respects his property right be b_i ($j \in N$: $j \neq i$ and j respects i's right) = 1.

In the *natural state*, where there are no institutions to establish and maintain property rights, each agent would get a positive payoff, $m \cdot b_i$, if m agents ($0 \leq m \leq n$) decided to respect his rights, but would pay $c_i = 1$ to respect the rights of others. Let $S_i = \{0,1\}$ (with $s_i \in S_i$) be the set of pure strategies available to each agent: he or she can pay the cost and respect the rights of others, $s_i = 1$, or decide not to bear the cost and ignore the rights of others, $s_i = 0$. I assume that agents do not discriminate among players: they either respect the rights of all players or respect the rights of no one.[6] Allowing for mixed strategies, the strategy space of each agent is $[0,1]$ with $\sigma_i = \text{pr}(s_i = 1) \in [0,1]$. That is, σ_i is the probability that i would respect the right of other agents in society. One can think of σ_i as the willingness, or level of commitment, of i to respect the rights of others.

[4] The n-person prisoners' dilemma is an extreme case in two different senses. First, Taylor (1987) and others (e.g., Palfrey and Rosenthal, 1984) argue in favor of other game theoretic representations of the problem of public goods. The most commonly mentioned is the "chicken game," or what I call "participation games" which I discuss in chapter 5. The prisoners' dilemma is extreme in this sense because alone in this type of game it has a unique, dominant strategy, Pareto inferior equilibrium (Rappoport and Guyer, 1966; Hardin, 1971: 28). "Chicken" or "participation" games have multiple equilibria, some of which are Pareto optimal. The second sense in which the way the problem is presented here is quite extreme has to do with the way economists tend to characterize the difference between public goods and private goods. By this account, the difference stems from the fact that in the case of private goods, for every consumer $i \in N$ $MRSi = MRT$, while in the case of public goods $\Sigma_{i \in N} MRSi = MRT$, where MRT is the marginal rate of transformation between the "bundle of all private goods" and the public good or, loosely speaking, the "price" of the public good, and $MRSi$ is the marginal rate of substitution, for individual i between the bundle of private goods and the public good, which is a measure of how much individual i values the public good (Varian, 1984: 253–6). This formulation of the problem yields the prediction that while public goods are always undersupplied, some level of public goods is always supplied. The prisoners' dilemma representation predicts that no units of public goods will ever be produced.

[5] My characterization of the n-person prisoners' dilemma is a variation on an earlier characterization due to Hardin (1971); see also Schofield (1985).

[6] Calvert (1995) proposed the most adequate formulation of this context, of which I am aware. In Calvert's formulation agents discriminate between other agents depending on past behavior of each agent. While the formulation is more adequate, it considerably

Let $\sigma = (\sigma_1, \ldots, \sigma_n) \in \sigma$ be a strategy vector that specifies the strategy σ_i that each agent $i \in N$ chose. The payoff for every agent $i \in N$ from any $\sigma \in \sigma$ is:

$$u_i(\sigma) = \Sigma_{j \neq i} b_j \cdot \sigma_j - c_i \cdot \sigma_i = \Sigma_{j \neq i} \sigma_j - \sigma_i \text{ (since } b_i = c_i = 1). \tag{4.1}$$

Regardless of what other agents do, each agent maximizes his or her utility at $\sigma_i = 0$. So, the unique dominant-strategy equilibrium vector is $\sigma^0 = (0, \ldots, 0)$, where all agents ignore each other's rights, with $u_i(\sigma^0) = 0 \; \forall i \in N$.

But note that if all agents respected each other's rights, each would get: $u_i(\sigma^1 = (1, \ldots, 1)) = b_i \cdot (n-1) - c_i \cdot 1 = (n-1) - 1 = n - 2$. If $n > 2$, we get the n-person analog of the two-person dilemma: since each agent, $i \in N$, prefers $u_i(\sigma^1) > 0$ over $u_i(\sigma^0) = 0$, σ^1 Pareto dominates the unique dominant-strategy equilibrium strategy vector σ^0. As explained in chapter 3, these are the features that characterize the prisoners' dilemma.

So, in the *natural state*, without government intervention, no one respects the rights of anyone. This is a formal representation of the original Hobbesian argument: in the absence of government, any human society is bound to degenerate into a "war of all against all" (cf. Taylor, 1987).

The question is: "what happens when governments intervene in this game?" Introducing government, we get a sequential game Γ in two stages:

STAGE 1: The government chooses a strategy $g \in \{0,1\}$ whether to pay a fixed cost c_g and grant the right, $g = 1$, or not, $g = 0$.

STAGE 2: Agents choose simultaneously the probability, $\sigma_i \in [0,1]$, with which to respect the rights of others conditional on the government decision in stage 1.

The game form of Γ is a triple (D, G, Π), where $D = D_1 X \ldots X D_m$, $d \in D$, $d_i \in D_i$, and $d = (d_1, \ldots, d_n)$. A strategy $d_i \in D_i$ is an ordered pair $((\sigma_i | g = 0), (\sigma_i | g = 1))$, specifying the probability $\sigma_i \in [0,1]$ that agent i will respect the rights of other agents, conditional on whether the government enforces the right or not. $G = \{0,1\}$ with $g \in G$, specifies the strategic choice of the government. A government can either grant property rights, solving the public good problem – we denote this choice as $g = 1$ – or leave the good in the public domain – denoted as $g = 0$. Π is a mapping $\Pi: DXG \Rightarrow U \subseteq R^{n+1}$. U denotes the *utility profile* or *utility space* of all the agents involved, including the government. Therefore U is a subspace

complicates the presentation. More importantly, Calvert demonstrates that if the game is modeled appropriately, then even in the infinitely repeated game it is extremely hard to obtain cooperation among agents whenever the number of members in the community is greater than 30 (on this point see also Olson, 1993). It is obvious that my concern in this book is with much larger societies.

of R^{n+1}. We denote a vector in this space as $u = (u_1, \ldots, u_n, u_g) \in U$. Such a vector specifies a utility level for each relevant agent. In this way $\Pi: DXG \Rightarrow U \subseteq R^{n+1}$ specifies the utility each relevant agent gets out of the realization of each strategic choice (d, g) of the $n + 1$ players in this game. The utility the government extract out of any strategic combination (d, g) is:

$$u_g(d,g) = t \cdot [\Sigma_{j \in N}(b_j \cdot (\Sigma_{i \in Ni \neq j}(\sigma_i | g))) - (\sigma_j | g) \cdot c_j] - g \cdot c_g. \tag{4.2}$$

One can think of t as a tax or as a marginal added political support. (4.2) states that the government levy a share, $0 < t < 1$, of the added utility that agents get from the government grant of the new property right. The government can grant the right, $g = 1$, imposing on every agent who disobeys the law a certain fine, f, or not, in which case $g = 0$ and $f = 0$.[7] Accounting for government's law enforcement the utility each agent $j \in N$ gets from any strategic combination (d, g) is:

$$u_j(d,g) = (1 - t) \cdot [b_j \cdot (\Sigma_{i \in Ni \neq j}(\sigma_i | g))] - [(\sigma_j | g) \cdot c_j - ((f | g) \cdot (1 - (\sigma_j | g)))]. \tag{4.3}$$

(4.3) states that the utility $u_j(d,g)$ any agent, j, gets from any strategic combination (d, g) is the utility derived from the sum of agents in society that chose to respect his or her property rights, depending on the government's policy of granting or not granting the property right, *less* the tax collected by the government: $(1 - t) \cdot [b_j \cdot (\Sigma_{i \in Ni \neq j}(\sigma_i | g))]$. From the expected benefits we subtract the price this agent pays to respect the rights of others, or the fine he or she has to pay if he or she fails to respect these rights, given the policy of the government – $[(\sigma_j | g) \cdot c_j - ((f | g) \cdot (1 - (\sigma_j | g)))]$.

ASSUMPTION 3: Complete information: n, c_g, b_j, c_j, f, t are common knowledge with: (i) $0 < t < 1$, (ii) $t + (f | g = 1) > 1$ and (iii) $b_j = c_j = 1 \forall i \in N$.[8]

---

[7] A comprehensive model should treat f as a function of c_g and compliance as a function of f. Since compliance in such a model is a function of the resources that the government invests in law enforcement, the government decision will not be whether to enforce the right or not, but rather to what extent to enforce the right. It all comes down to treating c_g and f as endogenous, while I treat them as exogenous.

[8] An additional implicit assumption is that the government strategy of granting rights dominates the strategy of central government ownership. To be perfectly accurate, a government has three basic options: (a) to take over the content of the right and manage it on its own, $(g = 2)$; (b) to grant property rights and collect taxes, $(g = 1)$; or (c) to leave the good in the public domain as a public good $(g = 0)$. I assume that $(g = 2)$ is dominated by the strategy of granting property rights to citizens $(g = 1)$ and derive conditions under which the government chooses to play $(g = 1)$ rather than $(g = 0)$. This assumption can be justified on three different grounds. First, there is no reason to believe that a government should have less hardship protecting its own rights than protecting the rights of other agents. Thus, c_g should be equal for both strategies. Second, to keep all goods, or all possible rents from production, to themselves requires

I relax the assumption of complete information in chapter 6. I justified assumptions (3.i–3.iii) elsewhere (Sened, 1990, ch. 4). These restrictions are of some technical importance but need not be elaborated here.

As a solution concept I use the standard *subgame perfect Nash equilibrium* (SPNE), defined in definition 4.2.

DEFINITION 4.1: A strategy vector (d,g) is a Nash equilibrium iff:

1. $u_i(d^*,g^*) \geq u_i(d_i^*,d_i,g^*), \forall i \in N$ and $\forall d_i \in D_i$
2. $u_g(d^*,g^*) \geq u_g(d^*,g) \forall g \in \{0,1\}$.

DEFINITION 4.2: A strategy vector, (d^*,g^*), is a *subgame perfect Nash equilibrium (SPNE) if:*

1. It is a Nash equilibrium for the entire game, as defined in definition 4.1; and
2. Its relevant action rules are a Nash equilibrium for every subgame.

Every SPNE is a Nash equilibrium. The converse is not true. Subgame perfection is one of the most commonly accepted refinements of the Nash equilibrium solution concept (Rasmusen, 1989: 87–8; Ordeshook, 1986: 141).[9]

Theorem 4.1 proves that, in equilibrium, governments grant property rights whenever the cost of enforcement is lower than the marginal benefit they expect in tax revenues and political support. This explains why governments are involved in the business of granting and enforcing property rights.

More importantly, it shows that the assumption of benevolent government that philosophers like Hobbes and Hume thought was necessary to guarantee that governments would implement law and order is not necessary. We can rely on perfectly selfish governments to protect property

governments to enforce their own property rights without the support of other right-holders. Finally, to grant rights to subjects induces private production, which is more efficient than centralized production. Since governments can use force to extract any rent they helped generate by enforcing property rights, they are better off granting rights and collecting taxes than supervising a centralized system of production. The collapse of eastern European economies in the late 1980s is a commonly cited empirical case of the deficiencies of government owned enterprises and other property such as land.

[9] A simple way to identify an SPNE is the method of backwards induction. One calculates what the last player to act would do, when he or she is called upon to act, and what would be the consequent payoff vector for all the agents, given the anticipated behavior of the last player. One then treats the anticipated behavior of the last player and its consequences as given, and repeats the exercise for the one-before-last player. One works his or her way up the game tree until one reaches the starting point of the original game. The proof of theorem 4.1 is a simple example of this method.

rights in society. This observation goes a long way towards the revival of traditional liberal theory of the social contract, in as much as it overcomes the main objection to this tradition: the objection stated in chapter 1, according to which governments cannot be assumed to be benevolent, and selfish governments cannot be trusted to implement adequate institutions of law and order. My analysis shows that selfish governments are likely to protect property rights to further their own interests.

THEOREM 4.1: Under assumptions 1–3,

(i)   If $t \cdot n^2 < c_g$, the unique *subgame perfect Nash equilibrium* (SPNE) outcome of the game is one in which the government *does not* grant the right and all agents ignore each other's property rights.

(ii) If $t \cdot n^2 > c_g$, then the unique *subgame perfect Nash equilibrium* (SPNE) outcome of the game is one in which the government *grants* the right and all agents respect each other's rights.

(iii) If $t \cdot n^2 = c_g$, then both outcomes described in 4.1i and 4.1ii are SPNE.

PROOF: By (4.3) and assumption 3ii, the best response [BR] to $g = 1$ for all agents is to respect the right and the BR to $g = 0$ is to ignore these rights. So, the unique dominant-strategy equilibrium for the subgame that starts if $g = 1$ is for all agents to respect the right, while the unique dominant-strategy equilibrium for the subgame that starts if $g = 0$ is for all agents not to respect those rights. Γ is reduced to a decision problem for the government on whether or not it will grant the right. If it does, agents will respect each other's rights, while if it doesn't no one will respect the property rights of anyone.   QED

In the following section I show that the classical norm that laws should be "common knowledge," has a straightforward positive explanation, a derivative of the model developed here. So, this model explains the emergence of political institutions at two separate levels. Theorem 4.1 explains why governments intervene at the "collective action level," and enforce property rights upon their constituents. Theorem 4.2 in the next section explains why governments "constrain" themselves at the "constitutional level" and make the code of civic law common knowledge.

In terms of the general approach developed in chapter 3, Γ is a special case of the class of complex games of type Γ^X discussed there. Here, the government is assumed to be a decisive coalition, due to its monopoly over the use of force and its special role in the legislative process. In the game Γ, discussed here, the government anticipates a game of collecting tax from productive citizens. It has to choose whether to impose well defined property rights before the production game begins. Theorem 4.1 describes in precise terms under what conditions it is an equilibrium behavior for a government to grant property rights: a government will impose well defined property rights if it expects that the improvement in productivity, due to the grant and subsequent enforcement of the property right, will be higher than the costs of granting and enforcing the right.

Why are laws made public knowledge?

Many democratic and non-democratic regimes adhere to the principle that laws must be made public. Normative justifications to this moral *maxim* exist (Kant, [1794] 1983: 135; Hegel, [1821] 1942 no. 1215), but positive explanations to the commonly observed *political institution* are harder to come by. In its different versions, this principle implies that governments must make their decisions on whether to grant and enforce any particular right *public* before agents decide whether to respect this right or not. This was an implicit assumption of the game specified in the previous section. What would happen if we assumed, instead, that governments do not publish their decisions on whether to enforce a right or not? I denote this game by Γ'.

The difference between Γ and Γ' is that in Γ' agents *do not* know what the decision of the government is when they make their strategic choices regarding whether or not to respect the rights of their fellow citizens. So, agents cannot make their strategic moves conditional on the government's policy.

The game form of Γ' is a triple (D',G',Π') where $D' = D'_1 X \ldots X D'_n$ and D'_i is the set of feasible strategies for player i. A strategy, $d_i \in D_i$, in Γ', is the probability $\sigma_i \in [0,1]$ that agent i will respect the right. Unlike the case in Γ, here, $\sigma_i \in [0,1]$, is not conditional on the government's strategy. $G' = \{0,1\}$ and Π' is a mapping $\Pi': D'XG' \Rightarrow U \subseteq R^{n+1}$ as specified in (4.2')–(4.3').

$$u_g(d,g) = t \cdot [\Sigma_{j \in N}(b_j \cdot (\Sigma_{i \in Ni \neq j}(\sigma_i))) - (\sigma_j) \cdot c_j] - g \cdot c_g. \tag{4.2'}$$

Agents' payoffs are:

$$u_j(d,g) = (1 - t) \cdot [b_j \cdot (\Sigma_{i \in Ni \neq j}(\sigma_i))] - [(\sigma_j) \cdot c_j - ((f \mid g) \cdot (1 - (\sigma_j)))]. \tag{4.3'}$$

THEOREM 4.2: Under assumptions 1–3, the only Nash equilibrium outcome of the game Γ' is one in which the government does not enforce the right and all agents ignore the rights of other agents, so that $u_g = u_i = 0 \forall i \in N$.

PROOF: Given the payoffs functions, defined in (4.2'), the government has a dominant strategy not to enforce the right. Since the government never enforces the right, by (4.3') $\sigma_i = 0$ is a dominant strategy $\forall i \in N$.
                                                                              QED

Without making the penal law public knowledge, governments cannot escape from becoming themselves entangled in the $(n+1)$-person prisoners' dilemma. So, the *norm* that requires that laws be made public knowledge is explained as an institutional solution adopted by governments that try to maximize their benefits as law enforcing agencies. In a very interesting way this institutional solution is "self-enforcing." If we augmented the game and let the government decide first whether to make laws public or not, and then play either Γ or Γ' depending on its choice, the government is always better off making its laws public, i.e. playing Γ. Thus, governments' commitment to publish their laws is not to be attributed to some moral respect of public interest but to the fact that it is in their best interest, as revenue maximizers, to make their laws public.[10] It is also a good example of how "constitutional level" institutions, such as the norm of publishing the code books of the civil law, can be explained using the same logic we use to explain "collective decision level" institutions, such as the grants and protection of property rights by central governments.

Theorems 4.1 and 4.2 clarify an important implication of governments' monopoly over the use of coercive force that is often overlooked: it allows them to make credible commitments to use force against reluctant duty-bearers. In a straightforward sense, the combination of theorem 4.1 and 4.2 supports Umbeck's (1981) claim that such a monopoly is a necessary condition for the emergence of property rights in society. But theorem 4.2 captures in a very precise way how making the law public knowledge is necessary to make the governments' threat to enforce property rights credible (cf. North and Weingast, 1989; Bianco and Bates, 1991).

It is important to note that, in equilibrium, the credibility of the threat allows governments to abstain from using coercive force. Umbeck's analysis implies that in a world without central governments, even if benefits do not totally dissipate as a result of entry, agents spend many resources on violent means to ensure that other agents don't rob them of their property. If we add the economies of scale which central governments exploit in the

---

[10] It is of great interest to cite from Hegel's discussion of this principle:

> 215. If laws are to have a binding force, it follows that . . . they must be made universally known . . . Rulers who have given a national law to their people in the form of a well-arranged and clear-cut legal code . . . have been the greatest benefactors of their peoples and have received thanks and praise for their beneficence. But the truth is that their work was at the same time a great act of justice. ([1821] 1942: 138)

My formal results also capture Kant's justification for his moral imperative, in the sense that if governments did not make the law public knowledge, there would be no law enforcement, given the unique equilibrium of the game. The meaning of law enforcement would, thus, be altered.

production and use of force, we realize that, contrary to the common neo-classical account, at least in this respect, central governments do not only induce efficiency by coordinating the complex transactions needed in advanced economies (North, 1990), but also by reducing the cost of violent means needed to protect private property.

But all of this induced efficiency is possible only if the government makes its threat to enforce the property rights credible, by publishing its intention to enforce the law.

The discussion in the next section uses the model developed in this chapter to explain, in precise terms, one origin of the concern of neo-classical economists about government intervention. I also use there a simple graphic illustration that may help clarify the central argument of this chapter.

The monopolist's tax schedule

If governments are better off granting property rights to agents, why don't governments collect all the rents that the production of rights generate? Whether governments keep all marginal rents to themselves or distribute them among right-holders depends on the value of the tax rate t that maximizes government revenues, and the value of political support. In this section I ignore the political support factor, in order to concentrate on the tax issue.

When we say that governments maximize their revenues by using optimal tax rates, we have to distinguish between the problem of monopolists who maximize rents, and the issue of whether the tax rate that governments impose gives the incentive to right-holders to maintain and get the most out of their private property.

My model analyses government as a monopolist who produces law enforcement of property rights and chooses a tax rate to maximize revenues and political support. It is not suited to address the issue of optimal taxation schemes and I do not intend to offer a theory of taxation (see, on this issue, Frohlich and Oppenheimer, 1974). The purpose of this discussion is to clarify the model and its implication for a neo-liberal theory of the state.

Suppose that we interpret the benefit that each agent receives if *all* agents respect his or her rights as the payment he or she gets when selling a good he or she produces. Suppose that the cost $c_j = 1$ is interpreted as the cost of respecting the rights of other agents in the economy by paying for goods in the market instead of stealing them. In my model, without law enforcement everyone steals everything so that no producer will ever produce anything. If governments protect the rights of producers, markets develop. Let us concentrate on "one output" markets and assume that the supply curve of the good is perfectly elastic ("flat") everywhere and the demand curve for the good is downwards sloping, as in figure 4.1.

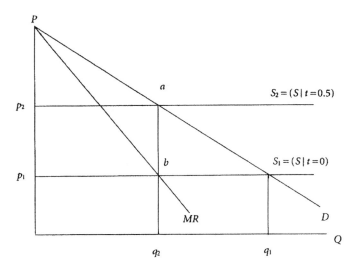

4.1 Property rights, production, and taxation

Without property rights everyone who needs a unit of the good steals it, thus the effective price is zero. In such an environment no one will produce and the utility of all agents involved in producing (right-holders), buying (duty-bearers), or taxing (government) the good (the content of the right), is zero. Now suppose that the government enforces the rights but does not impose any tax. In the example illustrated in figure 4.1, q_1 units of the good will be produced and sold in the market at price p_1. However, as a monopolist, the government maximizes its revenues by imposing a tax that forces producers to produce at a point at which marginal revenue equals marginal cost. In figure 4.1 this can be achieved at a 0.5 sales tax. Such tax shifts the supply curve to S_2, prices will increase to p_2, and the number of units produced in the market will go down to q_2. This will yield a tax revenue of $q_2 \cdot (p_2 - p_1)$ for the government.

If $q_2 \cdot (p_2 - p_1) > c_g$ then the government would enforce the right, imposing a penalty, $f > p_2$, on anyone who steals the product. Producers will produce and sell at a price of p_2 and pay the government a tax $(p_2 - p_1)$ on every unit they sell.

This illustration reveals an important missing piece in the neo-classical account of the structure of economic markets. Note that without a government or any other law enforcing agency, no production takes place, because the benefits of production are not protected (Olson, 1993). To induce production, the property rights of the producers must be protected. It is the premise of this book, and a rather common observation, that in most modern societies it is the role of governments to protect the property rights of producers and consumers alike.

I have explained in the previous chapters why well defined and properly enforced property rights are unlikely to evolve in the absence of central governments. I have explained above why we should expect governments to grant and enforce property rights. At the same time, I have just shown that governments' intervention in the grant and protection of property rights is unlikely to be efficient from a social welfare perspective.

The prediction that the above graphic illustration of my model implies fits nicely with the reality in most contemporary nation-states. In well organized, be it more or less developed, countries we observe, almost without exception, that governments tend to overcharge producers and consumers alike for the protection of their respective property rights. This overcharge is evident in excessive tax rates and the excessive costs of army and police forces who serve as central agents of the government in its role as granter and enforcer of property rights.

In the next section I provide a numerical example for this implication of the model, while "revisiting" Coase's "problem of social cost" from the perspective of the model I developed here.

Coase's "problem of social cost" revisited

The main contribution of "Coase's Theorem" is the observation that if property rights are well defined then, in the absence of transactions costs, the efficiency of – and resource allocations for – production are not affected by the initial distribution of property rights. This result generated a body of literature known as the "transaction costs' theory of institutions."

Unfortunately, most of this literature is based on two very problematic assumptions (North, 1990: 1–2):

1. *Instrumental rationality* – "actors either have correct models by which to interpret the world around them or receive information feedback that will lead them to revise and correct their initially incorrect theories."
2. The notion that "political markets" are as efficient as any competitive "economic" market.

In chapter 5 I look at some shortcomings of assumption 1 by studying a model of political interaction between governments and constituents where government officials have incomplete information regarding the consequences of their decisions. In this section I illustrate why the assumption or expectation that political institutions yield efficient allocation of resources is problematic. Using Coase's argument, I provide a numerical example that includes a rational, revenue maximizing government.

Coase's argument is best illustrated by his own example:[11] Suppose we live in a world where legal institutions generate perfectly competitive markets and reduce transaction costs to zero. Consider two agents: a farmer, growing corn in his field and his neighbor, a cattle rancher raising cows. The problem is whether it makes any difference whether the cattle rancher is liable or not for the damage done by her cows to the farmer's corn fields. Such damages are often referred to by welfare economists as "externalities."

Externalities are often mentioned as a justification for government intervention. The argument behind such justification is that the cattle grower does not include the damage her herd causes to her neighbor's fields of corn when she calculates the maximand of her production cost function, and therefore produces "more than she should." A government can impose a tax on the cattle grower to force her to take these costs into account and reduce the size of the herd to an optimal size, taking into account the damage caused to the farmer.

Coase's rejection of this argument is known as "Coase's Theorem," and is best understood through his example: the expected revenue of the farmer without damage is $p \cdot q$, where p is the market price for corn and q is the quantity of corn produced. Since we assumed perfectly competitive markets, the price of corn and steers is unaffected by the amount produced by our farmer or cattle raiser. For the sake of the numerical example, assume that the price of 1 tonne of corn is $1.00 and that the farmer would have produced 100 tonnes of corn if his crop was not damaged by the herd of steers raised by the cattle raiser. Suppose, further, that the damage to the farmer and the benefits, total and marginal, to the cattle raiser, given different sizes of herds of steers are as summarized in table 4.1. Since $p = 1$ in our example, the losses to the farmer are expressed in tons or dollars interchangeably.

Note that marginal revenues are linearly decreasing while marginal losses are linearly increasing. By standard neo-classical analysis these implicit assumptions are not very restrictive. It is clear that if the cattle raiser is liable for damage he or she will raise a herd of 12 steers. What previous analysts did not recognize, and Coase pointed out, is that the same is true if the cattle raiser is not held liable. This is true because the farmer can pay $ 6.00 to the cattle raiser "bribing" her not to raise the size of her herd beyond 12 steers. The cattle raiser is indifferent between raising 16 steers or raising just 12 and getting the forgone marginal benefit of increasing the

---

[11] I have modified the numerical example, following a discussion with David Carney and Randall Calvert, to allow the richer analysis that my argument requires, but in essence I have not deviated from Coase's original presentation of the problem.

Table 4.1. *Total and marginal benefits to farmer and cattle raiser*

No. of cattle heads	Tons/$ of crop lost	Marginal loss in crop	Net return to cattle raiser	Marginal returns to cattle raiser with no liability (with liability)	Total social return ($)
7	0	0	79	9 (9)	100 + 79 = 179
8	0	0	87	8 (8)	100 + 87 = 187
9	0	0	94	7 (7)	100 + 94 = 194
10	1	1	100	6 (5)	100 + 100 − 1 = 199
11	3	2	105	5 (3)	100 + 105 − 3 = 202
12	6	3	109	4 (1)	100 + 109 − 6 = 203
13	10	4	112	3 (−1)	100 + 112 − 10 = 202
14	15	5	114	2 (−3)	100 + 114 − 15 = 199
15	21	6	115	1 (−5)	100 + 115 − 21 = 194

herd as a bribe from the farmer. Hence Coase's Theorem as stated above.[12]

Given this analysis it does not matter if the government taxes the rancher in order to reduce her production to the optimal level, if the rancher is made liable for the damages by law, or if the law does not put any liability on cattle raisers. Table 4.2 summarizes the rest of the argument. Since, by the previous analysis, it is already clear that the legal structure of rights concerning liability for damage is not going to affect the allocation of scarce resources in the market, we can concentrate on the efficient outcome, which in our example is an outcome where the cattle raiser raises 12 steers.

Table 4.2 more or less concludes Coase's argument. There is one missing link in this argument: why would the government tax the cattle raiser at $ 4

[12] Recently, several conjectures have been made concerning the extent to which Coase's Theorem is as generally applicable as previously thought (most notably Aivazian and Callen, 1981; Aivazian *et al.*, 1986). Instead of entering into this debate, I prefer to quote the conclusion of Coase's comment (1981: 187) on one of these attempts:

> I would not wish to conclude without observing that, while consideration of what would happen in a world of zero transaction costs can give us valuable insights, these insights are, in my view, without value except as steps on the way to the analysis of the real world of positive transaction costs. We do not do well to devote ourselves to a detailed study of the world of zero transaction costs, like augurs divining the future by the minute inspection of the entrails of a goose.

Table 4.2. *Optimal resource allocation under different ownership designs*

Alternative regulation, using alternative structures of property rights	Net return to cattle raiser	Net return to farmer	Net return to government	Total social return including government's tax revenue
Liability on cattle raiser	103	100	0	100+103=203
No Liability	109 + 6 = 115	100 − 12 = 88	0	115+88=203
One firm management	—	—	0	100+103=203
Government taxes cattle at a rate of $4 per steer	109 − 48 = 61	100 − 6 = 94	48	61+94+48=203

per steer? Welfare economists would respond that the answer is trivial: this is the efficient tax rate. It is the efficient tax rate since if the tax is higher the cattle raiser will reduce production below the efficient output and the total social return will decrease below the optimal of $203, while if the tax is lower the cattle raiser will raise more than the optimal number of steers. But why should governments be concerned to maximize total social revenues? We know for a fact that they are not. Governments maximize toward diverse goals: possession of resources, tax income, policy goals, benefits of being in office and the like (North, 1981; Levi, 1988; Riker and Sened, 1991; Laver and Schofield, 1990).

Governments, as independent actors who maximize their own utility, are almost always absent from this type of analysis (Buchanan, 1986). Models of social choice either ignore them or assume them away (North, 1990). Two separate assumptions hide behind this neglect. First, there is the efficiency assumption we discussed above. There is no reason to assume that government officials try to maximize social welfare, and we know, for a fact, that they don't.

The second more or less implicit assumption in Coase's argument is of much greater interest to us here. This is the assumption that property rights are well defined and enforced. Earlier works in neo-classical theory made

Table 4.3. *Resource allocations with governments that maximize revenues*

Alternative regulations, using alternative structures of property rights	Net return to cattle raiser	Net return to farmer	Net return to government	Total social return including government's tax revenue
Government taxes cattle at a rate of $8 per steer	$87 - 64 = 23$	100	64	$23+100+64=187$

the assumption that such rights are guaranteed by governments explicit (Stigler, 1942: 22). Recent works tend to make this assumption implicit. But almost all of this literature depends crucially on this assumption (Eggertsson, 1990: 38–9).

If governments are crucial players in this context, we must include them in the story as rational agents with their own utility functions that they try to maximize (Hammond and Miller, 1987). What would be the consequences of including governments in the analysis as independent utility maximizing agents? If governments grant and enforce property rights, and since enforcement is not costless, they must collect taxes to pay law enforcement costs. As utility maximizers with a monopoly on the production of law enforcement, they can enforce whatever tax rates they wish. If governments maximize revenues then, in the context of our example, they will collect $8.00 per steer. This tax rate would reduce production below the efficient level of output to 8 steers. The wealth distribution will now be as specified in table 4.3.

This is an inefficient outcome as far as social welfare goes. But this "inefficiency" is induced by a government, without which it is unrealistic to hope that any market transactions could take place uninterrupted by violence. We cannot keep eating the cake and leave it whole.

On democratic competition

Given what I have established thus far, we can now discuss the claims concerning the proximity of democratic political institutions to economic competitive markets. In the last two sections we observed how monopolistic governments might deviate from optimal designs of property rights' institutions in their will to maximize their own utility, or simply their tax revenues. Democratic political institutions certainly alleviate this problem, through the introduction of some competition into the political arena (Olson, 1993).

To see how this may be the case, consider the simple model of uni-dimensional political competition (Shepsle, 1990) between two candidates in a plurality rule electoral competition, discussed in chapter 3.

RECAP: the set of outcomes, X, is a subset of the policy m-dimensional space: $X \subseteq R^m$. Every vital, political issue is represented as one dimension of this space. We represent ideal policy positions of agents and alternative policy positions as points in this space. The utility, u_i, that agent i derives from a policy position, $x \in X$, is assumed to be a function of the Euclidean distance between x and the ideal policy point of agent i which we denote by ρ_i, i.e. $u_i(x) = \phi_i(\parallel x - \rho_i \parallel)$. Each agent seeks to realize policy points as close as possible to his or her ideal point. The central solution concept in this paradigm, the "core" or "simple majority equilibrium," is defined, as in definition 3.6 (p. 63), as:

DEFINITION 4.3: $x^* \in R^m$ is a *simple majority equilibrium* if, for any other feasible alternative $y \in R^m$, at least half of the agents prefer x to y.

THE MEDIAN VOTER THEOREM: In uni-dimensional political settings, using plurality rule, if voters have single-peaked preferences, if voters and candidates have complete information about voters' preferences and candidates' positions, in equilibrium, candidates will endorse the ideal point of the median voter as their platform (Black, 1958; Feddersen *et al.*, 1990; Shepsle, 1990).

The general implications of this result are quite remarkable (Shepsle, 1990). For our purposes, two implications are of particular interest. First, as Ledyard (1984) notes, if candidates converge to the same median voter's ideal point, voters should be indifferent about who wins, and abstain from voting. Second, if the rationality of voters and candidates forces both candidates to offer the median voter's ideal point, on every salient ideological dimension that preoccupies voters at the moment, how can the candidates possibly compete? One way to compete is by promising to grant special privileges to special interests, and to lower taxes.

Such competition forces candidates to support more efficient institutional structures of property rights. In order to give more property rights to more interests, governments must reduce the cost of enforcement. Furthermore, in their attempt to reduce taxes, governments may lower taxes below the monopolistic prices discussed in the previous sections (on this issue, see also Frohlich and Oppenheimer, 1974; Olson, 1993).

This is why, so often, before national elections, in almost every democratic country, we see candidates converge on the general issues and begin to dispute, in public debates, who will reduce taxes more effectively, and who will protect better, the rights of the poor, the elderly, the farmers, and other interests in society.

Yet, as discussed in chapter 3, the tendency of political debates to be multi-dimensional is likely to lead to intransitivities in the policy space which, in turn, leads to uncertainty and other types of efficiency losses. Politicians can use asymmetries of information to renege on their promises which, of course, they do all the time. Politicians are rarely held responsible for the long-term consequences of their policies. One well documented consequence of this fact is "pork-barrel politics" (Shepsle, 1986: 69):

> In the policy game in a legislature, . . . there is an attitude of live and let live. Each legislative agent seeks to obtain benefits for his constituency, and [with] some exceptions, the general rule does not impose sanctions on those who seek to place the distributive and regulatory powers of the state in the service of their constituents.

As Shepsle and Weingast eloquently note (1984b: 356):

> Expenditure policies are, therefore biased so as to be larger than the economically efficient scale. The very label "pork barrel," connotes economically unwarranted projects.

It is not the purpose of this chapter to discuss at any length the reasons why efficient institutional structures of property rights in democratic regimes are unlikely. Actually, it is quite odd, given the state of the art on the subject, that some scholars still try to put forward such arguments (e.g. Wittman, 1989, 1995).

The purpose of this chapter is to assert, in clear terms, the role that governments play in the evolution of political institutions that protect individual rights in general, and property rights in particular. The discussion in this section is meant only to highlight the relevance of my model to the debate on the issue of the economic efficiency of social institutions, and how democratic competition may put some constraints on the government as a monopolistic producer of law enforcement of private property and related individual rights (Olson, 1993).

An historical illustration: the Northwest Ordinance[13]

The passage of the Northwest Ordinance of 1787 is a nice example of the means by which governments create credible property rights.

The Northwest Ordinance was a miniature constitution relevant to what later became the states of Ohio, Michigan, Indiana, Illinois, and Wisconsin. The Ordinance comprised three sections. The first established clear, simple laws of inheritance and (inexpensive) transferal rights. The second section established guidelines concerning the creation of territorial governments, and the means by which they could become state governments. The last section provided a "bill of rights" for these territories (North and Rutten, 1987: 22):

> (1) freedom of religion; (2) the use of writs of habeas corpus jury trials, the common law and bail . . . prohibition against cruel and unusual punishment, the seizure of property without due process of compensation, or laws interfering with contracts; (3) the encouragement of schools and the means of education . . . (4) the obligation of the territories to the United States, including remaining in the United States, sharing in the payments of the federal debt, not interfering with the federal land sales . . . (5) the division of the territories into states, which were to have republican governments and to be admitted into the United States after reaching specified populations.

Many of these rights reflect compromises and bargained outcomes between states that had diverse needs for the uncolonized territories. Yet, the key issue for the study of the political institution of property rights is the means by which this immense tract of public land was set under an institutional structure of a formidable design by the central federal government in what is often regarded as America's "first privatization movement" (Anderson and Hill, 1975).

A second, related issue, which the North and Rutten (1987) study indirectly highlights, is the important linkage between "pure property rights" and other civil rights like "freedom of religion" and "the encouragement of schools." In this book most of my evidence (chapter 7) and terminology come from the literature on property rights. I discuss at length two "civil rights" which are the "right to know your rights" discussed in this chapter, and the right for "freedom of speech" discussed in chapter 5. What the above quote from the North and Rutten (1987) study of the Northwest Ordinance nicely illustrates is the interdependence between "pure property rights" and more general civil rights. It is quite clear why these rights were incorporated in the Ordinance. It was the

---

[13] I owe an important debt to Steve Lewis who helped me work out this historical example. The main references for short recounts of the study are: North and Rutten (1987), Anderson (1987), Onuf (1987), and North (1990: 97–100).

intention of the federal government to enhance economic growth in the territories in order to pay its war debts. To do this, the government had to create favorable conditions for investment and resettlement. To attract new settlers from the old to the new lands, the government had first to ensure reasonable mechanisms to enforce and protect property rights. But it also had to ensure that the civil rights protected in the established states of the United States, particularly Virginia and Massachusetts who had well defined bills of rights in their constitutions, were protected. Otherwise the incentives of potential new settlers would be severely compromised. There was no "deep moral" intention involved. It was only a matter of setting up the institutional design of the new governments in a way that would be attractive for future investors.

To go back to the issue of the government grant of property rights over land that was previously publicly owned, the government faced competing claims for the means and ways of privatizing these lands. Large states which still had much undeveloped public land within their borders favored a slow plan of selling off the new territories in order to maintain the value of their own land. States that controlled tracts of land in the new territory – e.g. Delaware that controlled tracts of land around Cleveland – favored means to increase the value of these assets. The remaining states preferred to sell the public lands in a way which gained the most revenue for the federal government (North and Rutten, 1987; Onuf, 1987).

The actual means by which these lands would be sold off was also subject to disagreement. The newly established federal government favored the quick selling off of the lands to large companies in order to pay off immense war debts, while some states preferred small-scale auctions which would maintain the value of the assets. Finally, the landless, including war veterans, preferred the establishment of squatters' rights. The Northwest Ordinance formalized none of these means. In the end, Congress ended up selling off large chunks to well connected land companies. But they also set up auctions and ended up recognizing some squatters' rights.

What is important in this story is that a newly established government sets up a formidable institutional design to protect property and a set of other human rights, only as a mean to pay its war debts. It is just as important to realize that everyone got something out of this government grant, even though the chief motivation for the government was to pay its war debts and, for some states, to make future monetary gains they hoped would materialize. As a symbol of just policy it was outrageously unjust; but as the blueprint for creating stable interactions between new local governments and individual agents in society it was effective, and became a source of much economic growth in the nineteenth century (North and Rutten, 1987; Anderson, 1987).

Concluding remarks: governments, property rights, and institutional design

For much too long, scholars have looked at what "should be" the institutional structure of individual rights, in normative terms. Without any convincingly justifiable, ethical theory of what should or should not be, they followed normative rhetoric in judging, designing and reforming institutions of individual rights. It is now time to identify the origin of these structures, and to judge them according to their real merits. We can no longer deny the crucial role that central governments play in designing complex, political, institutional structures to protect property and related individual rights. It is the purpose of this chapter in particular, and of this book in general, to allow a better understanding of the logic of why such institutional structures are designed by central governments in the first place. With all the discussion on individual rights in past and present literature, it is amazing how little attention has been given to the simple fact that most institutions that protect meaningful individual rights almost invariably depend on the "good will" and "designing skills" of central governments. So it is about time that we paid more attention to the origin of this "good will" and to the art and science of institutional designs, as well as to their limits, which is the "raison d'être" of this book in general, and this chapter in particular.

This chapter explored the role of governments in the evolution of private property and related individual rights. I argued that in situations where agents tend to settle for Pareto inferior, equilibrium outcomes, governments tend to intervene and help free them of such dilemmas by granting and enforcing property rights. Since governments have many ways to extract a fraction of the benefits they help generate in this way, through taxes and other forms of political support, we expect governments to seek opportunities to grant such rights.

This claim goes at least as far back as Hobbes. What was often ignored in the literature, however, is that governments are rational players themselves (Buchanan, 1986: 36–7) and that enforcing rights is not costless. Governments weigh the benefits of granting rights (North, 1981; Levi, 1988) against the cost of enforcement. Rational governments will grant rights only when the expected benefit outweighs the expected cost of enforcement. The main goal of this chapter was to characterize, in precise terms, our expectations regarding the behavior of rational government officials who have to consider the possibility of granting individual rights, under conditions of complete information regarding the consequences of such decisions.

It is realistic to assume that governments possess relatively accurate estimates of the costs of enforcement, but to assume that governments have complete information regarding other agents' preferences is less realistic. One reason why governments fail to seize opportunities to enrich society and themselves by creating property rights, and why they often grant property rights that only impoverish society, is that they do not have complete information. It is for this reason that ordinary citizens have an important role to play in the evolution of individual rights. In order to understand the role of citizens in the evolution of rights we had to specify, in precise terms, the role of governments in this process. Now that we have established what citizens should expect from their government, we can study their strategic behavior, given these expectations.

If a government overestimates its expected benefits from granting a right, then the actual enforcement of the right will result in a loss of revenue. The government will realize this, and correct its mistake. There are many examples of governments who stopped enforcing property rights because they could not cover the costs. The lack of law enforcement in the urban centers of the USA is but one obvious example.

But what happens if some agents believe that they can benefit from the right while the government is reluctant to grant it? Agents can petition governments to grant the right, trying to convey to government officials the information that the government would be better off granting the right. Unfortunately, conveying information to the government is costly. In addition, the problem of contributing to such petitioning efforts is, in and by itself, a complex, strategic problem for potential right-holders. This is the subject of chapter 5.

There are (at least) three important features of the evolution of rights that I have not dealt with in this chapter. First, preferences are not equal across individuals. Some rights may enrich some agents while imposing a cost on other agents. Second, governments do not have complete information about the preferences of their constituents. Third, governments are uncertain about the consequences of their policies (Austen-Smith and Riker, 1987; Krehbiel, 1992). In chapter 5 I deal with these issues by introducing into the model uncertainty with respect to the number of constituents that are expected to benefit from the grant of any particular property right. This allows me to include in the model (1) different types of preferences, (2) asymmetric information: agents know what their preferences are, but governments do not; and (3) governments' uncertainty about the consequences of their policies: they do not know how many of their constituents are potential right-holders, and are thus uncertain about the economic consequences of granting the right.

5

A neo-liberal theory of the social contract: the role of autonomous individuals in the evolution of property rights

Introduction

Governments in my model act as political entrepreneurs who enter the business of granting property rights in order to make profits (Frohlich *et al.*, 1971; Ainsworth and Sened, 1993). Without social institutions, humans often end up in a Hobbesian "war of all against all" – a very unproductive state of affairs. By granting and enforcing property rights, governments can improve productivity. Such improvements help them gain more tax revenues and other forms of political support. In chapter 4, I used a simple model to specify conditions under which governments would grant and enforce property rights.

The model explored in chapter 4, however, assumed that all the agents in the game have complete information. In this chapter I relax the assumption of complete information to unveil the role of individual agents in the evolution of institutions that structure the social contract by committing central governments to protect the private property and related individual rights of their constituents.

Consider the case of a government that, based on its beliefs, does not expect to gain from granting certain property rights. Agents who expect to benefit from such rights could be made better off by petitioning the government to grant them. If government officials receive enough petitions to convince them that they could benefit from granting the right, they might do so. Petitioning, however, is not only costly, it also involves a collective action problem: since property rights are public goods, once they are granted, all beneficiaries benefit from the protection of the rights regardless of whether they participated in petitioning for them or not.

Schotter (1981: 28) notes that:

if the social institutions we are investigating are created by a social planner [or a government], their design can be explained by maximizing the value of some objective function existing in the planner's mind. Such an exercise, as Hayek (1945) has pointed out is of less theoretical interest . . . unless the problem of preference revelation exists.

The analysis in chapter 4 shows that Hayek and Schotter underestimated the interest of the first problem. Whatever the case may be, in this chapter I enrich the analysis by looking at the case where a problem of preference revelation does exist.

In the first section I review work by Palfrey and Rosenthal that characterized the collective action problem that individual agents face in environments similar to the ones discussed in this book. In the next section I model the interactions between governments and their constituents, by which the "social contract" between them evolves. In the third section I derive equilibrium conditions for this type of interaction. In the fourth section I show that, *ex ante*, governments and constituents expect to be made better off by playing this game. The fifth section tells the story of King John's signature of the Magna Carta, in 1215, as an historic illustration to the central argument of this chapter.

The collective action problem of challenging existing institutions

Suppose an agent can benefit from the grant of a property right. If the government is not informed about the benefits of granting the right and, therefore, does not grant the right, the agent could be made better off by petitioning the government to grant the right. Petitioning, however, is costly. Petitioning also involves a collective action problem. As discussed in chapter 4, property rights are public goods: once granted, all of the potential beneficiaries of such rights would benefit, regardless of whether they paid the cost of petitioning for these rights, or not.

To explain the problem in more precise terms we need some formal notation. Let $s_i = 1$ denote the strategy of petitioning for a right, and $s_i = 0$ denote the strategy of not petitioning. Let $A^1 \subseteq N$ be the set of agents who actually petition. That is A^1 is a group of individuals or economic firms that pay some petitioning cost, which we will denote by "c," to obtain the grant and protection of the property right in question.

Suppose there was an integer threshold value, ω, so that if the number of petitioners, $\alpha = |A^1|$, is greater than this threshold, i.e. if $\alpha \geq \omega$, government officials would update their beliefs, realize that they could benefit from granting the right and grant it, while if $\alpha < \omega$, these officials would continue to believe that the cost of enforcing the right would offset the expected benefits of granting it. Lemma 5.7 in the appendix and corollary 5.1 on p. 112 show that such a threshold always exists. Theorem 5.1 shows how agents in society use their expectations about such thresholds to make strategic choices on whether or not to petition the government to change the institutional structures that protect property and other individual rights. This often leads to a positive turnout of interested agents who petition for change. These petitions eventually lead to structural changes in the make up of institutions that protect property and other individual rights.

Enforcement agencies can solve the prisoners' dilemma of mutual respect of rights. But, in most cases, it is up to individual agents to solve the collective action problem of conveying to government officials the information that any property right could be enforced to the benefit of citizens and government officials. If government officials had had this information they would have enforced the rights for their own benefit, as shown in chapter 4. But when government officials have prior beliefs that imply that the government cannot benefit from granting the right, they are unlikely to search for such information on their own.

Even when economic organizations and other social agents have information that indicates clearly that the government and most agents in society could benefit from the grant and enforcement of a property right, they still have to overcome the difficulty that conveying this information involves a collective action problem. They may believe that the government and so many agents will be better off if the right is granted, but each agent prefers that others pay the cost of conveying this information to the government. This collective action problem is the subject of this chapter.

Palfrey and Rosenthal (1984, 1988) studied such participation games with the following characteristics: each agent $i \in N$ expects a payoff of $b_i = 1$ if a public good is provided. The public good is provided only if at least ω agents contribute a cost of $0 < c < 1$ each. The basic structure of this game is described in table 5.1.

The collective action problem here is straightforward: if the number of contributors, except i, α_{-i}, is smaller than the threshold number by more than one, i.e. if $\alpha_{-i} < \omega - 1$, then agent i is better off not contributing because, with or without his or her contribution, the public good is unlikely to be provided. If the number of contributors except i, α_{-i}, is greater than or equal to the threshold number, i.e. if $\alpha_{-i} \geq \omega$, then agent i is better off not contributing because, with or without his or her contribution, the public good is provided. Only if $\alpha_{-i} = \omega - 1$, is agent i better off contributing, because without his or her contribution the public good will not be provided, while with his or her contribution the public good will be provided.

Palfrey and Rosenthal show that for any threshold, ω, there are three

Table 5.1. *N-person participation game*

We assume that	Player i's strategy	Number of contributions from		
$b-c>0$		$\alpha_{-i} < \omega - 1$	$\alpha_{-i} = \omega - 1$	$\alpha_{-i} \geq \omega$
$1 > c > 0$	Contribute	$-c$	$b-c$	$b-c$
$b-1$	Do not contribute	0	0	b

types of equilibria. One in which no one contributes: $\alpha = 0$. In the second type of equilibria, exactly ω agents contribute: $\alpha = \omega$. In this type of equilibria, however, identical agents who face the same game play different strategies. In addition, there is an implicit coordination problem since agents cannot predict who of the n agents will contribute, and who will free ride. The third type of equilibria are "mixed-strategy" equilibria.

Of particular interest to us here are symmetric mixed-strategy equilibria. The attractive feature of "symmetric equilibria" is that each agent uses the same strategy believing, "correctly," that all the other agents are using the same strategy as he or she does. In symmetric mixed-strategy equilibria all the agents use that same "mixed" strategy, which makes all agents indifferent between contributing and not contributing. It is because of this indifference that each agent may, just as well, use the mixed strategy that everyone else uses. This is the intuitive logic behind such equilibria.

In participation games, as modeled by Palfrey and Rosenthal, there is no role for a government. Once enough agents contribute, the public good is provided by some implicit benevolent provider or by a firm that specializes in producing such goods. Here, I am concerned with governments as political entrepreneurs providing institutional structures that protect private property and related individual rights to interested agents to garner political support from them. In the next two sections, I model this interaction formally, incorporating a government with incomplete information. Some of the analysis is technical, and readers who are not familiar with this type of technical argument can skip the technical paragraphs and read only the verbal explanations that follow.

Challenging governments to change structures of property rights

To introduce uncertainty about agents' preferences, I distinguish between agents of type $b_i = 1$, who expect a positive benefit from the grant of the right, and agents of type $b_i = 0$, who expect no benefit from the grant.

Each agent can choose between petitioning, and not petitioning. Let $S_i = \{0,1\}$ denote agent i's pure strategy set, where $s_i \in S_i$ is a particular strategic choice, $s_i = 1$ denoting "petition" and $s_i = 0$ denoting "not petition." A normalized strategy σ_i is a mapping σ_i: $\{0,1\} \Rightarrow [0,1]^2$ or an ordered pair $\sigma_i = (\mathrm{pr}(s_i = 1 \mid b_i = 1); \mathrm{pr}(s_i = 1 \mid b_i = 0))$. The normalized "mixed" strategy σ_i, is the probability that agent i will petition. It is conditional on i's type, b_i. Agent i's normalized strategy set, or choice set, is $\sigma_i = [0,1]^2$.

Thus, the strategic choice of an agent consists of choosing the probability he or she would petition if he or she is of type $b_i = 1$ and the probability of petitioning if he or she is of type $b_i = 0$. The strategy space of the entire society is denoted as $\sigma = \sigma_1 X \ldots X \sigma_n$. A particular combination of strategic choices by the n players is denoted as $\sigma = (\sigma_1, \ldots, \sigma_n)$ with $\sigma \in \sigma$. Each agent chooses σ_i, the probability of petitioning conditional on the agent's type, but eventually he or she either petitions ($s_i = 1$), or not ($s_i = 0$). Thus, s_i is the realization of σ_i. We denote by $s = (s_1, \ldots, s_n)$, the realization of σ. $A^1(\sigma) = \{i \in N: s_i = 1 \mid \sigma\}$ is the set of agents who petition in a particular realization s of σ. Let α denote the number of agents that turned out to petition in this realization: i.e. $\alpha = |A^1|$. Let $0 < c < 1$ denote the cost of petitioning. For simplicity, we assume that this cost is the same for all petitioners.

[Re]Introducing government

A strategy for a government is a mapping g: $\{0,1\}^n \Rightarrow \{0,1\}$, where $g(A^1) = 1$ denotes granting the right upon observing the group A^1 of petitioners that turned out and $g(A^1) = 0$ denotes not granting it, after observing the group of petitioners. The government's benefits, b_g, from granting a property right, are assumed to be a linear function of β, the number of potential beneficiaries of the right, $b_g = t \cdot \beta$, where $0 < t < 1$ may be interpreted as a tax rate or as "good will" dividend toward the next election. Again, c_g denotes the government's costs of enforcing the right. I assume that c_g, c, and t are common knowledge. I assume that all the agents and the government have common prior beliefs about the probability, q, that any agent is of type $b_i = 1$, $q = \mathrm{pr}(b_i = 1)$. Let $b = (b_1, \ldots, b_n)$ be a particular realization of n independent draws of $b_i \in \{0,1\}$ by the n agents, with a probability q that each draw yields $b_i = 1$. Let $B^1(b) = \{i \in N: b_i = 1 \mid b\}$ denote the set of potential beneficiaries, and β denote the number of potential beneficiaries, or agents of type $b_i = 1$. All players start with a common prior belief $f(\beta)$, where $f(\beta)$ is a discrete multinomial probability density function defined by q and n that assigns to every value of

Table 5.2. *Agents' payoffs*

i's payoff $u_i =$	i's type $b_i =$	i's pure strategy $s_i =$	Government's strategy $g=$
$(1-t) - c$	1	1	1
$(1-t)$	1	0	1
$-c$	0	1	$g \in \{0,1\}$
$-c$	1	1	0
0	0	0	$g \in \{0,1\}$
0	1	0	0

$k \in Z = \{0,1,\ldots,n\}$ a probability that $\beta = k$. So, $f(\beta)$ is the belief all agents have about the probability that the number of potential beneficiaries, β, from the grant of the right is any number $k \in Z = \{0,1,\ldots,n\}$.

The game, denoted as Γ, is a four-stage sequential game:

STAGE 1: Each agent chooses his or her strategy $\sigma_i \in \sigma_i = [0,1]^2$.

STAGE 2: Each agent learns from nature his or her type $b_i \in \{0,1\}$ and acts according to the strategy he or she chose in stage 1.

STAGE 3: Government officials choose whether to grant the right $g(A^1, f(\beta)) = 1$, or not $g(A^1, f(\beta)) = 0$, depending on the set of petitioners that turned out, A^1, and the prior beliefs, $(f(\beta))$, about the number of potential beneficiaries β.

STAGE 4: Agents decide whether to respect the right or not, given g.

From chapter 4 we already know the expected outcome of stage 4: if the government officials decide to grant and enforce the property right, all agents will respect it, and if the government does not enforce the right, the right will be worthless because no one will respect it. Thus, we can now roll back to stage 3. Let $g \in \{0,1\}$ denote the government strategic choice $g(A^1, f(\beta)) \in \{0,1\}$. Theorem 4.1 from chapter 4 implies the following payoff structure of the game Γ: if the government grants the right, i.e. if $g = 1$ then the government payoff is $u_g(g=1) = (t \cdot \beta) - c_g$. If the government does not grant the right, then the payoff it gets is zero: $u_g(g=0) = 0$. The payoff structure for the agents, depending on the different possible contingencies in the game, is specified in table 5.2.

By theorem 4.1, if the government enforces the right, all agents respect it. Thus, any agent that is a potential beneficiary of the right gets some positive utility if the government chooses to grant the right. For the sake of simplicity I standardize this utility to be $u_i(b_i = 1 \mid g = 1) = 1$. Agents then have to pay taxes. If the agent is of type $b_i = 1$ and he or she did not petition, i.e. $s_i = 0$, then he or she ends up with a strictly positive payoff of $u_i(b_i = 1 \mid g = 1, s_i = 0, t) = (1 - t)$. If the agent petitions, he or she also pays the cost of petitioning so that $u_i(b_i = 1 \mid g = 1, s_i = 1, t) = (1 - t) - c$, which we also assume to be strictly positive, or else no one would ever petition.

If the agent does not stand to benefit anything from the right, i.e. if $b_i = 0$, then if he or she petitions then, regardless of what the government does, he or she loses the cost of petitioning. If he or she does not petition, he or she saves the cost of petitioning.[1] If the government does not enforce the right, then each agent gets $-c$ if he or she petitions and 0 if he or she does not. Therefore, agents of type $b_i = 0$ never petition (lemma 5.1 in the appendix, p. 124). The government's payoff is $t \cdot \beta - c_g$, given any number of β beneficiaries, if it grants the right, and 0 if it does not.

Define $v_g(A^1, \sigma) = E(u_g \mid \mu(\cdot \mid A^1, f(\beta), \sigma))$. v_g denotes the expected utility to the government, after observing the set of petitioners, A^1, that turned out, and given its updated, or posterior beliefs $\mu(\cdot \mid A^1, f(\beta), \sigma)$, defined as:

$$\mu(\beta \mid A^1, f(\beta), \sigma) = \left(\frac{\mathrm{pr}(A^1 \mid \beta, \sigma) \cdot \mathrm{pr}(\beta \mid q, n)}{\displaystyle\sum_{\beta'=0}^{n} (A^1 \mid \beta', \sigma) \cdot \mathrm{pr}(\beta' \mid q, n)} \right). \tag{5.1}$$

(5.1) states that government officials use Bayes' rule to update their beliefs. Using Bayes' rule to update one's beliefs means that one uses prior beliefs, together with incoming information — in this case, the fact that a group of petitioners, A^1, turned out to petition for the grant of the right — to form his or her posterior beliefs. This mechanism will become clearer as I unfold the model and the results, in this and the next section.

If the government does not grant the right then its expected payoff is zero: $v_g(g = 0 \mid A^1, \sigma) = 0$. If the government decides to grant the right, its expected payoffs are as specified in (5.2):

$$v_g(g = 1 \mid A^1, f(\beta), \sigma) = \sum_{\beta=0}^{n} \beta \cdot t \cdot \mu(\beta \mid A^1, f(\beta), \sigma) - c_g. \tag{5.2}$$

Substituting (5.1) in (5.2) we get:

$$v_g(g = 1 \mid A^1, f(\beta), \sigma) = \sum_{\beta=0}^{n} \beta \cdot t \cdot \left(\frac{\mathrm{pr}(A^1 \mid \beta, \sigma) \cdot \mathrm{pr}(\beta \mid q, n)}{\displaystyle\sum_{\beta'=0}^{n} (A^1 \mid \beta', \sigma) \cdot \mathrm{pr}(\beta' \mid q, n)} \right) - c_g \tag{5.3}$$

[1] Technically, we assume that the payoff 0 that agents of type $b_i = 0$ get takes into account the cost of respecting the rights of others.

(5.3) states that the payoff the government expects if it grants the right, $v_g(A^1,f(\beta),\sigma)$, is the sum, over all $\beta \in \{0,1,\ldots,n\}$, of the payoff the government expects, $t\cdot\beta$, given any β, times the probability that there are β potential beneficiaries – according to the government posterior beliefs, $\mu(\cdot\,|\,A^1,\sigma)$, less the cost of enforcement c_g.

Let $W(g) = \{A^1 \subseteq N: (g\,|\,A^1) = 1\}$ be the set of all the possible groups of petitioners that will bring the government to grant the right, if they turned out to petition for it. The expected payoff for any agent in this game, is:

$$v_i(\sigma,g,b_i) = E(u_i\,|\,\sigma,g,b_i) = [(1-t)(b_i)\cdot\text{pr}(A^1 \in W(g)\,|\,\sigma)] - c\sigma_i. \quad (5.4)$$

In words: the expected payoff of an agent of type $b_i = 1$ is $(1-t)$ times the probability that the government grants the right, less c, the cost of petitioning, times the probability, σ_i, that the agent would turn out to petition and pay the cost of petitioning. If the agent is of type $b_i = 0$, the first term of the right hand side (RHS) of (5.4) cancels out because $b_i = 0$, and the expected payoff is the probability of petitioning, σ_i, times the cost of petitioning, c. Definition 5.1 defines the central equilibrium concept used in solving this type of signaling game.[2]

DEFINITION 5.1: A sequential equilibrium [SE] is a triple $(\sigma^*,g^*,\mu(\cdot))$ such that:

1. $\forall i \in N, \forall b_i \in \{0,1\}, v_i(\sigma^*,g^*) \geq v_i(\sigma^*_{-i},\sigma_i,g^*)\forall \sigma_i \in \sigma_i$.

2. Given $\sigma^*, \forall A^1 \subseteq N, g^*(A^1) = \arg\max_{g\in\{0,1\}}\{g\cdot v_g(g=1\,|\,\mu(\cdot\,|\,A^1,f(\beta),\sigma^*))\}$.

3. $\forall \beta \in \{0,1,\ldots,n\}$, if $\text{pr}(\beta\,|\,A^1\sigma^*) > 0$, then

$$\mu(\beta\,|\,A^1,f(\beta),\sigma) = \left(\frac{\text{pr}(A^1\,|\,\beta,\sigma^*)\cdot\text{pr}(\beta\,|\,q,n)}{\sum_{\beta'=0}^{n}(A^1\,|\,\beta',\sigma^*)\cdot\text{pr}(\beta'\,|\,q,n)}\right).$$

Condition 1 says that the strategy chosen by any agent, σ_i^*, must, in equilibrium, maximize i's utility, given the strategies of the government and other agents. Condition 2 states that the strategy chosen by government officials, g^*, must, in equilibrium, maximize the government's expected

---

[2] The classical reference is Kreps and Wilson (1982). More accessible discussions are found in Cho (1987), Cho and Kreps (1987), and Banks and Sobel (1987). The definition I use is adopted from Banks (1991: 7). It is easy to see that the game I analyze here can be reinterpreted as a signaling game with the government being the "receiver" (R), each agent $i \in N$ being a sender (S) with two types $b_i \in \{0,1\}$ and two messages $m \in \{0,1\}$ where 0 is the message of not petitioning and 1 the message of petitioning. I do not use this terminology in the text to save on notations and technicalities that are not needed for the sake of the argument.

utility given its posterior beliefs $\mu(\cdot)$, that are based on its prior beliefs and the observed group of petitioners, A^1. Condition 3 says that the government's beliefs are consistent with σ^* in the sense that the government's posterior beliefs, $\mu(\cdot \mid A^1, \sigma^*)$, are determined by Bayes' rule according to its prior beliefs, $f(\beta)$, the observed group of petitioners, A^1, and the strategy vector σ^*.[3]

The essence and substance of the social contract

This section characterizes the set of agent-symmetric sequential equilibria [SSEs] for the game Γ. Lemma 5.1 in the appendix (p. 124) shows that agents of type $b_i = 0$ never petition in equilibrium. I can, thus, limit my analysis to the behavior of potential right-holders, i.e. agents of type $b_i = 1$. (Lemma 5.2–5.6 are important mainly for the sake of completeness and were, therefore, omitted from the text. The interested reader can find them in the appendix.)

Corollary 5.1 shows that for every agent's strategy vector, the government's strategy in equilibrium is a threshold strategy, i.e. there exists an integer ω so that if the government observes a number of petitioners, α, equal or greater than this threshold, it grants the right and if it observes a number of petitioners smaller than the threshold, it does not grant the right.

Lemma 5.8 specifies the equilibrium strategy vector for potential right-holders, given any such threshold. The probability, ρ, that any potential right-holder would turn out to petition for the right, anticipated by the government, induces a threshold integer, ω, as the government's best response. This threshold value, ω, induces, in turn, a value of ρ as the agents' mixed-strategy best response.

Theorem 5.1 shows that, *in equilibrium*, these two values must be consistent with each other. This means that the equilibrium threshold, ω^*, induced by the equilibrium value of ρ^*, must induce the same ρ^* as the best response of potential right-holders, in terms of the probability that they turn out and petition (the proofs of lemma 5.1–5.8 and theorem 5.1 are in the appendix, pp. 124–32).

---

[3] This definition specifies the government's beliefs only "along-the-equilibrium path." This poses a problem if a government observes an event that according to its beliefs occurs with probability zero. This can happen if $\sigma = (1, \ldots, 1)$, but $A^1 = 0$. I use the Intuitive Criterion (IC) (Cho and Kreps, 1987) to deal with this problem. IC requires that off-the-equilibrium-path beliefs place zero probability on the event that types who can only lose from defection will defect. Here it implies that $\mu(b_i = 0 \mid s_i = 1) = 0$, i.e. government's out-of-equilibrium beliefs put zero probability on the event that a type $b_i = 0$ petitions.

DEFINITION 5.2: $(\sigma^*, g^*, \mu(\cdot))$ is an agent's *symmetric sequential equilibria* (SSE) if $\forall i, j \in N \sigma_i^* = \sigma_j^*$.

The attractive feature of symmetric equilibria is that they depend on the premise that each agent expects all other agents to behave in the same way he or she does when they face the same payoff structure and have the same prior beliefs. Restricting attention to SSEs simply means looking only at those equilibria where all agents play the same strategy in equilibrium.[4]

DEFINITION 5.3: Anonymity: for every two sets $A^1, A^{1'}$, with $|A^1| = |A^{1'}|$ if $A^1 \in W(g)$, then $A^1 \in W(g)$.

Anonymity requires that all agents be treated the same regardless of who they are. Restricting the analysis to SSEs implies anonymity: since all agents use the same mixed strategy in equilibrium, it is not an equilibrium behavior for government officials to interpret the behavior of different agents as resulting from different strategies. This would violate condition 5.13 of the definition of sequential equilibrium. Thus, without loss of generality, I use α instead of A^1 as the argument of the government's posterior beliefs $\mu(\alpha, f(\beta), \sigma)$. (5.5) redefines expression (5.3) using α instead of A^1:

$$v_g(g = 1 \mid \alpha, f(\beta), \sigma) = \sum_{\beta=0}^{n_i} \beta \cdot t \cdot \left(\frac{\mathrm{pr}(\alpha \mid \beta, \sigma) \cdot \mathrm{pr}(\beta \mid q, n)}{\sum\limits_{\beta'=0}^{n} (\alpha \mid \beta', \sigma) \cdot \mathrm{pr}(\beta' \mid q, n)} \right) - c_g. \qquad (5.5)$$

In the remainder of this section I limit my discussion to cases where the minimum number of petitioners needed to convince the government to grant the right is greater than one. Lemma 5.6 (see appendix, p. 127) implies that in such cases there is always one equilibrium in which no one petitions and the government does not grant the right, regardless of the number of potential beneficiaries in the population at large. This is an equilibrium because no single potential right-holder can change this unfortunate deadlock. In chapter 6 I discuss work with Ainsworth (Ainsworth and Sened, 1993), where we demonstrate that one important role of political entrepreneurs, such as lobbyists and party activists, is to move agents away from such "unfortunate" stalemates.

Corollary 5.1 (implied by lemma 5.7 in the appendix) states that the government's strategy in equilibrium, is always characterized by a threshold ω such that $g^*(\alpha) = 1$ if $\alpha \geq \omega$, and $g^*(\alpha) = 0$ if $\alpha < \omega$. In words: for every strategy vector, σ, of all the potential beneficiaries, the government's strategy in equilibrium must be a threshold strategy, so that there exists an

---

[4] The results of Palfrey and Rosenthal (1988) imply that non-symmetric equilibria will look very much like symmetric equilibria, only that different subsets of players will use different mixes, or probabilities to turn out.

integer, ω, so that if government officials observe a set of petitioners equal or greater, in number, than this threshold, it grants the right, but if they observe a number of petitioners smaller that the threshold, they do not grant the right.

COROLLARY 5.1: A government's strategy in an SSE is always character-ized by a threshold, ω, so that $g^*(\alpha) = 1$ if $\alpha \geq \omega$, and $g^*(\alpha) = 0$ if $\alpha < \omega$.

Given that this is what agents anticipate from government officials, we can now roll back to the first stage of the game. Lemma 5.8 characterizes the symmetric equilibrium response of the agents for each possible threshold strategy.

LEMMA 5.8: If $(\sigma^*, g^*, \mu(\cdot))$ is a mixed-strategy[5] SSE then the following must hold:[6]

$$c = (1-t) \cdot \sum_{\gamma=\omega-1}^{n-1} \left[\binom{\gamma}{\omega-1} \rho^{\omega-1}(1-\rho)^{\gamma-\omega-1} \right] \cdot \left[\binom{n-1}{\gamma} q^{\gamma}(1-q)^{n-\gamma-1} \right]. \quad (5.6)$$

The meaning of lemma 5.8 is discussed below, but it is of some interest to notice that lemma 5.8 implies that if $c > (1-t)$, no one petitions in equilibrium. It provides a formal statement of a well known concern about taxation: high taxes tend to compromise economic growth because they reduce the incentives for economic entrepreneurs to invest in the economy. Lemma 5.8 proves a special case of stagnation brought by high taxes. It implies that if taxes are too high or, alternatively, petitioning for change is too costly, agents will abstain from petitioning for changes in the institutional structure of property rights.

The discussion of the merits of promoting freedom of speech, on pp. 116–19, suggests that such conditions hurt both governments and economic entrepreneurs by discouraging agents of change that tend to promote economic growth. Thus, a byproduct of lemma 5.8 is a precise specification, albeit of just one aspect, of how high taxation impedes innovation and change.

Let h be a correspondence that assigns zero, one or two values of $\rho \in (0,1)(0 < \rho < 1)$, to each threshold value, ω, of the set of integers, $Z = \{0,1,2,3,\ldots,n\}$. So $h: Z \Rightarrow (0,1)$ is defined as $h(\omega) = \{\rho \in (0,1) \mid \rho$ solves for (5.6) of lemma 5.8, given $\omega\}$. Define $y: \rho \in (0,1) \Rightarrow Z$ as $y(\rho \in (0,1)) = \min\{\omega \in Z \mid v_g(1 \mid \mu(\cdot \mid \alpha, \sigma), \alpha = \omega) > 0\}$. That is, y assigns a threshold value, ω, to each value of ρ. In technical terms, y and h are best response (BR)

[5] For completeness, the case of $\rho = 1$ is covered in n. 7.
[6] For every value of ω there exist zero, one or two solutions to the symmetric equilibrium condition characterized by lemma 5.8. This follows immediately from lemma 5.8, and proposition 2 and corollary 2.1 in Palfrey and Rosenthal (1984).

functions. Theorem 5.1 characterizes the set of SSE equilibria as $SSE = \{(\omega,\rho) \mid \omega = y(\rho) \text{ and } \rho \in h(\omega)\}$, which is the intersection between y and h or the set of ordered pairs $\{(\omega,\rho)\}$ so that $\omega = y(\rho)$ and $\rho \in h(\omega)$. In words: condition (5.8) of theorem 5.1 guarantees that the government will use a BR threshold strategy, given ρ. Condition (5.7), which repeats (5.6) of lemma 5.8, guarantees that, given the threshold strategy of the government, every agent is using a mixed strategy, ρ, s.t. if all agents use the same strategy, each agent is indifferent between contributing and not contributing. Given this indifference he or she can use the mixed strategy that everyone else uses, which is the intuitive logic behind corollary 5.1, lemma 5.8, and theorem 5.1.

THEOREM 5.1: The triple $(\sigma^*, g^*, \mu(\,\cdot\,))$ is a mixed-strategy[7] SSE iff:

(i) $\forall i \in N \sigma_i^*(0) = 0$.

(ii) $\forall i \in N \sigma_i^*(1) = \rho, g^*(\alpha) = 1$ iff $\alpha \geq \omega$, and the pair (ω,ρ) satisfies simultaneously:

$$c = (1-t)\cdot \sum_{\gamma=\omega-1}^{n-1} \left[\binom{\gamma}{\omega-1} \rho^{\omega-1}(1-\rho)^{\gamma-\omega-1} \right] \cdot \left[\binom{n-1}{\gamma} q^{\gamma}(1-q)^{n-\gamma-1} \right] \quad (5.7)$$

$$v_g(1 \mid \rho,\alpha) = \sum_{\beta=\alpha}^{n} (t\cdot\beta - c_g) \cdot \frac{\left[\binom{n}{\beta} q^{\beta}(1-q)^{n-\beta} \right] \cdot \left[\binom{\beta}{\alpha} \rho^{\alpha}(1-\rho)^{\beta-\alpha} \right]}{\sum_{\beta'=\alpha}^{n} \left[\binom{n}{\beta'} q^{\beta'}(1-q)^{n-\beta'} \right] \cdot \left[\binom{\beta'}{\alpha} \rho^{\alpha}(1-\rho)^{\beta'-\alpha} \right]} \geq 0 \text{ iff } \alpha \geq \omega. \quad (5.8)$$

Theorem 5.1 captures a crucial aspect of the meaning of the social contract that is essential to the neo-liberal theory that I promote in this book. Contracts between governments and their constituents seem to rely

---

[7] By a mixed-strategy SSE we mean $\rho \in (0,1)$, thus the cases of $\rho = 1$ and $\rho = 0$ are left out. For the sake of completeness I state without proof theorem 5.1', for the case of $\rho = 1$:

Theorem 5.1': The triple $(\sigma^*, g^*, \mu(\cdot))$ is a SSE iff:

(i) $\forall i \in N \sigma_i^*(b_i = 0) = 0$.

(ii) $\forall i \in N \sigma_i^*(b_i = 1) = 1$. $g^*(\alpha) = 1$ iff $\alpha \geq \omega$, and the pair (ω,ρ) satisfies simultaneously

$$c = \binom{n-1}{\omega-1} q^{\omega}(1-q)^{n-\omega-1} \text{ and } \omega = \min\{k \in Z: k\cdot t \geq c_g\}.$$

To see this, simply substitute 1 for ρ in theorem 5.1 in the text and solve. As for the case of $\rho = 0$, as stated in the text, there will usually exist a symmetric equilibrium where $\sigma^* = \sigma^0 = (0,0,\ldots,0), g^*(\alpha < 2) = 0$. In this equilibrium, no one petitions and the government does not grant the right. It is an equilibrium (depending on the prior beliefs $f(\beta)$) because, when $g^*(\alpha < 2) = 0$, and $\sigma^* = \sigma^0 = (0,0,\ldots,0)$, no agent can unilaterally change the outcome by petitioning and paying the cost of petitioning (Ainsworth and Sened, 1993: 844, n. 10).

Table 5.3. *Equilibria and expectations with* $N=10$, $q=0.4$, $c_g=1.0025$, $c_i=0.2$

Equilibrium pair $\{\omega^\star, \rho^\star\}$	$\{\omega=3, \rho=0.36\}$	$\{\omega=4, \rho=0.68\}$	$\{\omega=5, \rho=0.996\}$
pr(right is granted) = pr($g=1$)	0.162	0.273	0.363
pr(right granted but $c_g > b_g$) $\sum_{\beta=\omega}^{\beta=5}\mathrm{pr}(\alpha \geq \omega)\vert\beta)\cdot\mathrm{pr}(\beta\vert q,n)$	0.093	0.148	0.197
pr(right granted and $c_g < b_g$) $\sum_{\beta=6}^{\beta=n}\mathrm{pr}(\alpha \geq \omega)\vert\beta)\cdot\mathrm{pr}(\beta\vert q,n)$	0.069	0.125	0.166
pr(right granted and $c_g < b_g$) $\sum_{\beta=6}^{\beta=n}\mathrm{pr}(\alpha < \omega)\vert\beta)\cdot\mathrm{pr}(\beta\vert q,n)$	0.097	0.041	~0.0
$E(\alpha)$	1.44	2.72	3.98

on a very fragile equilibrium of expectations and behavior. Governments constantly write and rewrite this contract, depending on their beliefs as to how they can best promote their own interests. These interests often coincide with the interests of their constituents inasmuch as most governments rely, in one way or another, on popular support and tax revenues. This reliance on popular support allows economic entrepreneurs and other individual agents to petition for changes in the structure of social institutions that regulate the activity of the market and other aspects of life. Consider the following quote from North (1990: 86):

> The process of institutional change can be described as follows. A change in relative prices leads one or both parties to an exchange, whether it is political or economic, to perceive that either or both could do better with an altered agreement or contract. An attempt will be made to renegotiate the contract. However, because contracts are nested in a hierarchy of rules, the renegotiation may not be possible without restructuring a higher set of rules . . . In that case, the party that stands to improve his or her bargaining position may . . . devote resources to restructuring the rules at a higher level.

The model developed here is a precise specification of this argument. "The parties that stand to improve their bargaining positions" are the agents I refer to as potential right-holders, or potential beneficiaries from the institutional change. Given the control of governments over the "rules at the higher level," the interested parties "devote resources to restructuring the rules at a higher level" in petitioning government officials to change the structure of property rights' institutions, as described by my model.

North never specified under what conditions this plea to change the "rules at a higher level" would be successful or not because, as I explained in chapter 2, North never really modeled the political game that determines the answer to this question. This is the task I took upon myself to complete. Theorem 5.1 generalizes theorem 4.1 from chapter 4, in stating that the plea of economic and other entrepreneurs to change the political institutional structure that endows members of society with property rights will be successful if and only if the government is convinced, by the petitioners, that it stands to gain from changing the institutional structure. One way in which such parties can make a convincing plea for an institutional change is by mobilizing enough petitions from enough interested parties to convince the government that the change will bring with it economic growth, or increase the government's political support. This is precisely the underlying logic behind theorem 5.1, and it seems to be a close enough approximation of how "the world we know" works.

A numerical example will help appreciate the implications of theorem 5.1. Let $n = 10$, $q = 0.4$, $c_g = 1.0025$, $t = 0.2$, $c = 0.25$. Solving for conditions (5.7) and (5.8) in theorem 5.1(ii) we get the set of equilibria. Table 5.3

(borrowed from Ainsworth and Sened, 1993) reports the probability that a right be granted, and the expected number of petitioners, given any of the three equilibria.

Table 5.3 points to four important implications of theorem 5.1:

1. We expect positive (at times substantial) participation rates even when common prior beliefs indicate that the expected number of beneficiaries is not enough to justify the granting of the right – e.g., with $q = 0.4$, and $n = 10$, $E(\beta) = 4$, and $E(b_g - c_g) = -0.2$.
2. We expect government officials to make two types of mistakes in equilibrium: try to enforce property rights that make them worse off, or fail to grant property rights that could make them better off.
3. A coordination problem remains, since the game has multiple equilibria. The multitude of equilibria is easy to interpret: if agents petition with low probability and government officials realize it, then they should grant the right, even upon observing a low number of petitioners. If the threshold number, ω, is high, a bigger number of petitioners will be needed to warrant the grant of the right, i.e. potential beneficiaries will have to petition with higher probability.
4. Finally, in this kind of equilibria, the number of petitioners, α, will rarely be the "efficient" number. Thus, "political action" in the pursuit of individual rights is "almost always" "wasteful" (cf. Lohmann, 1993a; Ledyard, 1984).

Inefficient but effective political institutions: freedom of speech

The first row of table 5.3 reports the probability that a right be granted, given any of the three equilibria. The second row reports the probability that the government grants the right even though, *ex post*, it would have been better off not granting it. The third row of table 5.3 specifies the probability that the government grants the right and be better off by so doing. The fourth row specifies the probability that the government fails to grant the right even though, *ex post*, it would have been better off granting the right. The last row gives the expected number of petitions, given any of the three equilibria.

Possible mistakes and inefficiencies of this type have often evoked the frustration of economic and political theorists. This frustration stems from the common mistake of comparing ideal "competitive markets with perfectly defined property rights and complete information" with the imperfect world of imperfect property rights and incomplete information in which humans always lived and apparently always will live. Political and economic games are never played in environments of complete information, perfectly well defined property rights, or zero transaction costs (Coase, 1981).

We should begin to realize that the political process is crucial for at least two important reasons that were highlighted here and in chapter 4. First, without political intervention, there is little chance that property rights, so crucial for the price mechanism to work its marvels in the market, would ever be established or maintained. In chapter 4, I emphasized that without the intervention of governments there would only be property rights in remote, unrealistic environments. Second, political institutions regulate the transition of crucial information. Without such regulations the operation of the market would be inefficient, and the structure of the economy would be slow to change in order to meet changing circumstances (North, 1990, 1993). This chapter elaborated this argument, showing how political institutions can encourage individual agents to reveal crucial missing information about their preferences, and how government officials can be expected to change the structure of legal institutions to protect property rights that better fit the preferences of their constituents.

This argument has some interesting empirical backing: Krehbiel (1992) has put forward a comprehensive argument on how the main function of the institutional structure of the US Congress is to promote the revelation of information concerning the consequences of government policies. This point is crucial for the understanding of the emergence and the evolution of institutional structures that enforce and protect property rights. Economists tend to assume environments with complete information. Inefficient and otherwise problematic political institutions seem to be instrumental mechanisms to reach a world that remotely resembles the world economists unwarrantedly assume, and apparently hope, to live in.

In this section I prove that in this imperfect world, playing the game of politics as formalized above makes both governments and their constituents better off. Both autonomous individuals and governments are made better off because in the process of the game – despite the mistakes and the misleading information that such processes often yield – the players obtain certain information that they did not know before, and would never have gained, without playing this game. For example, agents who turn out to petition reveal their preferences. Alternatively, once a government enforces property rights, whether it gains or loses in the process, those who stand to benefit from these rights, as well as the benefits associated with granting and exploiting such rights, become known.

Proposition 5.1 shows that political action, as modeled here, makes individual agents and government officials better off. In this way, the model captures both the rationale behind political action, at the same time as it provides important insights into the complexity and difficulties associated with political activism and governments' response to popular demands.

PROPOSITION 5.1: The *ex ante* payoffs of this game are always positive for the government, and for each individual agent.

Proposition 5.1 (see the appendix, p. 131 for the proof) has a simple substantive interpretation: governments and citizens benefit from institutions that allow agents to petition for property rights. What drives this result, and my optimistic interpretation of it, is that in the process of petitioning for new rights, citizens reveal valuable information to their governments. They do not intend to reveal information, but in the hope of obtaining valuable benefits from new property rights, they help government officials make decisions by "partially" revealing their preferences. This conclusion provides another example of how institutions at the "constitutional level," that seem to rely on deep moral premises, can be explained by the positive theory of institutional emergence and institutional change promoted here.

This conclusion provides a partial explanation for the success of democratic institutions in western democracies in the last two centuries. The model of the neo-liberal polity that emerges out of the discussion so far predicts that such institutions will often yield "undesired" results in the short run. But in the long run, they should have beneficial consequences in the process of the evolution of individual rights in general, and property rights in particular.

A numerical example will further clarify this claim: to get a better feel for the implications of this model I constructed a simulation that reproduces theorem 5.1, in analytical equations that allow for the use of the simulation package.[8] To use one particular example, the following parameters were used: I let the number of individuals be $n = 1000$. The prior beliefs about the probability that any agent would turn out to be a potential beneficiary was set to be $q = 0.49$, which means that the expected number of beneficiaries is 490. The benefit that any potential beneficiary expects to get was set to be $b(b_i = 1) = \$1.00$, and the cost of petitioning was set at \$0.01. The tax rate was set at 0.2, assuming that this rate maximizes the government's tax revenues. The cost of enforcing the right was set to be \$100. Given the prior beliefs, the government has no reason to grant the right prior to the game. The expected benefits from granting the right is smaller than the cost of enforcement: $E(\beta) \cdot t = \$490 \cdot 0.2 = \$98.00 < \$100.00$. Note that while the expected number of potential beneficiaries is 490, depending on the "luck of the draw" it could be higher or lower.

The simulation generates the probabilities of different values of β that could occur – given the probability 0.49 that any of the $n = 1000$ agents would turn out to be a potential beneficiary. It then computes, given the equilibrium behavior computed from (5.7) and (5.8) in theorem 5.1, the

---

[8] The simulation was constructed and run with the much appreciated help of Simon Jackman.

expected payoffs to individual players and the government. Recall that proposition 5.1 proves that these payoffs will always be positive. The following is just a simulated example.

The set of equilibria in this example is: $\{133 < \omega < 1145, \rho \in [0.235, 0.259]\}$. Using one equilibrium pair $(\omega = 139, \rho = 0.247)$, for example, we get the following results: the equilibrium pair means that the threshold that will prompt the government to grant the right is 139. That is, if the government observes 139 people or more petitioning, it will grant the right. Note that the government is willing to grant the right even when it observes a relatively small number of petitioners, much smaller than the 500 needed to guarantee positive payoff for the government. The reason why this threshold makes sense is that the equilibrium probability that potential beneficiaries, agents of type $b_i = 1$, petition is 0.247. The expected number of petitioners is 121 $E(\alpha \mid (\omega^* = 139, \rho^* = 0.247) = 121)$. This number is lower than the government threshold. The probability that the government's threshold be attained and the right will be granted, is 0.049 $(\text{pr}(g = 1) = E(\text{pr}(\alpha > 139 \mid \rho = 0.247)) = 0.049)$. The probability that the government will end up getting negative payoffs, *ex post*, in playing this game, given this particular equilibrium pair is 0.02 $(\text{pr}(b_g < c_g) = \text{pr}(g = 1 \mid \omega^*, \rho^*, \beta < 500) = 0.02)$. The probability that the government would obtain positive payoffs is 0.0274 $(\text{pr}(b_g > c_g) = \text{pr}(g = 1 \mid \omega^*, \rho^*, \beta > 500) = 0.0274)$. More importantly the expected payoff to the government of playing the game is $0.026: E(v_g) = 0.026$, the expected payoff to any potential beneficiary in this game is $0.019: E(v_i) = 0.019$. The *ex ante* expected payoff to all individual agents together from playing this game is $9.31. Combined with government's benefits, the *ex ante* expected payoff to society from playing this game is $9.336. Of this, only less than 0.3% goes to the government and the remaining 99.7% is distributed among its constituents.

This example clarifies a central argument of this book: we do not have to rely on "benevolence" to get governments to generate policies that benefit the society as a whole. At the same time, this discussion demonstrates that politics is rarely efficient: it usually evolves in environments with incomplete information, imperfect property rights, and faulty decision making mechanisms, that generate all types of social welfare waste. Nevertheless, democratic political institutions can often be very effective in achieving different social goals, including economic growth.

An historic illustration: the Magna Carta[9]

The central argument of this chapter is that property rights are granted by governments through a bargaining process with their constituents. The

[9] I am grateful to Steve Lewis for helping me out in putting this illustration together. The main references are: North and Thomas (1973), Holt (1985, 1992), and Harriss (1975).

governments want to gain tax revenues and political support, while their constituents want to gain secure private property and related individual rights.

Perhaps the most important historical example of this process is the set of property and related individual rights that emerged from the events surrounding the establishment of England's Magna Carta. As political historians have noted, the Magna Carta saw the beginning of the practice whereby English kings had to exchange privileges for revenues (North and Thomas, 1973: 83), eventually leading to the rise of the powerful English mercantilist order (Levi, 1988). The Magna Carta is the source of common law and civil liberties in England to this very day, so much so that it is often referred to as the informal English Constitution (Holt, 1985). Yet, this remarkable charter was only intended to regulate the means by which a powerful monarch, King John, might reign (Harriss, 1975).

I have already referred in this book to the remarkable tax collecting machine that the Norman kings set up as soon as they took over the island. This machine depended on what is known as *The Domesday Book*, commissioned by William the Conqueror and published in 1087:

> Domesday Book is remarkable because it includes detailed information on the "ownership" income, resources, and fiscal responsibilities of every manor in Norman England in 1086. (McDonald and Snooks, 1986: 3)

William the Conqueror commissioned this remarkable survey for the purposes of tax collection. Actually, the king was not doing anything that the local gentry did not do.

> Domesday Book had its "satellite" private surveys, just as the Exchequer Pipe rolls were mirrored in the Pipe rolls of the bishopric of Winchester. (Holt, 1992: 33)

The tax collecting machine built by the Norman kings explains much of Henry II's success in building his kingdom. Now his son, King John, had to finance the maintenance of this kingdom. Unlike Henry II, though, his son had to deal with the much more powerful new king of France, Philip II, and with growing costs of warfare in general. To finance his wars, the king relied on two types of taxes. There were the traditional feudal taxes levied on a customary basis. But the issue that brought about the rebellion that resulted in the signing of the Magna Carta was the other type of taxes, levied on "special occasions" for special purposes, the most important and frequent of which was the event of war. Given his growing expenses, King John abused this norm and began to levy "war" taxes on almost a yearly basis. The barons responded in their famous "rebellion."

In 1215, the king negotiated, and then signed, the Magna Carta. This is exactly the type of bargained agreements that makes for "the social contract" I refer to in this book. Above all, the Magna Carta constrained the arbitrary taxing power of the king; from this point on, the king had to get the permission of the barons to levy special taxes. This is probably the first instance, in modern history, of accepting the idea of the fiscal power of a group of constituents. Such agreements were not infrequent between barons and kings at the time, but the barons' agreement was much wider in scope and influence, which gave it its name: Magna Carta.

The king signed this accord to regain the power of government he had lost in the war that had preceded the agreement. At the time of the signature, London and some of the most lucrative estates of the king were occupied by the rebellious barons, who would not give them back to the king unless Magna Carta was signed. As in the case of the Glorious Revolution (1688), discussed elsewhere in this book, the barons did not want to rid themselves of the king. In spite of the fact that they just won the war, all they asked for, in return for the king's territories, was a better "social contract."

Had the king known the result of the barons' rebellion prior to the war he would in all likelihood have settled the issue with the barons, as he has done so often before. Rebellion against royal tax authority was common both before and after the Magna Carta (Holt, 1985). What made this case different, was that, as the main argument of this chapter goes, the king underestimated the barons' concern with his frequent tax levies. As my argument further stipulates, the response of the 25 barons who led the rebellion was to use whatever means they had at the time, to petition the king to alter the structure of property rights that determined the relations between king and barons, and allowed the king to levy these frequent taxes. The king learned the hard way to appreciate the resolve with which the barons insisted on altering the "social contract" between them.

As was the case with the Northwest Ordinance, discussed in chapter 4, it is interesting to note that here, too, the change in the structure of property rights was closely tied to changes in the structure of other rights we usually regard as "human" rights. At that early stage of history we do not expect to find the grant of a right like the "freedom of speech" discussed in this chapter. We do find a similar, limited right of representation: by the Magna Carta, some incorporated boroughs were to elect leaders for self-adminis-tration (Holt, 1992: 57–60).

Of a lesser historical consequence, but of a greater interest for the argument here, is a special right granted to women by the Magna Carta. From now on, widows could refuse to obey the order of the king as to whom, and when, they were to be remarried. They could actually refuse to get remarried altogether. This very basic human right to have the "freedom" to choose when, and to whom, a widow would marry, has a clear link to property rights. The reason the barons insisted on including this right in the charter had nothing to do with moral principles – one need only look at other references to women's rights and rights of minorities in the charter, to appreciate fully how far the barons were from any such principles. The barons wanted to avoid any repetition of cases in which the king had abused his power to decide on these matters, to rob the barons of their properties by marrying their daughters to his allies or otherwise preferred associates (Holt, 1992: 53–5).

Holt (1992) appropriately stresses the fact that the above-mentioned rights, as well as other, similar "human" rights, included in the charter, could be bought from the king, for a ransom of sort, long before 1215. The difference is that now they were part of the new "social contract" formalized by the Magna Carta and applied to all women or boroughs of the relevant status group.

Concluding remarks: a neo-liberal theory of the social contract

In their historic study of the evolution of rights in western Europe, North and Thomas (1973) provide evidence that the remarkable development of effective private property rights in England and the Netherlands, compared to the cases of France and Spain, explains the observed difference in growth rates in the sixteenth and seventeenth centuries, which was remarkable in England and the Netherlands and stagnating in Spain and France. North and Thomas explain the difference in the momentum in the development of property rights' institutions by the fact that commercial interests were politically stronger in England and the Netherlands (Libecap, 1989: 2–3). They overlook, however, the fact that in both the Netherlands and England political institutions existed, due to precedents like the Magna Carta in England, that allowed these interests to be heard. Such institutions were virtually absent in Spain and France.

More generally North and Thomas (1973) show that the evolution of property rights is not a smooth progression from less to more efficient institutions of property rights. Libecap (1989: 2) describes this as follows:

> a continuing puzzle is why we observe so much variety in . . . property institutions . . . [S]tudies . . . reveal that differences in property rights institutions across societies with otherwise similar resource endowments contributed importantly to observed variations in economic performance.

This chapter provides a partial solution to this diversity in property rights' institutions. A key to a possible solution is that, according to the model developed here, in equilibrium, governments make mistakes: they grant rights they "shouldn't" and fail to grant rights they "should." The reason for this is the imperfect mechanism through which governments and individual agents in society bargain for changes in the structure of property rights, and the environment in which this process take place, which is characterized by incomplete and imperfect information.

The approach presented here seems more realistic than most game theoretic accounts of the evolution of property rights, inasmuch as it treats property rights' institutions not as equilibria in games among equal agents, but as equilibria in games among players who control old institutions and agents who challenge these institutions with new demands. This approach provides a rich analytical framework for the study of the evolution of property rights, providing straightforward explanations to the emergence of such institutions at two different levels: it explains why property rights are granted and enforced by central governments and, at the same time, it explains the emergence of more fundamental institutions that protect individual rights such as "the right to know your rights," or the fundamental civil right to petition for new property rights.

Governments enforce such institutions, not because these rights are a part of a list of "natural" rights, and not because they are committed to moral principles or economic growth, or because they are moral or benevolent actors. Rather, they enforce institutions that protect the private property of their constituents because such institutions allow them to obtain from their constituents crucial information that helps them improve the structure of institutions that protect private property and related individual rights which, in turn, makes for a more affluent society. By making society more affluent, governments hope to increase tax revenue and enhance the support they receive from their constituents.

According to this neo-liberal social contract theory, the social contract is not a contract to which we are obligated by moral, logical, or historical bounds. It is a contract that is constantly renewed by citizens of every polity in their continuing attempt to affirm and confirm the respect of governments of their individual rights. These rights are not derivatives of moral or "natural" origins, but the expression of individual unalienable preferences, that individuals try to satisfy through the promotion of institutional structures that would accommodate them.

Governments do not erect such structures out of benevolence or moral concern. They grant and protect rights in order to promote their own interests. But in doing so, they fulfill two crucial social functions. The function of maintaining law and order that is a necessary condition for economic growth and affluence, and the function of arbitrage between conflicting interests. The former was discussed at length in this chapter, the latter is discussed in chapter 6.

As a liberal theory of the state, my model suggests, and the story of the events surrounding the signature of the Magna Carta illustrates, how the state can promote the autonomy of individual agents while regulating interactions among them. The state promotes individual rights through a bargaining process in which the government is not an outsider benevolent, moral, grand legislator, but a self-interested broker who is sensitive to the interests of its clients – constituents only inasmuch as they promote the interests of the government.

However, this bargaining process is more complicated than the model, as developed so far, suggests. It usually involves conflicting interests that petition in opposite directions on each issue. In chapter 6 I discuss some of the issues associated with the competitive nature of pluralistic society by introducing into the analysis political entrepreneurs as intermediaries between the government and these competing interests. I show that while such competing interests seem to considerably complicate the interaction, current theoretical knowledge allows us to incorporate them quite naturally into the analysis modeled in this chapter. Using an extension of my model, developed by Ainsworth and Sened (1993), I conclude my theoretical argument by showing the dual role that political entrepreneurs play in alleviating the collective action problem of potential right-holders, on the one hand, and providing both their constituents and government officials with crucial information that can reduce the problem of coordination and improve the efficiency of the interaction among government and particular interests in society, on the other.

Appendix: proofs of lemma 5.1–5.8, theorem 5.1, and proposition 5.1

Lemma 5.1 states that agents of type $b_i = 0$, that stand to gain nothing from the grant of the right will never petition because, regardless of what the government does, such agents will always lose the cost of petitioning, c, if they petition. Thus, they have a dominant strategy not to petition.

LEMMA 5.1: If $(\sigma^*, g^*, \mu(\cdot))$ is a SE, then $\forall i \in N, \sigma_i(0) = 0$.

PROOF: $\forall i \in N, v_i(s_i = 1 \mid b_i = 0) = -c < v_i(s_i = 0 \mid b_i = 0) = 0$, regardless of σ^*_{-i}, and g^*. Thus, by condition (1) of the definition of a SE, $\sigma_i^*(b_i = 0) = 0 \forall i \in N$, is a necessary condition for $\{\sigma^*, g^*, \mu(\cdot)\}$ to be a SE.   QED

Lemma 5.2 shows that a government will grant the right if "enough" agents petition so that $\alpha > c_g/t \Rightarrow A^1 \in W(g^*)$. I show below that the converse is not true. So, $\alpha > c_g/t$ is a sufficient, but not a necessary, condition for the grant of a property right. This result is quite intuitive, since, by lemma 5.1, all agents that petition must be potential beneficiaries, and so the fact that $t \cdot \alpha > c_g$ guarantees the government a positive payoff.

The fact that government officials often grant rights even if $t \cdot \alpha < c_g$ (see below), is of much greater interest.

LEMMA 5.2: In an SSE satisfying IC, $\alpha > c_g/t \Rightarrow A^1 \in W(g^*)$.

PROOF (by contradiction): Assume for simplicity that c_g/t is not an integer. Suppose contrary to lemma 5.2 that $\alpha > c_g/t$, but $A^1 \notin W(g^*)$. By condition 2 of the definition of a SE,

$$\arg\max_{g \in \{0,1\}} \{g \cdot v_g(1 \mid \mu(\cdot \mid A^1,\sigma^*))\} = 0$$

i.e., the government's best response (BR) upon observing α petitioners is not to grant the right. By lemma 5.1 and the IC refinement the government's beliefs upon observing A^1 are $\mu(\beta \geq \alpha \mid A^1,\sigma^*) = 1$, regardless of $f(\beta)$ or σ^*,

$$\arg\max_{g \in (\{0,1\})} \{g \cdot v_g(1 \mid \mu(\cdot \mid A^1,\sigma^*))\} = 1$$

by (5.5), since

$$v_g(1 \mid \mu(\cdot \mid A^1,\sigma^*)) > 0 \text{ while } v_g(0) = 0.$$

Thus, upon observing $\alpha > c_g/t$ the government is better off granting the right, a contradiction.   QED

Let $\sigma^0 = (\sigma \in \sigma \mid \sigma_i(1) = 0 \forall i \in N)$, $\sigma^1 = (\sigma \in \sigma \mid \sigma_i(1) = 1 \forall i \in N)$,

$\sigma^0_{-i} = (\sigma \in \sigma \mid \sigma_j(1) = 0 \forall j \in N, j \neq i)$, $\sigma^1_{-i} = (\sigma \in \sigma \mid \sigma_j(1) = 1 \forall j \in N, j \neq i)$.

In words: σ^0 denotes a strategy combination in which no one petitions; σ^1 denotes a strategy vector where everyone petitions; σ^0_{-i} denotes a strategy vector in which no one petitions and i's strategy is not specified; finally, σ^1_{-i} denotes a strategy vector in which everyone petitions and i's strategy is not specified.

Lemma 5.3 implies that if government officials granted rights even if no one petitioned, then in equilibrium no one would petition. While the result itself is straightforward, it has an interpretation of some consequence: if government officials become "too liberal" in granting property and other individual rights, they will lose this important tool of assessing the popular support for such grants.

LEMMA 5.3: If $(\sigma^*, g^*, \mu(\cdot))$ is a SE and $\varnothing \in W(g^*)$, then $\sigma^* = \sigma^0$.

PROOF: If the government's strategy is to grant the right even if no one petitions then it is a dominant strategy for all players not to petition, even if they are of type $b_i = 1$, since they can avoid the cost of petitioning. QED

Lemma 5.4 states that government officials will grant property rights without any petitioning if, and only if, by their prior beliefs, they expect benefits to exceed the costs of enforcing the rights in question. Thus, lemma 5.4 restates theorem 4.1 of the complete information model developed in chapter 4 as a special case of the general model with incomplete information developed here.

LEMMA 5.4: If $g^*(0) = 1$, then $(\sigma^0, g^*, (\cdot))$ is a SSE iff $E(\beta) = q \cdot n \geq c_g/t$.

PROOF: *Necessity.* By condition 5.13 of the definition of a SSE, if $\sigma^* = \sigma^0$, then upon observing A^1 of cardinality $\alpha = 0$, the government should maintain its prior beliefs $f(\beta)$, since $pr(A^1 = \varnothing \mid B^1, \sigma^0) = 1$ for any $B^1 \subseteq N$ (substitute accordingly in the expression of Bayesian updating in condition 5.13 of the definition of a SE). Thus, $g^*(0) = 1$ is BR given $\mu(\cdot \mid \varnothing, \sigma^0)$ only if $E(\beta) = q \cdot n \geq c_g/t$. If $g^*(0) = 1$, by lemma 5.3, any $\sigma_i > 0$ for any $i \in N$ is not BR, s.t. $g^*(0) = 1 \Rightarrow \sigma^* = \sigma^0$.

Sufficiency. If $E(\beta) \geq c_g/t$, then $g^*(\varnothing \mid \sigma^0) = 1$ is BR, $g^*(0) = 1 \Rightarrow \sigma_i^* = 0 \forall i \in N$ is the unique BR. Thus, $E(\beta) \geq c_g/t \Leftrightarrow \{\sigma^* = \sigma^0, g^*(\alpha \geq 0) = 1, \mu(\cdot)\}$ is a SSE.   QED

Lemma 5.5 states that if one petitioner is necessary and sufficient to convince the officials of the government to grant a property right then, in equilibrium, some potential right-holders always petition. This amounts to what is known in the literature as the "privileged group," in which the free rider problem does not really exist (Olson, 1965; cf. lemma 5.6 below to understand the importance of this lemma).[10]

---

[10] Lemma 5.5 and 5.6 below require one more restriction on government officials' "out-of-the-equilibrium path" beliefs. The restriction known as the Intuitive Criterion, introduced in n.3 of chapter 5, implies that $\mu(b_i = 1 \mid s_i = 1, \sigma^* = \sigma^0) = 1$ and $\mu(b_i = 0 \mid s_i = 1, \sigma^* = \sigma^0) = 0$. In words, when an agent is observed to petition for a right we assume he or she is of type $b_i = 1$, even if her or his action were not expected to occur on "the equilibrium path" (being, $\sigma^* = \sigma^0$). We assume so because we would argue that an agent may be miscalculating her or his actions, but is unlikely to act when he can only lose from so acting (Cho and Kreps, 1987; Banks, 1991). For Lemma 5.5 and 5.6, I must further assume that $\mu(b_i = 1 \mid s_i = 1, \sigma^* = \sigma^0) = q$ and that $\mu(b_j = 0 \mid s_j = 0 \mid s_j = 1, \sigma^* = \sigma^0) = (1-q)$. In words, when government officials and other agents see any agent petitioning, even when the equilibrium path is $\sigma^* = \sigma^0$, so that no one is expected to petition, they all believe that the agent is of type $b_i = 1$, but regard the event that "should not have happened," as an aberration. Therefore, they keep their

LEMMA 5.5: If $g^*(0) = 0$ and $g^*(1) = 1$, then $\sigma^* \neq \sigma^0$ is a SE.

PROOF: Given the assumptions about the government's beliefs, and the hypothesis of lemma 5.5, one petitioner is enough to convince the government to grant the right. Thus, if $\sigma^* = \sigma^0$, any agent of type $b_i = 1$ is better off petitioning. QED

Lemma 5.6 states that if more than one petitioner is necessary to convince the officials of the government to grant a property right, then the case in which no one petitions and the governement fails to grant the right is always a SSE.

LEMMA 5.6: If $g^*(0) = g^*(1) = 0$, then $(\sigma^0, g^*, \mu(\cdot))$ in a SSE iff $1 + (q \cdot (n+1)) < c_g/t$.

PROOF: Lemma 5.6 implies that $1 + (q \cdot (n+1)) < c_g/t$ is necessary.

Sufficiency: If $1 + (q \cdot (n+1)) < c_g/t (\Rightarrow q \cdot n < c_g/t)$, then $g^*(0) = g^*(1) = 0$ is BR for the government given the out-of-equilibrium beliefs specified in n. 10. If $\sigma_{-i}^* = \sigma_{-i}^0$, and $g^*(0) = g^*(1) = 0$, then $v_i^0(\sigma^*, g, \mu(\cdot)) = 0$ while $v_i^0(\sigma_{-i}^*, \sigma_i > 0, g^*, \mu(\cdot)) = -\sigma_i \cdot c$. Therefore, it is BR for all agents not to respect the rights of others, and so: $\sigma^* = \sigma^0$. QED

Lemma 5.3–lemma 5.6 characterize all the equilibria where no petitioning occurs. The triple $\{\sigma^0, g^* = 1, \mu(\cdot)\}$ is a SSE when no one petitions and the government grants the rights if and only if the prior beliefs of the government officials $(f(\beta))$ are such that they estimate that they stand to benefit from the grant. This is just a repetition of theorem 4.1 of chapter 4. There is some merit in the fact that the more sophisticated model presented here, with incomplete information, yields as a part of its theoretical consequences the simpler model with complete information. It guarantees theoretical consistency.

Lemma 5.7 implies corollary 5.1, that states that the strategy of the government officials in equilibrium must be a threshold strategy, so that there must exist an integer, ω, so that if the officials observe a set of petitioners, the number of which is equal or greater than this threshold, they will grant the right, while if the number is smaller than the threshold the officials will not grant the right.

LEMMA 5.7: $v_g(1 \mid \alpha, \rho) > 0 \Rightarrow v_g(1 \mid (\alpha+1), \rho) > 0$.

PROOF: By (5.5) reproduced (using combinatory equivalents) below:

prior beliefs with respect to all the other agents so that while they now believe that agent i is of type $b_i = 1$, they maintain their beliefs that any other agent $j \neq i$ may turn out to be of type b_j with probability q and of type $b_j = 0$, with probability $(1-q)$. The need for this assumption should be apparent from the proofs of Lemma 5.5 and 5.6.

$$v_g(1 \,|\, f(\beta), \alpha, \rho) = \sum_{\beta=\alpha}^{n} (t \cdot \beta - c_g) \cdot \frac{\left[\binom{n}{\beta} q^\beta (1-q)^{n-\beta} \right] \cdot \left[\binom{\beta}{\alpha} \rho^\alpha (1-\rho)^{\beta-\alpha} \right]}{\sum_{\beta=\alpha}^{n} \left[\binom{n}{\beta} q^\beta (1-q)^{n-\beta} \right] \cdot \left[\binom{\beta}{\alpha} \rho^\alpha (1-\rho)^{\beta-\alpha} \right]}. \tag{5.50}$$

We have to prove that

$$v_g(1 \,|\, f(\beta), \alpha, \rho) = \sum_{\beta=\alpha}^{n} (t \cdot \beta - c_g) \cdot \frac{\left[\binom{n}{\beta} q^\beta (1-q)^{n-\beta} \right] \cdot \left[\binom{\beta}{\alpha} \rho^\alpha (1-\rho)^{\beta-\alpha} \right]}{\sum_{\beta=\alpha}^{n} \left[\binom{n}{\beta} q^\beta (1-q)^{n-\beta} \right] \cdot \left[\binom{\beta}{\alpha} \rho^\alpha (1-\rho)^{\beta-\alpha} \right]} > 0 \text{ implies} \tag{5.51}$$

$$v_g(1 \,|\, f(\beta), \alpha+1, \rho) = \sum_{\beta=\alpha+1}^{n} (t \cdot \beta - c_g) \cdot \left[\frac{\left[\binom{n}{\beta} q^\beta (1-q)^{n-\beta} \right] \cdot \left[\binom{\beta}{\alpha+1} \rho^{\alpha+1} (1-\rho)^{\beta-\alpha-1} \right]}{\sum_{\beta=\alpha+1}^{n} \left[\binom{n}{\beta} q^\beta (1-q)^{n-\beta} \right] \cdot \left[\binom{\beta}{\alpha+1} \rho^{\alpha+1} (1-\rho)^{\beta-\alpha-1} \right]} \right] > 0. \tag{5.52}$$

To prove that (5.51) implies (5.52) it is enough to prove that

$$\sum_{\beta=\alpha}^{n} (t \cdot \beta - c_g) \cdot \left[\binom{n}{\beta} q^\beta (1-q)^{n-\beta} \right] \cdot \left[\binom{\beta}{\alpha} \rho^\alpha (1-\rho)^{\beta-\alpha} \right] > 0 \text{ implies} \tag{5.53}$$

$$\sum_{\beta=\alpha+1}^{n} (t \cdot \beta - c_g) \cdot \left[\binom{n}{\beta} q^\beta (1-q)^{n-\beta} \right] \cdot \left[\binom{\beta}{\alpha+1} \rho^{\alpha+1} (1-\rho)^{\beta-\alpha-1} \right] > 0. \tag{5.54}$$

But (5.54) can be rewritten as

$$\frac{\rho}{(\alpha+1) \cdot (1-\rho)} \left[\sum_{\beta=\alpha}^{n} (t \cdot \beta - c_g)(\beta - \alpha) \cdot \left[\binom{n}{\beta} q^\beta (1-q)^{n-\beta} \right] \cdot \left[\binom{\beta}{\alpha} \rho^\alpha (1-\rho)^{\beta-\alpha} \right] \right] > 0. \tag{5.55}$$

Thus, we only have to prove that (5.53) implies (5.55). Let β^0 be the largest value of the index in (5.53) for which $t \cdot \beta - c_i \leq 0$, then (5.55) implies (5.56).

$$\sum_{\beta=\alpha}^{\beta^0} (t \cdot \beta - c_g) \cdot \left[\binom{n}{\beta} q^\beta (1-q)^{n-\beta} \right] \cdot \left[\binom{\beta}{\alpha} \rho^\alpha (1-\rho)^{\beta-\alpha} \right]$$

$$< \sum_{\beta=\beta^0+1}^{n} (t \cdot b - c_g) \cdot \left[\binom{n}{\beta} q^\beta (1-q)^{n-\beta} \right] \cdot \left[\binom{\beta}{\alpha} \rho^\alpha (1-\rho)^{\beta-\alpha} \right]. \tag{5.56}$$

Multiplying each summand on each side by $(\beta - \alpha)$ leaves inequality (5.56) true, since the RHS is increased more than the LHS. Multiplying both sides by $\rho/(\alpha+1)(1-\rho) > 0$ does not alter the relation in the inequality either. We get:

$$\frac{\rho}{(\alpha+1)\cdot(1-\rho)}\left(\sum_{\beta=\alpha}^{\beta^0}(t\cdot\beta-c_g)(\beta-\alpha)\cdot\left[\binom{n}{\beta}q^\beta(1-q)^{n-\beta}\right]\cdot\left[\binom{\beta}{\alpha}\rho^\alpha(1-\rho)^{\beta-\alpha}\right]\right)$$
(5.57)

$$<\frac{\rho}{(\alpha+1)\cdot(1-\rho)}\left(\sum_{\beta=\beta+1}^{n}(t\cdot\beta-c_g)(\beta-\alpha)\cdot\left[\binom{n}{\beta}q^\beta(1-q)^{n-\beta}\right]\cdot\left[\binom{\beta}{\alpha}\rho^\alpha(1-\rho)^{\beta-\alpha}\right]\right).$$

Which, rearranging terms, yields (5.55).   QED

COROLLARY 5.1: The government's strategy in a SSE is characterized by a threshold

$\omega \in Z$ so that $g^*(\alpha) = 1$ if $\alpha \geq \omega$, and $g^*(\alpha) = 0$ if $\alpha < \omega$.

PROOF: Since we consider only SSEs, if $\rho \in (0,1)$ then lemma 5.7, conditions (2) and (3) of the definition of SE (in equilibrium the government uses a BR, and consistency of beliefs) imply corollary 5.1. If $\rho = 0$, corollary 5.1 follows from lemma 5.4, given the assumed "out-of-equilibrium" beliefs.   QED

LEMMA 5.8: If $(\sigma^*, g^*, \mu(\cdot))$ is a mixed-strategy SSE, then the following must hold

$$c = (1-t)\cdot\sum_{\gamma=\omega-1}^{n-1}\left[\binom{\gamma}{\omega-1}\rho^{\omega-1}(1-\rho)^{\gamma-\omega-1}\right]\cdot\left[\binom{n-1}{\gamma}q^\gamma(1-q)^{n-\gamma-1}\right].$$

PROOF: To play mixed strategies in equilibrium agents must be indifferent between petitioning and not petitioning. Thus $\forall i \in N$, (5.9) below must hold:

$$(1-t)\cdot\mathrm{pr}(g=1\mid\rho_i=0)=(1-t)\cdot[\mathrm{pr}(g=1\mid\rho_i=1)-c_i.$$
(5.9)

By lemma 5.1, in equilibrium, only agents of type $b_i = 1$ ever petition. Every agent, $i \in N$, upon observing that he or she is of type $b_i = 1$ updates his or her beliefs so that:

$$\mathrm{pr}=(\mid B^1\mid=\beta\mid b_i=1)=\left[\binom{n-1}{\beta-1}q^{\beta-1}(1-q)^{n-\beta}\right].$$

S/he thus believes that:

$$\text{pr}(g=1 \mid \rho_i = 1) = \sum_{\alpha=\omega-1}^{n-1} \sum_{\gamma=\alpha}^{n-1} \left[\binom{\gamma}{\alpha} \rho^\alpha (1-\rho)^{\gamma-\alpha} \right] \cdot \left[\binom{n-1}{\gamma} q^\gamma (1-q)^{n-\gamma-1} \right],$$

$$(5.10)$$

and

$$\text{pr}(g=1 \mid \rho_i = 0) = \sum_{\alpha=\omega}^{n-1} \sum_{\gamma=\alpha}^{n-1} \left[\binom{\gamma}{\alpha} \rho^\alpha (1-\rho)^{\gamma-\alpha} \right] \cdot \left[\binom{n-1}{\gamma} q^\gamma (1-q)^{n-\gamma-1} \right].$$

$$(5.11)$$

So, (5.9) can be rewritten as:

$$\left(\sum_{\alpha=\omega-1}^{n-1} \sum_{\gamma=\alpha}^{n-1} \left[\binom{\gamma}{\alpha} \rho^\alpha (1-\rho)^{\gamma-\alpha} \right] \cdot \left[\binom{n-1}{\gamma} q^\gamma (1-q)^{n-\gamma-1} \right] \right) - c_i/(1-t)$$

$$= \sum_{\alpha=\omega}^{n-1} \sum_{\gamma=\alpha}^{n-1} \left[\binom{\gamma}{\alpha} \rho^\alpha (1-\rho)^{\gamma-\alpha} \right] \cdot \left[\binom{n-1}{\gamma} q^\gamma (1-q)^{n-\gamma-1} \right]. \qquad (5.12)$$

Subtracting

$$\sum_{\alpha=\omega}^{n-1} \sum_{\gamma=\alpha}^{n-1} \left[\binom{\gamma}{\alpha} \rho^\alpha (1-\rho)^{\gamma-\alpha} \right] \cdot \left[\binom{n-1}{\gamma} q^\gamma (1-q)^{n-\gamma-1} \right]$$

from both sides of (5.12) above and multiplying by $(1-t)$ and adding c to both sides we get:

$$c = (1-t) \cdot \sum_{\gamma=\omega-1}^{n-1} \left[\binom{\gamma}{\omega-1} \rho^{\omega-1} (1-\rho)^{\gamma-\omega-1} \right] \cdot \left[\binom{n-1}{\gamma} q^\gamma (1-q)^{n-\gamma-1} \right].$$

QED

THEOREM 5.1: A triple $(\sigma^*, g^*, \mu(\cdot)\}$ is a mixed-strategy SSE iff:

(i) $\forall i \in N \sigma_i^*(0) = 0$

(ii) $\forall i \in N \sigma_i^*(1) = \rho, g^*(\alpha) = 1$ if $\alpha \geq \omega$, and $g^*(\alpha) = 0$ if $\alpha < \omega$, and (ω, ρ) satisfies:

$$c = (1-t) \cdot \sum_{\gamma=\omega-1}^{n-1} \left[\binom{\gamma}{\omega-1} \rho^{\omega-1} (1-\rho)^{\gamma-\omega-1} \right] \cdot \left[\binom{n-1}{\gamma} q^\gamma (1-q)^{n-\gamma-1} \right].$$

$$(5.7)$$

$$v_g(1 \mid f(\beta), \rho, \alpha) = \sum_{\beta=\alpha}^{n} (t \cdot \beta - c_g) \cdot \frac{\left[\binom{n}{\beta} q^\beta (1-q)^{n-\beta} \right] \cdot \left[\binom{\beta}{\alpha} \rho^\alpha (1-\rho)^{\beta-\alpha} \right]}{\sum_{\beta=\alpha}^{n} \left[\binom{n}{\beta} q^\beta (1-q)^{n-\beta} \right] \cdot \left[\binom{\beta}{\alpha} \rho^\alpha (1-\rho)^{\beta-\alpha} \right]} \geq 0$$

iff $\alpha \geq \omega.$

$$(5.8)$$

PROOF: *Sufficiency:* If condition (5.8) holds, then, by lemma 5.7, g^*, as specified in (ii) is BR for the government, satisfying condition (5.12) of the definition of a SE. By lemma 5.8, (5.7) characterizes the equilibrium response of any agent of type $b_i = 1$ to the government threshold strategy g^*. If both (5.7) and (5.8) hold simultaneously, then the government's beliefs are consistent with the strategies of the agents, satisfying condition (5.13) of the definition of a SE, and the agents are playing a BR satisfying condition (5.11) of the same definition.

Necessity: Lemma 5.8 implies that condition (5.7) is necessary. By lemma 5.7 and corollary 5.1, the only strategy that the government ever uses, in equilibrium, is a threshold strategy. If the threshold ω that defines such a strategy does not satisfy condition (5.8), then g^* is not a BR, since it would grant a right expecting negative payoffs, or not grant it expecting positive payoffs, which violates condition (2) of the definition of a SE. Thus, condition (5.8) is necessary. If (5.7) and (5.8) do not hold simultaneously, condition (5.13) of the definition of a SE is violated. Thus, condition (ii) is necessary for $(\sigma^*, g^*, \mu(\cdot))$ to be an equilibrium. (5.1(i)) is necessary by lemma 5.1. QED

PROPOSITION 5.1: The *ex ante* payoffs of this game are always positive for the government and for each individual agent.

PROOF: Assuming that every player plays a strategy corresponding to the same equilibrium, the *ex ante* expected payoff for the government, $E^a(V_g)$, is:

$$E^a(v_g) = \sum_{\alpha=\omega}^{n} \sum_{\beta=\alpha}^{n} (t \cdot \beta - c_g) \cdot \left[\binom{\beta}{\alpha} \rho^{\alpha} (1-\rho)^{\beta-\alpha} \right] \cdot \left[\binom{n}{\beta} q^{\beta} (1-q)^{n-\beta} \right].$$

(5.13)

By condition (5.8) of theorem 5.1 and lemma 5.7, $E^a(V_g)$ is always non-negative in equilibrium. Let ∇b_i denote "net benefit to agent i." The *ex ante* expected payoffs for each agent $i \in N$ in this game is:

$$E^a(v_i) = (1-q) \cdot (E(\nabla b_i \mid b_i = 0) + q \cdot E(\nabla b_i \mid b_i = 1)). \quad (5.14)$$

By construction and lemma 5.1 (agents of type $b_i = 0$ never petition) the first term of this equation is always zero s.t.:

$$E^a(v_i) = q \cdot E(\nabla b_i \mid b_i = 1) = q \cdot (\rho \cdot E(\nabla b_i \mid b_i = 1, s_i = 1) + (1-\rho) \cdot E(\nabla b_i \mid b_i = 1, s_i = 0)) \quad (5.15)$$

$$\Rightarrow E^a(v_i) = (1-t) \cdot q \cdot [\rho \cdot (\mathrm{pr}(g=1 \mid s_i = 1) - c_i) + (1-\rho) \cdot \mathrm{pr}(g=1 \mid s_i = 0)]. \quad (5.16)$$

But, by lemma 5.8, in equilibrium $\mathrm{pr}(g=1 \mid s_i=1) - c_i = \mathrm{pr}(g=1 \mid s_i=0)$.

$$\Rightarrow E^a(v_i) = (1-t) \cdot q \cdot (\rho + (1-\rho)) \cdot \mathrm{pr}(g=1 \mid s_i=0). \qquad (5.17)$$

Thus, in equilibrium:

$$E^a(v_i) = (1-t) \cdot q \cdot \mathrm{pr}(g=1 \mid s_i=0), \qquad (5.18)$$

which is always non-negative.   QED

6

Political entrepreneurs: the linkage between autonomous individuals and central authorities

Introduction

The chapters 4 and 5 promote a simplistic picture of society inasmuch as they imply a polity where rulers rule over – and bargain with – citizens directly, with no role for mediators, parties, special interests or, in general, political entrepreneurs. This chapter introduces political entrepreneurs as generic players in the positive model of the polity promoted in this book. For the sake of the argument, I make no distinction among different types of political entrepreneurs such as party activists, lobbyists, or other paid and volunteer political activists.

In an earlier work with Scott Ainsworth (Ainsworth and Sened, 1993),[1] we argued that political entrepreneurs play a triple role in fulfilling a linkage function between constituents and government officials. First, they help individuals form and crystallize preferences about different possible outcomes. Second, they alleviate the collective action problem of groups of individuals, by providing information about the likelihood that any given property right will be granted and "focal points" regarding the most likely action to be taken by members of the group. Finally, they provide information about the costs and benefits of government action on one side, and group members on the other.

In the first section I introduce the subject of this chapter. In the second section I review work by Ainsworth and Sened (1993). Our work is "neo-institutional" in the sense that we have made an effort to explain the emergence and the essence of the role of political entrepreneurs in the context of a broad structure of political institutions (cf. Ainsworth, 1993),

---

[1] The second section of this chapter is based on work with Scott Ainsworth, previously published in the *American Journal of Political Science* (1993).

using the theoretical foundations discussed in chapter 3. In the third section I use a model, developed by Olson (1995), to explain how political entrepreneurs serve as nexuses of information and coordination in the polity. The fourth section uses the privatization process in Russia as an illustration of the central argument of this chapter. The concluding remarks sum up my general argument as to how individual rights in general, and property rights in particular, evolve in polities that are characterized by central governments, networks of political entrepreneurs, and active individual citizens. By this, I conclude the construction of my neo-liberal theory of the political institution of private property and related individual rights.

Explaining the institution of political entrepreneurs

To be successful, entrepreneurs must interact with two distinct sets of individuals: members and potential members of interest groups and government officials. An entrepreneur attracts members by helping them to mobilize around a common interest that is often formed and articulated by the entrepreneur, and by alleviating the collective action problem. The ability of entrepreneurs to influence government officials affects the groups' ability to compete successfully with other groups over different structures of institutions that promote and protect individual rights that governments consider for implementation. A structure of property rights affects the well being of group members, depending on the interest of the members in the rights implied by this structure.

Studies of interest groups typically focus on the strategic interaction between entrepreneurs and one of these groups of agents (cf. Milbrath, 1963). Olson (1965), Frohlich *et al.* (1971), Moe (1980), among others, concentrated their analyses on the group side because it was at the heart of the collective action problem they were studying. Other studies focused more directly on the influence of entrepreneurs on the government side, paying little attention to how the political entrepreneur affects the maintenance of interest groups. Bauer *et al.* (1968), Austen-Smith and Wright (1992), and Ainsworth (1993) emphasized the lobbyists' direct interaction with legislators. Bauer *et al.* described the lobbyists' roles as communicators providing important information to legislators. Ainsworth, Austen-Smith, and Wright developed signaling games to model the credibility of lobbyists' communication of electorally relevant information.

In our work (Ainsworth and Sened, 1993), we argued that it is misleading to separate the analysis of the role of political entrepreneurs into these two components because the effect of political entrepreneurs on the polity cannot be understood without careful examination of their interaction with the group of individuals they represent. At the same time, their influence on the way the group operates cannot be well understood without careful consideration of how political entrepreneurs affect the decisions of government officials. In order to study political entrepreneurs in a realistic environment, we took the model developed in chapters 4 and 5 and inserted in it a generic entrepreneur, to see how such a player would affect the final outcomes. This exercise allowed us to achieve two separate goals. First, we believe that by studying the role of entrepreneurs in this realistic environment we provide a better understanding of their activity. Second, by showing how outcomes in a society "with entrepreneurs" differ from outcomes in a society without them, we proposed a neo-institutional explanation of political entrepreneurs as political institutions. This is the subject of the second section.

One of the drawbacks of our 1993 analysis is that we have only one entrepreneur active in our model. In the third section I discuss a model developed by Olson (1995) that includes multiple entrepreneurs that act in competition with one another. In the last section of the chapter I use the insights gained from this discussion to explain the role of entrepreneurs in the emergence and evolution of property rights.

In chapter 5 I noted that theorem 5.1 has two important implications. First, it turns out that, in equilibrium, governments often end up enforcing some property rights even though the marginal benefits from enforcing these rights falls short of the costs of enforcement. Second, governments may fail to enforce other property rights that could yield benefits to government officials that exceed the costs of enforcement.

We argue (Ainsworth and Sened, 1993) that such inefficiencies help to explain the appearance of political entrepreneurs as a crucial element in the structure of the institutional build up of the modern polity. In the following section I introduce the model we developed to explain the argument.

Recall that the major problem in the model without political entrepreneurs, developed in chapter 5, was the difficulty in the assessment of the number of citizens who might benefit from amending the structural build up of institutions that protect property rights and the collective action problem of organizing the group of interested citizens to petition for such amendments. Ainsworth and Sened (1993) show that political entrepreneurs alleviate the collective action problem of groups of individuals, by providing information about the likelihood of obtaining a right, and "focal points" concerning the likely mode of action of the group members. Political entrepreneurs also provide crucial information about the costs and benefits of endorsing different structures of property rights to group members and government officials (Ainsworth and Sened, 1993). By doing so, entrepreneurs increase the probability that government officials endorse those structures of property rights that could be beneficial to members of society and government officials and reduce the probability that governments would enforce property rights that could be detrimental to different agents in society. Political entrepreneurs make interested citizens and government officials better off by reducing the uncertainties involved in the political process through which individual property rights come to exist.

The underlying premise of our model is that the expertise of political entrepreneurs allows them to observe the number of potential right-holders, β. By providing this knowledge about β to group members of the interest group as well as government officials, entrepreneurs reduce the uncertainty about the number of potential right-holders. We show that, regardless of what the entrepreneur may claim β to be, government officials and members of interest groups can deduce from his or her willingness to promote the interests of the group, that he or she observed a β that was higher than a certain minimum $\underline{\beta}$.

The decision of an entrepreneur to represent an interest serves, in a sense, as a self-fulfilling prophecy. If he or she decides to promote the induction of an individual right into law, he or she improves the chances that the government will react favorably to the plea of the group. On the other hand, if the entrepreneur chooses not to promote the induction of a property right into law, he or she sends a message that could considerably limit the turnout of group members and practically rule out a favorable reaction of the government to the group's plea. Political entrepreneurs "accomplish" this without doing anything beyond deciding to represent or not represent an interest group of potential right-holders.

Introducing political entrepreneurs in the model

Introducing a political entrepreneur into the model developed and analyzed in chapter 5, we (Ainsworth and Sened, 1993) obtain a new game that we denote by Γ^E which is a nine-stage sequential game:

STAGE 1: Strategy choices: Each agent chooses his or her strategy $\sigma_i \in \sigma_i$, where σ_i is a mapping: $\sigma_i: \{0,1\} X \{0,1\} \Rightarrow [0,1]$. The first set represents the agent's type $b_i \in \{0,1\}$. The second set represents the entrepreneur's message space $M = \{0,1\}$. The third set represents the set of all possible values of ρ, where $\rho \in [0,1]$ denotes the probability that i will petition for a change in the institutional structure of property rights. The entrepreneur chooses a strategy, λ, which is a mapping from $T = \{0,1,\ldots,n\}$, the set of types, with $\beta \in T$, to the message space M, $\lambda: \{0,1,\ldots,n\} \Rightarrow \{0,1\}$. The government chooses a strategy which is a mapping $g: \{0,\ldots,n\} X \{0,1\} \Rightarrow \{0,1\}$. The first set is the set of all possible values of $\alpha \in \{0,1,\ldots,n\}$ which is the number of actual petitioners, the second set is the message space, and the third set is the strategy space of the government, where 1 denotes granting the right and 0 denotes not granting it.

STAGE 2: Each agent $i \in N$ learns his or her type $b_i \in \{0,1\}$.

STAGE 3: The political entrepreneur observes his or her type $\beta \in T$.

STAGE 4: The entrepreneur sends a message $m \in M = \{0,1\}$, based on λ and β.

STAGE 5: The government and the agents update their beliefs given m.

STAGE 6: Each agent acts according to the strategy he or she chose in stage 1.

STAGE 7: The government updates its beliefs after seeing m and α.

STAGE 8: The government chooses its action given g, and depending on m and α.

STAGE 9: The payoffs are distributed as specified below.

Strategies and payos

Recall from chapter 5 that in our model we have n members of the general public, $N = \{1, \ldots, n\}$ with $i, j \in N$, denoting arbitrary members of the set N. Again, let c be the cost of petitioning, assumed to be equal across all members of society. Agent i's type, $b_i \in \{0,1\}$, characterizes his or her expected benefits from the structural change of institutions that protect and enforce private property rights. Agents of type $b_i = 1$ expect to benefit from the change, while agents of type $b_i = 0$ expect no benefit. The government and all the agents have common prior beliefs about the probability q that any agent $i \in N$ is of type $b_i = 1$. That is, the probability, $q = \mathrm{pr}(b_i = 1)$, that any agent in society turns out to be a potential beneficiary of the grant of a new property right. Let $b = (b_1, \ldots, b_n)$ denote a particular realization of n independent draws of $b_i \in \{0,1\}$. Thus, b represents an actual vector or combination of draws, for all relevant players, 1 through n, of their types that may be $b_i = 1$, or $b_i = 0$. β represents the number of agents that ended up being of type $b_i = 1$. Everyone starts with a common prior belief $f(\beta)$, a discrete multinomial probability density function defined by q and n that assigns to every value of $k \in \{0,1, \ldots, n\}$ a probability that $\beta = k$.

Let $S_i = \{0,1\}$ denote agent i's pure strategy set, where $s_i = 1$ denotes the choice to petition and $s_i = 0$ denotes the choice not to petition. Agents' strategies are conditional on their type and the message they receive from the entrepreneur, about his or her willingness to represent the group. Therefore, a strategy σ_i, of agent i, is a mapping $\sigma_i : \{0,1\} X \{0,1\} \rightarrow [0,1]$,[4] or an ordered quadruple:

$$\sigma_i = (\text{pr}(s_i=1 \mid b_i=1, m=0); \text{pr}(s_i=1 \mid b_i=0, m=0); \text{pr}(s_i=1 \mid b_i=1, m=1);$$
$$\text{pr}(s_i=1 \mid b_i=0, m=1)),$$

that assigns a certain probability to the likelihood that agent i will petition depending on his or her type and on whether the entrepreneur had decided to represent the plea of the group or not. Intuitively, if a group of potential beneficiaries learns that an entrepreneur has announced that he or she will represent them and try to obtain the grant of the right that is important to them, they should be more willing to turn out and petition for the grant of the right. We know from chapter 5 that agents of type $b_i = 0$ never petition.

So, σ_i denotes i's strategy set, where $\sigma_i \in \sigma_i$ denotes a specific strategy which is a probability $\rho(b_i, m) = \text{pr}(s_i = 1 \mid b_i, m)$, that i will petition depending on his or her type, $b_i \in \{0,1\}$, and the message, m, he gets from the entrepreneur. Let $\sigma = \sigma_1 X \sigma_2 X, \ldots, X\sigma_n$ be the strategic space of all members of society and $\sigma = (\sigma_1, \ldots, \sigma_n)$ be one strategy vector $\sigma \in \sigma$. A strategy vector, $\sigma \in \sigma$, specifies a particular strategic choice to every member in society. The strategy space, σ, is the set of all possible strategy vectors, or the set of all possible combinations of strategic choices by all the individual agents in society.

Let u_i denote the utility each individual member of society derives from this complex interaction then, as in chapter 5, u_i is defined as in table 6.1.

Recall that $W(g) = \{A^1 \in N : (g \mid A^1) = 1\}$. That is, $W(g)$ is the set of subsets of agents, such that if the government sees any one of these subsets petition for the property right, it grants the right. We defined the expected payoff of any agent as:

$$v_i(\sigma, m, g, b_i) = E(u_i \mid \sigma, m, g, b_i) = [(1-t)(b_i) \cdot \text{pr}(A^1 \in W(g) \mid \sigma, m)] - c \cdot \sigma_i.$$
$$(6.1)$$

In words: the expected payoffs of every agent in this game is a function of his or her type, as well as the probability that the government grants the right, given the strategic decision of the political entrepreneur to promote the interest of the group and the willingness, or strategic choice, of members in the group to petition for the right.

Again, let $s = (s_1, \ldots, s_n), (s_i \in \{0,1\})$ denote a particular realization of σ. $A^1 = \{i \in N : s_i = 1 \mid s\}$, denotes the group of individuals who actually petition and α denotes the size of A^1, or the number of agents who actually petition the government to grant the new property right. A strategy for the government is a mapping $g: \{0,1,\ldots,n\} X\{0,1\} \Rightarrow \{0,1\}$, where $g(\alpha, m) = 1$ denotes granting the right and $g(\alpha, m) = 0$ denotes not granting it after observing α and m. As before, the government's benefits, b_g, from granting a property right are assumed to be a linear function of β, $b_g = t \cdot \beta$, with $0 < t < 1$, and c_g denotes the government's costs of granting the right. We assume c_g and c to be common knowledge. The utility that the government

Table 6.1. *Agents' payoffs*

i's payoff $u_i =$	i's type $b_i =$	i's pure strategy $s_i =$	Government's strategy $g =$
$(1-t)-c$	1	1	1
$(1-t)$	1	0	1
$-c$	0	1	$g \in \{0,1\}$
$-c$	1	1	0
0	0	0	$g \in \{0,1\}$
0	1	0	0

expects from granting a property right, given any number of potential beneficiaries, β, is:

$$u_g = t \cdot \beta - c_g. \tag{6.2}$$

The expected payoffs to the government from granting a right, after observing the message, m, of the political entrepreneur and a number, α, of petitioners, is:

$$v_g(\alpha, m \mid \lambda^*, \sigma^*) \equiv E(u_g \mid \mu_2(\cdot \mid \alpha, m, \lambda^*, \sigma^*)). \tag{6.3}$$

$\mu_2(\cdot \mid \alpha, m, \lambda^*, \sigma^*)$ denotes the government's posterior beliefs about the number of potential right-holders after observing α and m, given the equilibrium strategy, λ^*, of the entrepreneur and the vector σ^* of equilibrium strategies of all the other agents. If a government grants the right, $g = 1$, its expected payoff is the sum, over all $\beta \in \{0, 1, \ldots, n\}$, of the payoff, $t \cdot \beta$, it expects if β is the number of beneficiaries of the right, times the probability that β is actually the number of beneficiaries, given the government's updated beliefs, $\mu_2(\cdot \mid \alpha, m, \lambda^*, \sigma^*)$, concerning the number of beneficiaries, after observing α and m, *less* the cost of implementation, c_g. Recall that the strategy of the government in equilibrium is bound to be characterized by a threshold, ω, such that if the number of agents that petition is greater than or equal to this threshold, the government grants the right, $g(\alpha > \omega) = 1$, while if it is smaller than this number the government does not grant the right, $g(\alpha < \omega) = 0$.

Let $0 < \delta < 1$, be the share of the cost of petitioning, c, that the entrepreneur keeps to himself or herself, and let c_E be the cost of establishing oneself as a political entrepreneur. The entrepreneur's payoffs are as in table 6.2.

After observing β, the entrepreneur can choose not to represent the group, $m = 0$, in which case his or her expected payoff is 0 by construction.

Table 6.2. *The entrepreneur's payoffs*

Entrepreneur's payoff u_E	Entrepreneur's message $m=$	Government's strategy $g=$
$\delta \cdot \alpha \cdot c - c_E$	1	$g \in \{0,1\}$
0	0	$g \in \{0,1\}$

If he or she decides to represent the group, $m=1$, then his or her expected payoff is:[2]

$$v_E(\beta, m=1) = [\delta \cdot c \cdot (\rho \mid m=1) \cdot \beta] - c_E. \qquad (6.4)$$

(6.4) states that the entrepreneur gets a share of the total receipt, expected to be paid by all the agents that are expected to join the entrepreneur and petition for change, *less* the cost, c_E, of his or her expenses.

Definition of a sequential symmetric equilibrium[3]

DEFINITION 6.1: A sequential equilibrium (SE) to the game Γ^E is a quadruple

$(\lambda^*, \sigma^*, g^*, \mu^*)$ such that:

1. $\forall \beta \in T, \lambda^*(m', \beta) > 0$ only if $m' \in \arg\max_{m \in M} v_E(\beta, m, \sigma^*(m), g^*(m, \sigma^*))$.

2. $\forall m \in M, \forall i \in N, \forall b_i \in \{0,1\}, v_i\{\sigma^*, g^*, \mu_1^*(m)\} \geq v_i\{\sigma^*_{-i}, \sigma_i, g^*, \mu_1^*(m)\} \forall \sigma_i \in \sigma_i$.

3. $\forall m \in M$, given $\sigma^*, \forall \alpha, g^*\{\alpha, m)\} = \arg\max_{g \in \{0,1\}} (g \cdot v_g(g=1 \mid \mu_2^*$

   $(\cdot \mid \lambda^*, m, \alpha, \sigma^*))$.

4. $\forall m \in M$, such that $\Sigma_{\beta \in T} \lambda^*(m, \beta) > 0, \mu_1^*(\cdot)$ satisfies:

$$\mu_1^*(f(\beta), m) = \left(\frac{\lambda^*(m, \beta) \cdot \text{pr}(\beta \mid n, q)}{\sum_{\beta' \in T} \lambda^*(m, \beta') \cdot \text{pr}(\beta' \mid n, q)} \right).$$

5. $\forall \beta \in T$, such that $\text{pr}(\beta \mid \mu_1^*(f(\beta), m)) > 0, \mu_2^*(\beta \mid \alpha, \mu_1^*(f(\beta), m), \sigma^*)$ satisfies:

---

[2] The choice of this simple message space where m can either be 0 or 1 is justified in Ainsworth and Sened (1993: 845–6).

[3] The usual reference is Kreps and Wilson (1982). More accessible discussions are found in Cho (1987), Cho and Kreps (1987), and Banks and Sobel (1987). The definition used in the text is adapted from Banks (1991: 7; cf. Ainsworth and Sened, 1993: 842, n. 6).

$$\mu_2{}^*(\beta \mid \alpha, \mu_1{}^*(f(\beta), m), \sigma^*) = \left(\frac{\mathrm{pr}(\alpha \mid \beta, \sigma^*) \cdot \mu_1{}^*(\beta, m)}{\sum_{\beta' \in T} \mathrm{pr}(\alpha \mid \beta', \sigma^*) \cdot \mu_1{}^*(\beta', m)} \right).$$

Condition 1 requires that the entrepreneur send a message with a positive probability only if it is a best response (BR), given his type, β, to the expected response of potential members of the group. Condition 2 states that $\sigma_i{}^*$ must maximize i's utility given his or her type, his or her updated beliefs, given the entrepreneur's message, and the strategies of the government and the other agents. Condition 3 states that g^* must maximize the government's utility given its twice updated beliefs. Condition 4 requires that the posterior beliefs, $\mu_1{}^*(\,\cdot\,)$, of the government and the relevant agents be consistent with λ^* in the sense that, after observing m, these beliefs are determined by Bayes' Rule according to the prior beliefs $f(\beta)$ and the equilibrium strategy of the entrepreneur λ^*. Condition 5 requires that the government's posterior beliefs, $\mu_2(\,\cdot\,)$, after seeing the message of the entrepreneur and the number α of agents that turned out and petitioned, be consistent with the equilibrium strategy vector of all the agents σ^*, in the sense that after observing α, $\mu_2{}^*(\,\cdot\,)$ is determined by Bayes' Rule according to $\mu_1{}^*(\,\cdot\,)$ and the equilibrium strategy vector of all the agents (except the entrepreneur and the government), σ^*.[4]

Definition 6.1 defines a sequential equilibrium (SE). A sequential equilibrium is symmetric (SSE) if all agents use the same strategy in equilibrium. Formally, $\forall i, j \in N, \sigma_i{}^* = \sigma_j{}^*$.[5]

[4] Definition 6.1 only specifies beliefs "along-the-equilibrium-path." No restrictions are imposed on the belief structure "off-the-equilibrium path." This poses a problem if the government observes an event that according to its beliefs should never occur. This could happen, for example, if $\sigma^* = \sigma^0$ where $\sigma^0 = (\sigma_i{}^* = 0 \forall i \in N)$, but $\alpha \neq 0$. What should government officials make of a case where they expect no one to petition and all of a sudden someone does petition? To deal with these cases, from the technical and substantive aspect, we use the Intuitive Criterion (IC) proposed by Cho and Kreps (1987). The IC requires that beliefs "off-the-equilibrium-path" place zero probability on the eventuality that agents that certainly stand to lose from deviating from the equilibrium behavior would ever do so. In our case, it implies that if government officials observe someone petitioning, they will assume s/he is of type $b_i = 1$. In other words, the government "off-the-equilibrium-path" beliefs put zero probability on the event that an agent of type $b_i = 0$ would ever petition because such an agent can only lose from petitioning in any possible circumstances.

[5] Following the norm in the literature (e.g. Palfrey and Rosenthal, 1984, 1988), we restricted our analysis to symmetric equilibria. Without imposing symmetry, the analysis of this type of game tends to become intractable. In addition, there is some value to the claim that we want to study agents as if they would react in the same manner to similar circumstances, which is precisely what the assumption of symmetric equilibria imposes. From a more technical point of view, if we do not impose symmetry it becomes very unrealistic to expect agents to satisfy the requirement of "consistency of beliefs."

Results and implications

LEMMA 6.1: (Ainsworth and Sened, 1993): If $(\lambda^*, \sigma^*, g^*, \mu^*)$ is an SSE as defined in definition 6.1, then λ^* is characterized by a threshold, z, such that:

$$\lambda^*(m=1 \mid \beta \geq z) = 1, \ \lambda^*(m=0 \mid \beta \geq z) = 0, \ \lambda^*(m=1 \mid \beta < z) = 0,$$
$$\lambda^*(m=0 \mid \beta < z) = 1.$$

In words: if the entrepreneur enters, potential members of the group and government officials can infer that the entrepreneur has observed a number of beneficiaries of the property right, β, that is greater than a certain threshold, z.

The intuition here is that if the entrepreneur enters, group members and government officials can infer that his or her expected benefits cover the cost of his or her expenses.[6] Since group members and government officials know everything except β, they can compute the least number of potential beneficiaries that the entrepreneur must have seen in order to decide to enter. Therefore, by lemma 6.1, when an entrepreneur sends any of the two message $m \in \{0,1\}$, potential group members as well as government officials should update their beliefs and, then, act along the lines of theorem 5.1 of chapter 5. Theorem 6.1 characterizes the set of all SSEs in Γ^E (the proof of lemma 6.1 and theorem 6.1 is found in Ainsworth and Sened, 1993; the logic of the proofs is the same as the logic of the proof of theorem 5.1 in the appendix to chapter 5, pp. 130–1).

THEOREM 6.1 (Ainsworth Sened, 1993): $\{\lambda^*, \sigma^*, g^*, \mu^*(\ \cdot\ )\}$ is a mixed-strategy SSE iff:

(i) $\forall i \in N \sigma_i^*(0) = 0$.
(ii) $\lambda^*(m=1 \mid \beta) = 1$ only if $\delta \cdot c \cdot (\rho \mid m=1) \cdot \beta \geq c_E$ otherwise $\lambda^*(m=1 \mid \beta) = 0$.

It is one thing to more or less expect all agents to do what all agents end up doing, but if we don't impose symmetry, we have to require, as part of the requirement of consistency of beliefs, that agents guess which of all the possible combinations of different strategic choices by a large number of agents is expected to materialize, which is a very unrealistic assumption. If we assume symmetry, the expected behavior of other agents can be literally computed from the given parameters of the game. As we have shown elsewhere (Ainsworth and Sened, 1993), in such cases, the number of possible equilibrium strategy vectors is limited. Therefore, it is quite realistic to expect agents to compute the expected equilibrium strategies and expect each other to choose one among the possible equilibrium vectors. If we do not impose symmetry, the number of equilibrium strategy vectors becomes infinite, and it makes little sense to expect agents to guess which of the infinite possible strategy combinations is to be chosen in the particular game at stake.

[6] Formally, it must be the case that $\delta \cdot c(\rho \mid m=1) \cdot \beta \geq c_E$. We assume that $\delta \cdot c n > c_E > 0$ to rule out equilibria where the entrepreneur always enters ($c_E = 0$) or never enters ($\delta \cdot c n \leq c_E$).

(iii) If $v_g(g=1 \mid \mu_1^*(\cdot)) > c_g$, then $\forall \alpha \in \{0,1,\ldots,n\} g^*(\alpha) = 1$ and $\forall i \in N \sigma_i^*(0) = \sigma_i^*(1) = 0$ and $\lambda^*(m=1 \mid \beta) = 0$ regardless of the size of β.

(iv) If $v_g(g=1 \mid \mu_1^*(\cdot)) < c_g$ then $\forall i \in N \sigma_i^*(0) = 0$, $\sigma_i^*(1 \mid m=1) = (\rho \mid m=1)$, $g^*(\alpha_1 \geq \omega \mid m=1) = 1$, $g^*(\alpha_1 < \omega \mid m=1) = 0$ and the pair $\{\omega,(\rho \mid m=1)\}$ simultaneously satisfies (6.5) and (6.6) below:

$$c = (1-t) \cdot \sum_{\gamma=\omega-1}^{n-1} \left[\binom{\gamma}{\omega-1} (\rho \mid m=1)^{\omega-1}(1-(\rho \mid m=1)^{\gamma-\omega-1} \right] \cdot \mathrm{pr}(\beta = \gamma \mid \mu_1^*(\cdot), b_i = 1).$$

(6.5)

$$v_g(g=1 \mid (\rho \mid m=1), \alpha_1) = \sum_{\beta=\alpha_1}^{n} (t \cdot \beta - c_g) \cdot \frac{\mathrm{pr}(\beta \mid \mu_1^*(\cdot)) \cdot \left[\binom{\beta}{\alpha_1}(\rho \mid m=1)^{\alpha_1}(1-(\rho \mid m=1))^{\beta-\alpha_1} \right]}{\sum_{\beta'=\alpha_1}^{n} \mathrm{pr}(\beta' \mid \mu_1^*(\cdot)) \cdot \left[\binom{\beta'}{\alpha_1}(\rho \mid m=1)^{\alpha_1}(1-(\rho \mid m=1))^{\beta'-\alpha_1} \right]} \geq 0 \text{ iff } \alpha_1 \geq \omega.$$

(6.6)

(v) If $v_g(g=1 \mid \mu_1^*(\cdot)) < c_g$ then $\forall i \in N \sigma_i^*(0) = 0$, $\sigma_i^*(1 \mid m=0) = (\rho \mid m=0)$, $g^*(\alpha_0 \geq \omega \mid m=0) = 1$, $g^*(\alpha_0 < \omega \mid m=1) = 0$ and the pair $\{\omega,(\rho \mid m=1)\}$ simultaneously satisfies (6.7) and (6.8) below:

$$c = (1-t) \cdot \sum_{\gamma=\omega-1}^{n-1} \left[\binom{\gamma}{\omega-1} (\rho \mid m=0)^{\omega-1}(1-(\rho \mid m=0))^{\gamma-\omega-1} \right] \cdot \mathrm{pr}(\beta = \gamma \mid \mu_1^*(\cdot), b_i = 1).$$

(6.7)

$$v_g(g=1 \mid (\rho \mid m=1), \alpha_0) = \sum_{\beta=\gamma 0}^{n} (t \cdot \beta - c_g) \cdot \frac{\mathrm{pr}(\beta \mid \mu_1^*(\cdot)) \cdot \left[\binom{\beta}{\alpha_0}(\rho \mid m=0)^{\gamma 0}(1-(\rho \mid m=0))^{\beta-\gamma 0} \right]}{\sum_{\beta'=\gamma 0}^{n} \mathrm{pr}(\beta' \mid \mu_1^*(\cdot)) \cdot \left[\binom{\beta'}{\alpha_0}(\rho \mid m=0)^{\gamma 0}(1-(\rho \mid m=0))^{\beta'-\gamma 0} \right]} \geq 0 \text{ iff } \alpha_0 \geq \omega.$$

(6.8)

Theorem 6.1 replicates theorem 5.1 from chapter 5, with the important difference that now we have an entrepreneur as an additional player in the game. The important achievement of our earlier effort (Ainsworth and Sened, 1993) is that we were able to show (in lemma 6.1, stated above) that the effect that the entrepreneur has is to reduce the uncertainty in the game, by providing additional information that is revealed by her or his strategic behavior. Given lemma 6.1, the decision of the entrepreneur to represent, or not represent the group's plea can considerably narrow the range of possible values of β, allowing both government officials and group members to make more educated decisions regarding their strategic actions. Given this additional information, they would act in one way if the entrepreneur decides to represent the group (condition (iv) of theorem 6.1), and act differently if the entrepreneur decides not to represent the group (condition (v) of theorem 6.1). The ability to distinguish between these two possible cases, based on the message sent by the entrepreneur, reduces the uncertainty in this environment and the loss in social welfare associated with it.

Condition (ii) of theorem 6.1 does not imply that entrepreneurs necessarily secure a positive payoff; it only implies that the expected payoffs are positive. This is quite important inasmuch as models of this sort must, as this model does, be able to account for political defeat, be it by an entrepreneur that fails to get a law passed that would grant his or her constituent group the right they pursue, or a political party that fails to secure a right that was promised to its voters, when the voters fail to turn out on election day.

This is probably what Moe (1980: 42) had in mind when he emphasized the importance of communication between entrepreneurs and their constituencies, arguing that the "link . . . can become useful to other individuals and [the entrepreneur] can charge . . . a fee in return for access to it."

We (Ainsworth and Sened, 1993) show that, in general, equilibria in environments with political entrepreneurs are more efficient than equilibria in the game without entrepreneurs. Though political entrepreneurs rarely reveal the value of β, by the very act of undertaking to represent a group, they send messages that are powerful enough to restrict the coordination problem among group members. In the absence of entrepreneurs, potential beneficiaries have to choose between many possible equilibria. In the game with entrepreneurs, they receive useful signals as to which equilibria are likely to be played. The presence of political entrepreneurs is proved to be valuable to government officials as well. Our model highlights the fact that entrepreneurs can improve the efficiency of the government policy making process, by helping agents to focus on equilibria with high levels of turnout. In so doing, political entrepreneurs reduce the probability that government officials make the mistake of granting a right when the government would be better off not granting it, and the mistake of failing to grant a right when it would be better off granting it. The reduced probability for such errors does not guarantee that only sound property rights will be granted, but the information revealed by political entrepreneurs about the likely number of potential right-holders helps government officials estimate when, and to what extent, the grant of any right is likely to gain support.

Even with the reduction in the number of equilibria, an equilibrium almost always exists wherein no potential beneficiary contributes, the entrepreneur stays out of the game, and the right is not granted, regardless of whether the number of potential beneficiaries warrants the grant of the right. Yet, the presence of self-interested entrepreneurs creates focal points away from the equilibrium in which no one petitions. After observing the entrance of an entrepreneur, no potential beneficiary will rationally conclude that the group is less viable than previously thought. On the other hand, if the entrepreneur shows a reluctance to enter, potential beneficiaries should conclude that either the cost of lobbying (which is common knowledge) is too high, or the number of beneficiaries observed by the entrepreneur is too small. In this way, a message from the entrepreneur helps members of the group to focus on a small set of possible equilibria.

Political entrepreneurs as a nexus of information and coordination

A central drawback of our model (Ainsworth and Sened, 1993), is that entrepreneurs rarely work in an environment devoid of competition from other entrepreneurs. In her recent work, Olson (1995) studied how competition among political entrepreneurs may affect the distribution of regulatory favors. Olson's (1995) model suggests that political entrepreneurs in a competitive environment serve as a nexus of information and coordination for competing groups.

Different interest groups, usually, have conflicting interests as to what structure of individual rights should be implemented, because each institutional design of property ownership promotes the interests of some groups of potential right-holders at the expense of other groups. Using a more traditional neo-classical analytical framework, Olson (1995) constructs a model of a polity where a multitude of interest groups compete to obtain regulatory favors from a relevant regulatory agency. In turn, the regulator maximizes the positive feedback from all of the agents involved, including politicians, industry groups, and consumer groups.

Olson (1995) draws on earlier works by Stigler (1971), Peltzman (1976), and Noll (1985) to offer a general formulation of a "regulator's objective function," but her model can be used in the context of my analysis by interpreting the "regulator" to be a central bureaucracy or government. Using this interpretation, I use Olson's work to complete the model of the polity developed here.

Olson suggests that we understand her model as a contribution to the "external signal theory" developed by Joskow (1974), Noll (1985), and others. A basic premise of this analytical framework is that the regulator chooses its action $a_j(p,b) \in A$ as a function of some general policy, p, and a budget constraint, b. Assume k different interest groups potentially affected by the government's policy, and organized by the k political entrepreneurs. Let $\{w_1, \ldots, w_k\}$ be a set of weights that the regulator places on the vector $m = (m_1, \ldots, m_k) \in M$ of signals received from the respective entrepreneurs representing the different interests in society with respect to the contemplated change in the structure of property rights in the polity. Let the regulator's or government's utility, u_g, be a function of the vector m of signals received from the political entrepreneurs and the weight w_k the regulators or, in our case, the government officials, attach to each signal m_k. These weights may be interpreted as updated beliefs of government officials concerning the number of individuals represented by each entrepreneur, their economic or political wealth, the likelihood that the group will be active in pursuing its goals, etc.

In this way we obtain the following objective function of a government:

$$u_g = \phi_g \left(\sum_{i=1}^{i=k} w_i \cdot m_i(a_g(p,b)) - c(a_g(p,b)) \right) \tag{6.9}$$

where $c(a_g(p,b))$ is the cost of choosing an action $a_g \in A_g$, which is a policy of granting a particular property right or maintaining a particular structure of property rights for the polity. $\sum_{i=1}^{i=k} w_i \cdot m_i(a_g(p,b))$ is the total sum of benefits the regulator or government official expect from enacting a policy, $a_g \in A_g$, concerning the structure of property rights in the polity. $m_i(a_g(p,b))$ is the expected signal, $m_i \in M_i$ of the entrepreneur of group $i \in K$, which is a function of the action $(a_g(p,b))$, taken by the government and affecting the structure of property rights in the polity. w_i is the weight that government officials attach to signals coming from any particular entrepreneur representing any particular group $i \in K$, depending, as stated above, on the number of individuals represented by the entrepreneur, their economic wealth or political power, their likelihood to be active in pursuing their goals and other parameters that are important to the government in power.

Finally, ϕ_g is just a government specific utility function of the benefits and costs involved in granting or protecting any specific structure of property rights for the polity, captured by $a_g(p,b)$. Too often, in this literature, it is assumed that all governments have the same utility functions, maximizing revenues, political support, or other objectives. But different government officials are likely to have different objective functions, depending on the personality of the leaders in charge (Doron and Sherman, 1995), the wealth and political prospects of the government in power, and so many other parameters. Government officials who are relatively sure of maintaining power for the foreseeable future can raise taxes through policies that may not be popular. Governments who struggle to remain in power may compromise their immediate tax revenues in an effort to maintain power.

It is quite remarkable how little reference one finds in the literature on the subject to the different utility functions government officials may try to maximize. If one is willing to accept the premise of this book, that government officials play a crucial role in inventing and structuring the structure of the institutional set up that protects and enforces property rights, one must be more careful in assigning goals and utility functions to government officials.

Government officials may try to maximize tax revenues (Levi, 1988), but they are just as likely to maximize their chances for reelection, the direct benefits of family or party members, and so many other objectives. We must start taking seriously the true motives of government officials.

Consider the following remark by Eggertsson (1990: 248, italics in the original):

> The economic growth and development of a country are basically unaffected by the type of government it has, if the cost of transacting in both the political and economic spheres is zero. However, when transaction costs are positive, the distribution of political power within a country and institutional structure of its rule-making institutions are critical factors in economic development.

Without keeping these observations in mind we risk trivializing the analysis of the important political aspect of the process by which property rights emerge and survive in the institutional structure of the polity. We tend to ignore the fact that $u_g = \phi_g\left(\sum_{i=1}^{i=k} w_i \cdot m_i(a_g(p,b)) - c(a_g(p,b))\right)$ is "government specific." This is why we succumb so often to the temptation to expect government officials to grant and enforce efficient property rights' institutions. I have already quoted North on this point (1990: 52):

> In North (1981), I revised the 1973 argument to account for the obvious persistence of inefficient property rights. These inefficiencies existed because rulers would not antagonize powerful constituents by enacting efficient rules that were opposed to their interests.

North acknowledges the non-trivial nature of the political game in determining the structure of property rights, but returns, all too often, to his earlier argument according to which "[i]nstitutions exist to reduce the uncertainties involved in human interactions" (North, 1990: 25). As Knight pointed out, institutional structures have distributional consequences that have little to do with reducing transaction costs, uncertainties, or inefficiencies (Knight, 1992: 33).

Using Olson's formulation of the problem, we should expect government officials to choose an action $a_g \in A_g$, such that $a_g(p,b)$ is the argument that maximizes $\phi_g\left(\sum_{i=1}^{i=k} w_i \cdot m_i(a_g(p,b)) - c(a_g(p,b))\right)$, $\forall a_g \in A_g$. In words: the action we should expect government officials to take is the action $a_g^* \in A_g$ that maximizes ϕ_g, given the anticipated reaction of the affected interests, as presented by the vector of signals $m(a_g)$ given any action $a_g \in A_g$, and the set of weights, w, that government officials attach to these anticipated signals. The vector of signals, $m(a_g)$, are the expected reactions that government officials expect from the interested parties, given any action a_g they may choose to take, that alters the structure of property rights in the polity. The weights attached to the signals represent the size, or influence, of the groups represented. It is easy to understand how such numbers translate into utility: regulators seek to maximize their chances to win the next elections, or to maximize future gains from tax revenues, or maximize other forms of economic and political gains (Riker and Sened, 1991). Government specific objectives are represented in this model by ϕ_g, that may differ considerably between one government to another.

Having established that government utility functions may differ considerably, depending on the utility function that characterizes the collective decision making process of the top government officials, it should be pointed out that all the other elements in $\phi_g\left(\sum_{i=1}^{i=k} w_i \cdot m_i(a_g(p,b)) - c(a_g(p,b)) \right)$, may vary considerably across governments as well. Different government officials will put more or less weight on pleas coming from the business community, from groups that advocate social justice, and from groups that struggle to provide minimum conditions for the poor in society. These differences may be due to ideological differences, the set of acquired prior beliefs with which every elected or non-elected official enters office, education, and other parameters that help form the individual characteristics of every government official. It is, therefore, not differences but similarities among different structures of institutions that protect property rights that should come as some surprise.

More importantly, for too long we have been led to believe that nature, market forces, historic determinism, and other obscure forces should be expected to forge for us some optimal structure of individual rights in general and property rights in particular. It is time to realize that institutional structures that protect property and related individual rights are determined by individual agents in society, through a complex bargaining process in which the regulator will choose a structure of individual rights that maximizes his or her utility, given his or her beliefs about the size and strength of different interest groups in society, and the extent to which these groups are active in the pursuit of rights they wish the regulator to impose.

An historic illustration: restructuring property rights in Russia[7]

The central argument of this book is that property rights are granted and protected by political institutions that emerge as the outcome of a political process of bargaining between governments and constituents. Chapter 5 introduced the role of incomplete and imperfect information in the environment of this bargaining process. It was shown, there, how constituents reveal their preferences through the process of petitioning for changes in the design of the institutional structures of property rights. It was also shown how imperfect this process of preference revelation is. This chapter focuses on the role that political entrepreneurs play in alleviating the problem by acting as intermediaries between government officials and potential beneficiaries of new property rights.

A remarkable, contemporary example for the role of political entrepreneurs in the process of designing and restructuring the network of institutions that grant and protect property rights is found in the annals of the privatization plans of the previously centralized, planned economies in Eastern Europe. Recent accounts of the process of redesigning the structure of property ownership in Eastern Europe and the former Soviet Union highlight the role of the different local actors in each case.

One major issue in recent years in most of these countries is the sale of state owned enterprises (SOEs). As one would expect, different countries found different ways to sell off these SOEs. Central governments had to choose between two major policies: free distribution of vouchers to the population at large, or a whole series of means to sell the SOEs to different agents in society in a way that would discriminate in favor of some interests and against others. In deciding how to design their policies, the role of entrepreneurs came to light.

The case of Russia is probably the best documented. A series of biographical notes recently published by leading economic and political advisers suggests that Yeltsin's government used the popular voucher program strategically. Facing a growing opposition from the old, planned economy, bureaucracy, the government distribution of vouchers, that came quite unexpectedly, was aimed to weaken the *nomenklatura* by eroding the resources they had under their control. The bureaucracy wanted to control privatization by centrally planning it, which would have given them an incredible amount of clout.

The five major organized interests in Russia in the early 1990s were: the

[7] I am grateful to Steve Lewis for helping me work out this illustration. Steve has been studying the politics of privatization in China and other centralized economies for the last five years. The role of entrepreneurs in the privatizations of China is just as fascinating as the case of Russia, but I leave it to Steve to publish his part of the story. The two main secondary resources we used are two recent biographical accounts of the events in the last five years in Russia: Åslund (1995) and Boycko *et al.* (1995).

managers, the workers, the bureaucrats, the local governments, and the military. The public at large expected Yeltsin to strike some sort of a compromise with these strong interests, but Yeltsin chose strategically the popular distribution of vouchers, which served not only to garner popular support from the electorate, but also to thwart the political designs of the opposition.

Yeltsin himself, at the moment of announcing the plan, declared: "we need millions of owners rather than a handful of millionaires" (Åslund, 1995: 235). By "we" Yeltsin referred to himself. *He* needed millions of voters and not a handful of millionaires that were likely to belong to the growing opposition to his regime.

But entrepreneurs played a crucial role in this. The biographical accounts of the events, put together by high-level economic and political advisers (Boycko *et al.*, 1995; Åslund, 1995) repeatedly relate to the constant wheeling and dealing between government officials and the entrepreneurs representing the competing interests involved, including the new entrepreneurs, literally created by the program: the directors and executives of the voucher investment funds.

These entrepreneurs played a crucial role in organizing the different interests, helping the government officials to assess the strength of the different interests, and then brokering the final deals.

We know little about how this privatization plan is actually working in practice, but we do know that each interest got some share of the pie. The managers and the workers obtained some guaranteed share of each enterprise, depending on the size of the enterprise and the sector of the economy. The local governments got the small enterprises (Boycko *et al.*, 1995).

The new structure of property rights was designed by government officials to serve Yeltsin in his attempt to weaken old opposition and build supportive new coalitions. To do that, the plan deprived his main opponents, the bureaucrats, of their resources, by a remarkable act of redistribution. Different political entrepreneurs were trying to impress government officials, and gained shares in the redistributed wealth if, and to the extent that, they were successful. The following two quotes from these accounts illustrate my argument better than can any words of mine:

> Gradually, the various lobbies managed to place their representatives in the government. At the end of May 1992, two former general directors of military–industrial enterprises, . . . , became deputy prime ministers . . . Simultaneously, the general director of Gazprom, Victor Chernomyrdin, became deputy prime minister for energy. . . Only in the spring of 1993, did . . . a true agrarian lobbyist, join the government as deputy prime minister for agriculture . . . [They] all fought for the interests of their lobbies . . .

State enterprise managers coalesced in enterprise associations, and most appear to have been members of several such groups. The most visible organization of enterprise managers was the Russian Union of Industrialists and Entrepreneurs . . . in early 1994, the Russian Association of Commodity Producers, led by Yury Skokov, became a powerful organization. Most enterprises fought on their own, often as branch lobbies and sometimes as united lobby . . . The whole industrial lobby campaigned for low energy prices and cheap credits, notably in the campaign against stabilization in the spring of 1992, which . . . was led by Volsky. He called the appointment of Victor Chernomyrdin as prime minister his victory in December 1992. But Volsky did not manage to deliver more rents to his favorites, the big automotive factories, than the agrarian and energy lobbies expropriated. The agrarian lobby was tightly organized all along as the agrarian Union, which also sponsored the Agrarian Party in the parliamentary elections in December 1992 . . . Volsky and Skokov were strong leaders and sophisticated politicians with excellent connections . . . but even so, the agrarian lobby won. (Åslund, 1995: 305–7)

From a somewhat different perspective Boycko *et al.* (1995: 151) concluded their account of the events:

But perhaps the most significant consequences of privatization are political. Privatization has created a class of property owners who have become the clear economic beneficiaries, and political supporters, of further liberalization of the Russian economy and society. This class is not limited to a few brokers and traders driving BMWs around Moscow, as some Western observers would like to believe. These property owners include the 40 million Russians holding shares in privatized firms and in mutual funds, who want their investment protected. They also include the millions of people working for the growing service sector. In a country of 100 million voters, these are significant constituencies, which will throw their weight behind such critical reforms as land privatization, stabilization, and free trade. More importantly, the new property owners support the economic reformers who continue their struggle against communists and nationalists. Privatization and reform have created powerful political interests that are injecting some liberalism into Russian politics.

Concluding remarks: the role of political entrepreneurs

The analysis here and in chapters 4 and 5 suggests a general model of the emergence and evolution of individual rights that diverges considerably from the traditional analysis. According to this model, individual rights are neither derivatives of moral theories nor do they result from the benevolence of social leaders or governments that use any such theory to construct them. Individual rights are not "natural" in any sense of the word and they do not emerge in any "natural" evolutionary process that establishes one or another legal or conventional code of laws and norms that, in turn, imply the set of individual rights that are commonly accepted and respected in society.

Instead, individual rights evolve after a central force that can grant and enforce such rights establishes its monopoly over the use of extreme forms of force. Such central agencies use their monopoly over the use of force to grant rights to individual members of society in order to maximize their egotistical interests. They do so to maintain the political and economic support every leader needs to maintain control over society, and to advance some very "personal" goals that are "specific" to every set of government officials.

The central point of chapter 4 was that governments, in their quest to further their selfish interests, have an interest to grant private property and related individual rights to their constituents in order to improve production, thus enlarging the tax base from which they can draw taxes, or simply "buy" political support by granting private property rights to potential supporters.

The central premise of chapter 5 was that government officials often operate under conditions of incomplete information regarding the interests of their constituents. Consequently, they often make mistakes, granting rights they would be better off not granting, or failing to grant property rights they could benefit from. The main argument of chapter 5 was that political activism and protest send messages to the central agency that amending the existing institutional structure of property rights could make some citizens, and eventually the central agency itself, better off. In the course of the argument I have established two points. First, I proved mathematically that, *ex ante*, governments are expected to benefit from provisions for freedom of speech and other forms of political protest, because these forms of expression help the government collect essential information concerning the benefits and costs of different institutional structures of individual rights it may want to implement in the polity. The second point was that the problem of collective action, and the possibility that the government may misinterpret by under- or overestimating the signals sent by the public, leaves much room for error by the government, even in an open society with solid norms of freedom of speech and of political protest.

The main point of this chapter was to show how political entrepreneurs serve as a link between special interests and the government. Political entrepreneurs help groups of individuals form and elaborate their interests and understand how these interests may be advanced or damaged by different institutional structures of individual rights. They also help individuals rally around a cause or a public figure that may help alter, in their favor, the legal structure of individual rights. Just as significant is the fact that political entrepreneurs help group members focus on one or another mode of action by sending signals to members concerning the chances for success and their evaluation of what other members in the group are most likely to do.

From the government's perspective, political entrepreneurs pass crucial information to government officials regarding the number of interested individuals they represent and their ability to provide government officials with electoral or different types of economic support. Again, this information becomes available not because of some genuine "truthfulness" of political entrepreneurs, but because the selfish interests of the political entrepreneur makes it easy, for group members and government officials alike, to extract from his or her behavior the private information he or she holds. After obtaining the information, government officials use their updated beliefs to assign weights to the signals sent by the different political entrepreneurs and construct an institutional structure of individual rights for the polity so as to maximize the political and economic support they can get from its members.

The incorporation of political entrepreneurs into my positive model of the political institution of individual rights is important for two reasons. First, it is empirically sound: groups are active in petitioning for and against particular structures of individual rights. The second reason is more profound: modern designers of social and economic reform often promote structures of property and related individual rights that are probably "just," or "efficient," according to some ideal model of the world. They then blame special interests for ruining their "plans" (e.g. Åslund, 1995; Boycko *et al.*, 1995). The organization of special interests in society is a fact of life. To assume that society could operate without the intervention of governments and special interests is to assume away the very problem of social order.

We cannot go on designing institutions for "ideal" worlds without politics. Politics is a crucial part of the process that structures political institutions that protect property and related individual rights. If we want to be of any help in designing such structures in the future, we must design them for the world as it is, with transaction costs, with special interests, and with central governments with selfish interests of their own.

In chapters 4–6 I made an effort to construct a positive theory of the political process through which structures of property and related individual rights emerge and evolve. It seems to me that future attempts to design and reform institutions that protect private property and related individual rights must rely on such positive theories, and not on abstract normative speculations.

Montesquieu ([1848] 1949: 152–60), made the important observation that the separation of powers vested in government is an important foundation for any healthy democratic society. Much less known, but just as important, was his argument that the maintenance of an "open society" depends on the existence of competing centers of power, centers that can challenge the central authority with the necessary rigor and force to generate the change and evolution that will follow the unavoidable changes within and in the environment of every polity in the course of its history ([1848] 1949: 168–70). In this chapter I used rigorous analytical tools to study the way in which such alternative centers of power like political entrepreneurs operate, providing some additional support to Montesquieu's famous claim.

7

A case study: the grant of private property rights in air slots[1]

Introduction

The division between the disciplines of economics and political science may give the impression that the subjects of their study are equally separate. Yet, economic and political affairs are inextricably intertwined. Most political disputes are, in fact, about economic affairs, Poole and Rosenthal's (1991) survey of roll-calls in the US Congress between 1789 and 1985, for example, clearly demonstrates this point. Such admixtures occur because attempts to gain market advantage need not end in market transactions, but may transfer to the political arena as attempts to change the constitution of markets.

Economic theory, as it has developed in the last two centuries, is a theory about price equilibria in markets. It assumes traders' control of goods in order to study exchange, but cannot be used to study the emergence of different types of ownership and the effect they have on markets (Demsetz, 1982: 6–9). This chapter presents a case study of the grant of private property rights in air slots to individual carriers in four "high-density" airports in the USA. It uses the general theoretical model developed in the previous chapters in an attempt to improve our understanding of how polities shape market activities by structuring ownership through institutions of common and private property.

In the following pages, I analyze the evolution of ownership institutions in landing/takeoff time slots at four high-density airports. This study offers important insights into how property rights' institutions evolve, and how

[1] This chapter is based on work done with the late William H. Riker. I am grateful to Elinor Ostrom and four anonymous referees for their comments on an earlier version of this chapter, published in the *Journal of Theoretical Politics* (Sened and Riker, 1996).

155

these institutions affect the evolution of markets. This case is a rare example of the evolution of different ownership structures that regulate the same scarce resource over a short period of time: slots were owned by the state until 1968. From 1969 to 1985 they were used under a common property ownership institution. In 1986 the slots became privately owned, and have remained so since then. These changes in the institutional structure of ownership permitted a careful examination of the political process through which markets actually develop. Since the events are so recent, it was possible to collect accurate data to assess the impact of these institutional changes on the market they were designed to regulate.

The central argument of this chapter comes down to two central assertions:

1. Decisions at the political arena, concerning the structure of property rights, affect economic phenomena such as market price structures, the efficient use of scarce resources as inputs to production, and consumers' welfare.
2. Individual or corporate actors occasionally shift their efforts to the political arena in order to obtain more promising ownership arrangements (Riker and Sened, 1991). But politicians and government officials often alter the institutions that protect different ownership structures to serve their own political agenda, paying more or less attention to the costs and benefits, as well as the expressed interests, of the economic players involved.

While the first assertion seems trivial, until very recently it was systematically ignored by economists who study the subject of the evolution of property rights (cf. Demsetz, 1982; North, 1990; Riker and Sened, 1991). The second assertion received more attention in recent years (Mitchell and Munger, 1991; North, 1990) but the literature on the subject remained quite abstract. In this chapter I use the insights gained in the previous chapters about the origin and evolution of property rights to explain the shift from (a) government control of takeoff and landing slots in high-density airports, to (b) industry self-regulation of slots under a regime of common property ownership, to (c) the establishment, by the US government, of a mechanism that endows individual airlines with private ownership of slots, with rights of transfer. Through this empirical case study I demonstrate how individual and corporate actors shift their efforts to the political arena and how government officials decide to introduce changes in the institutional structures of ownership in the market.

The first section summarizes the story of the institutional change as it unfolded over the last three decades (cf. Riker and Sened, 1991). It examines the incentives of the players involved, and makes qualitative evaluations of the impact that strategic agents had on the events. The second section examines the impact of privatization on the market structure. The third section is a quantitative study of the effect that privatization had on the efficiency of the use of air slots. The fourth section examines some welfare consequences of the institutional change. Above all, it shows how privatization reduced transaction costs in the air transportation sector, which allowed carriers to maintain services to cities that would otherwise have had to be abandoned. The fifth section reexamines the incentives faced by the central actors – i.e., the main airlines and the government – that brought about the institutional change. The concluding remarks discuss the relevance of the findings to the general theoretical model developed in this book.

The development of private property in air slots

In this section I recount briefly (cf. Riker and Sened, 1991) the history of ownership of landing/takeoff time slots at the four US high-density airports: LaGuardia and Kennedy in New York, National in Washington DC, and O'Hare in Chicago.

Until 1969, the Federal Aviation Administration (FAA), acting as an agent for the owner, the USA, used the principle of "open skies" to allocate slots. This meant that air traffic controllers – employees of the FAA – organized queues on the ground and in the air on a first-come, first-served basis.

In the late 1960s, the queues at the four airports became excessively long, partly because of growth in traffic volume and partly because of each carrier's effort to operate at peak hours. As a result, a committee of carriers' executives recommended the establishment of users' committees to allocate slots "fairly." After obtaining assurances from the Department of Justice that exempted the carriers from anti-trust prosecution, the Civil Aeronautics Board (CAB, the regulator of carriers' routes, fares, etc.) and the FAA encouraged carriers to implement this solution.

The committee system was a form of common ownership. It gave the carriers, jointly, the right to allocate the slots among themselves. Each carrier, at each airport, had one vote on the airport allocation committee, and the committees used a unanimity rule in their decisions. The incentive to agree was the threat of possible FAA (political) reallocation in case of default. In this way, the carriers gradually adjusted their use of resources, accommodating each other's changing business plans. Initially, this system improved the efficiency of the use of the scarce resources inasmuch as it shortened the queues. As long as the CAB restricted entry into the industry by new airlines, established carriers' shares of slots remained stable.

The committees worked reasonably well until deregulation (1978 and after) and the air traffic controllers' strike (1981). As long as the CAB allocated routes and restricted entry into the cartel, the unanimity rule helped to maintain a stable size relationship among carriers at each airport. Carriers could not be forced to give up slots. They would give up slots only if the reallocation was advantageous to them. The semi-annual allocations were, usually, within marginal adjustments of the status quo. Initially the eleven carriers (then, by consolidation, nine) retained about the same relative position throughout the eleven years up to 1980 (Riker and Sened, 1991).

Starting in 1979, the air transportation sector in the USA entered a period of deregulation, started by the Carter administration and strongly endorsed by the Reagan administration that took over in 1980. One major institutional change that was initiated by the Carter administration was the elimination of the CAB as a federal agency. While the FAA continued to regulate safety aspects, including airport safety, the carriers could no longer rely on the CAB to restrict entry into the business by regulating the allocations of inter city routes. In this way, deregulation encouraged new entrants who had rights to membership on the committees of airports they served. Once on the committees, they refused to agree to any new allocations of air slots unless they obtained desirable slots. Gradually, large carriers gave in to demands for slots from new carriers, resulting in a major reallocation.

Why did the established carriers agree to new allocations in which they lost slots? They probably feared invoking the default implementation of alternative methods of reallocation that could result if the committees ever reached an unbreakable impasse. These were: (a) "open skies" – with queues; (b) auctions or lotteries – with uncertain results; and (c) arbitrary FAA assignment – with, doubtless, much Congressional input. Given these default options, an equilibrium of this game is an allocation that: (a) is at least as good as the expected outcome under the default rule, and (b) no other allocation is preferred to it by everyone (Grether *et al.*, 1981).

Deregulation brought in ten new carriers who gradually obtained slots from the largest carriers. The old carriers were thus forced to accept equilibria that were closer to what they probably believed was the worst the FAA could do. To take Washington National airport as an example of the general trend between 1980 and 1984, the number of slots held by Eastern Airlines went from 147 slots to 107, United Airlines' holdings went from 96 to 34, and American Airlines from 82 to 30 (for a detailed account of this trend, see Riker and Sened, 1991).

By 1984 all proposed reallocations were, evidently, worse than the large carriers expected from the FAA, so they defaulted. When the FAA did nothing to break the deadlock, the status quo turned out to be the sole equilibrium. The tragedy of the commons, which the committees were intended to resolve, reappeared.

No reform in the system occurred until the end of 1985. The main reason for the delay was a dispute about the appropriate reform: in carrying out President Reagan's political agenda of freeing up market forces, his agent, the Office of Information and Regulatory Affairs (OIRA) within the Office of Management and Budget (OMB), favored immediate privatization. The OIRA had an important bargaining chip, namely, the authority to veto new regulations.

Only the Department of Transportation (DOT) had the authority to initiate procedural reform, but it was internally divided. Its Office of Policy favored privatization while the FAA favored open skies. The latter was reluctant to release control of slots which was valuable in dealings with Congress and the carriers. Thus, the DOT favored privatization under Drew Lewis (1981–3) and open skies under Elizabeth Dole (1983–8). The preferences of the latter may have reflected the fact that she and her husband, Senator Robert Dole are from Kansas, a manufacturing center for general aviation. The general aviation lobby favored open skies, because small aircraft had much to lose from any procedural reform. Small aircraft need a long time to land, and they carry few passengers. Open skies treated equally small aircraft and big jets, that take a shorter time to land, and carry more passengers. Reform was expected to change this equal treatment and reduce the use and demand for small aircraft, therefore, any reform was expected to have a negative effect on the manufacturing industry. The general aviation lobby was strong because it had prosperous, well connected members in every Congressional district. The large carriers, on the other hand, were silent. They were probably frightened by the Grether *et al.* report (1981) that recommended auctions as a guideline for reforms. The carriers may have feared that the OMB under David Stockman would welcome the income from auctions. Thus, after 1983, OIRA was the only significant force that favored reform.

With this impasse of interests, it is unlikely that reform would have occurred had it not been for the committee defaults and the continually worsening gridlock in the high-density airports. In an attempt to break this deadlock, the OIRA published a letter, in 1983, which made it clear that it favored privatization but did not favor auctions. Thus reassured, those airlines that expected to benefit from privatization supported it before Congress (see pp. 172–4 for an analysis of the "revealed" and "concealed" preferences of the major airlines).

With this new array of interests, with the oversight committee of the House impatient for some reform, and with the DOT constrained by OIRA's authority to veto, DOT finally issued a "buy/sell" rule for the high-density airports on December 20 1985 (50 FR 52180-52201). It included a "grandfather" clause to protect slots of current holders and appointed the FAA to keep a register of holdings. It allowed the FAA to recall slots for Essential Air Services (for small communities) or operational necessity, and provided for FAA takeover of slots used less than 65% of the time in a two-month period (few slots have ever reverted to the FAA from low usage). Probably out of deference to the FAA, the rule also stated that slot holdings were "an operating privilege not a property right."[2] This did not alter the fact that slot-holders acquired an exclusive, alienable right, with reservations not significantly different from those to which owners of land are exposed for failure to pay taxes or for failure to obey zoning regulations.

The main lesson that this short history teaches us is the crucial role that politicians and government officials play in the process of structuring and restructuring institutions that define, grant, and enforce different owner-ship rights. Unlike the common picture promoted by the economic literature, we see very little effect of "market forces" on the shaping and reshaping of property rights' institutions. The main actors here are government officials who respond to political initiatives and ideologies and to perceived costs and benefits that different structures of property right institutions may entail for them. These officials certainly take into account the expected responses of different economic and public interests, as modeled in chapter 6. These interests, to the extent that they are organized and heard, play the role of petitioning for change, or against it, as the case may be. But it is government officials who, in the end, decide how and when to redesign the structures of property rights in the market.

If anyone really suffered from the inefficient allocations of air slots for landing and take off, it was the big carriers and the general public. But none of these very potent actors was very active or had much influence on the decisions of the officials, in President Reagan's administration, concerning the structure of ownership that was finally chosen to endow the carriers with private property rights of air slots. It was mainly the initiative of top government officials at the OIRA of the OMB that brought about the grant of private property rights.

As my model suggests, the different interest groups were definitely active in trying to shape, or change the shape, of the institution, as it was being "fabricated" by DOT and OIRA officials. As stated above, it seems that the lobbying efforts of the interest group of general aviation, representing the interests of builders and users of small aircraft, may have actually been successful in delaying the institutional change. By constantly opposing the change, they have brought powerful political figures to realize that the anticipated change was going to hurt their interests.

[2] The FAA was to monitor usage and, in event of a return, to conduct a lottery for reallocation. The FAA occasionally reclaims slots temporarily at O'Hare for operational reasons, but carriers can, and do, protect themselves against such reclaims by buying slots with low priority numbers.

Later on, representatives of the general public became more vocal in opposing the change in Congressional hearings. Political entrepreneurs who represented these interests raised three main issues: safety, price hikes, and abandonment of services to smaller communities (Hearing 99-33, 1985; Hearing 99-746, 1986; Hearing 99-59, 1986; cf. Report 99-299, 1986, submitted by Senator Danforth of the Committee on Commerce, Science and Transportation, US Senate, May 14). But in the end it was, again, government officials who weighted the costs and benefits to the government and the general public and decided to go ahead and grant private property rights to the carriers.

In lengthy interviews we conducted in the summer of 1989, these officials repeatedly responded that they did what they did because they were trying to solve the gridlock that had emerged in the relevant airports, and because they were guided by President Reagan's declared policy to favor privatization in any way possible. This was a politically calculated initiative. It was meant to ensure the political success of President Reagan. But it was based on the belief that privatization would make many American citizens better off, through the improved efficiency of the use of scarce resources it was supposed to promote.

Below, I evaluate the merits of these beliefs using data on the use of these scarce resources, before and after the grant of private property rights, but at this stage it is important to emphasize that our interviews leave no room for doubt that these beliefs held by top government officials were the driving force behind the institutional change that these officials initiated and implemented, to grant private property rights in air slots to the major air carriers servicing these airports.

The second–fourth sections provide a quantitative analysis of the consequences of this grant of property rights in slots to individual carriers. Grether *et al.* (1981) claimed, using standard microeconomic theory, that the common property "scheduling committees'" mechanism of slot allocation was inefficient, and that creating private property rights would result in welfare gains. As stated above, such claims, accepted by the top government officials at OIRA, brought them to initiate and carry on the institutional change that resulted in the grant of private property rights in air slots. Opponents of privatization feared that without government supervision carriers would practice cartel pricing, and predicted net welfare losses. The analysis below sheds light on this controversy.

Beyond the attempt to determine whether the grant of private property rights resulted in social welfare benefits or losses, this analysis offers a general method of evaluating, *ex ante*, or *ex post*, the benefits and costs of granting different forms of property rights as a public policy. I have stated repeatedly in this book that we have been blinded by normative and ideological claims on the merits and defaults of different structures of ownership rights. For too long, we have designed our institutions based on unwarranted claims about the consequences of one or another institutional structure. This chapter is a modest contribution towards the construction of a more scientific approach, that would allow us to evaluate the real merits of different institutional designs that are implemented to grant and protect different structures of property rights.

Before engaging in the analysis of the consequences that the grant of property rights had on the use of air slots, I must demonstrate that this change made a difference. The following section examines evidence on how the institutional change in the structure of property rights, after the grant of private ownership in air slots, affected exchange behavior in the market.

Exchange behavior following the transition to private ownership

The previous section demonstrated how government officials used their political power to alter the institutional structure of ownership rights in the market. The point of this section is to find out whether the institutional change made a difference. From a methodological point of view, in order to establish causality, we must first show that an active market developed. If only a few slots changed hands after the grant of private property rights, it would be hard to argue that any causal effect could be established to explain subtle changes in the economics of air slots by the institutional changes in the structure of ownership rights induced by the US government.

In chapter 3, I explained that institutional change is expected when powerful agents in society expect a visible change in the outcome under the new institutional design, as opposed to the status quo. If those *different* outcomes are expected to favor a decisive coalition of players, when compared to the status quo, then we would expect this coalition to initiate the institutional change. In this section I demonstrate that the Reagan administration was correct to anticipate that the institutional change would generate an important change of the market. The consequences of these changes are evaluated in the following sections.

The FAA established 4700 air slots. Two random samples were drawn out of this pool: one of 70 slots out of 670 slots at Washington National, and one of 175 slots out of 2245 slots at O'Hare airport in Chicago. Apparently, three different modes of exchange of air slots developed in the market:

1. *Trading*: Carriers trade slots, temporarily or permanently, to obtain more flexibility in scheduling.
2. *Leasing*: Carriers "rich" in slots and "poor" in profitable operations find it rewarding to lease slots. Such carriers did not sell these slots

Table 7.1. *Exchanges in the market for air slots between 1986 and 1988*

Type of transaction	Trades				No. (%) of slots that were	n – size of the
Airport	Perma-nent	Temp-orary	Leasing	Sales	never traded	sample
Washington National	22	27	25	28	34 (49%)	70
Chicago O'Hare	49	65	78	37	70 (40%)	175
Total	71	92	103	65	104 (42%)	245

because they did not find buyers, or because they hoped to increase operations in the future, and were concerned about future availability of slots.

3. *Selling*: There were two types of sellers: (a) non-viable carriers which sold all their slots, and went out of business; (b) carriers which sold (or bought) slots in order to reduce (expand) operations.

Table 7.1 summarizes the activity in the market during the first three years (1986–8) following the grant of private property rights. Nearly 50% of the slots of the Washington sample, and 40% of the slots sampled from O'Hare, changed hands between January 1986 and June 1988. While permanent and temporary exchanges could also have been made under the common ownership regime of the scheduling committees, from 1983 until the grant of private property rights, carriers did not reach any agreements on such exchanges. Thus, the grant of property rights in air slots appears to have resulted in significant market activity. It is now appropriate to consider to what extent this activity in air slots trades improved the efficiency of the use of this scarce resource.

Improved efficiency of exploitation of resources: statistical evidence

I now turn to a quantitative welfare analysis of the consequences of the transition to private ownership of air slots, in order to determine whether it actually improved the efficiency of their use. The data set includes observations on the allocations of the scheduling committees before, and FAA official records of ownership after, the grant of private ownership rights.[3] To test whether the change in the legal status of slots resulted in more efficient allocations, I regress the marginal changes in the number of slots held by each carrier on variables that measure the carrier's economic performance. As independent variables I include: size $[x_1]$, efficiency $[x_2]$, and profits $[x_3]$ and a set of dummy variables $\{D_1, \ldots, D_5\}$ for five of the major carriers.[4] Let i and t be indexes for carriers and years[5] respectively and e_{it} be the error term. Let S_{it} be the number of slots that carrier i had in year t. The underlying substantive equation for each observation is:

$$(S_{it+1} - S_{it}) = I_{it} \cdot (\alpha_1 + \beta_1 X_{1it} + \beta_2 X_{2it} + \beta_3 X_{3it} + \gamma D_{it}) + (1 - I_{it}) \cdot (\alpha_2 + \beta_4 X_{1it}$$
$$+ \beta_5 X_{2it} + \beta_6 X_{3it} + \gamma D_{it}) + \delta Y_{it} + e_{it}. \qquad (7.1)$$

Substantively, I assume that tomorrow's allocations are a function of today's values of the independent variables, X, that measure the economic "well being of the firm" in terms of efficiency and margin of profits. This specification is appropriate since under both institutional structures of property rights – the scheduling committees' system and the private owneship system – the acquisition of slots had to be planned in advance. Table 7.2 summarizes the operational definition of the variables.[6]

[3] Charles Plott was kind enough to share with me his data on slot allocations before the rule was enacted. The FAA was kind enough to let me use the data they have gathered since the rule was enacted.

[4] The substantive interpretation of the dummy variables is that each carrier has particular characteristics that are not captured by other independent variables. air transportation is a heterogeneous good. Some carriers provide quality services for higher prices, others have comparative advantages in the places they fly to, or their reputation. We would expect, for example, carriers who operate services at very low prices to be more aggressive in purchasing (and selling) slots than high-quality expensive carriers, because the revenues of the former may be more sensitive to actual load factors (ALF). The dummy variables capture the effects of these "managerial styles." I owe this interpretation of the substantive meaning of the dummy variables to Larry Bartels.

[5] I have two observations for each year, since slots were allocated twice a year for the summer (Jul. 1) and winter (Jan. 1) seasons. To avoid seasonal effects I compare S_{it+1} with S_{it} Separately for each season.

[6] The structure of the data set is known in the literature as "pooled time series" (Pindyck and Rubinfeld, 1976: 202–11; Sayrs, 1989; Ostrom, 1990). When using such data we anticipate two main problems: time-series auto correlation and cross-section heteroskedasticity. To test for heteroskedasticity I ran the regression described by (7.1). I then sorted the observations by year and plotted the residuals of each set of observations corresponding to a single point in time, using the size variable as the horizontal axis. After observing the plots I see no reason to suspect or correct for any problem of heteroskedasticity. For further detail on the use of this method, see Berry and Feldman (1985: 73–82). I also ran a WLS model using the size variable to create the weighted matrix, but this specification did not fare nearly as well as the OLS model, the results of which are reported in table 7.4 in the text. To check for the possibility of autocorrelation I separated six different carriers and plotted the residuals of the regression reported below for every carrier using the year variable as the horizontal axis. For more detail on the use of this technique to check for autocorrelation, see Ostrom (1990). The underlying model has a lagged dependent variable on the RHS:

Table 7.2. *Operational definitions of variables*

Dependent variable
$(S_{it+1} - S_{it}) \equiv$ Change in total number of slots allocated to the carrier
Independent variables
$X_1 \equiv$ Size of carrier, measured by: Total Available Seat Miles [ASM]
$X_2 \equiv$ Efficiency of carrier, measured by: Actual Load Factors [ALF]
$X_3 \equiv$ Profitability of carrier, measured by:
$\quad x_{31} \equiv$ Net Operating Income [NOI}
$\quad x_{32} \equiv$ Net Operating Income [NOI]/Total Operating Costs [TOC] $\Rightarrow$ NOI/TOC
$D \equiv$ A vector of dummy variables for five major carriers with γ being the vector of the respective regression coefficients
$Y \equiv$ A vector of dummy variables for specific years with δ being the vector of the respective regression coefficients
$I \equiv \begin{Bmatrix} I_{it} = 1 \text{ before the grant} \\ \quad = 0 \text{ after the grant} \end{Bmatrix}$ with $\begin{Bmatrix} \alpha_1 = \text{Intercept before the grant} \\ \alpha_2 = \text{Intercept after the grant} \end{Bmatrix}$

1. *Source:* Protocols of scheduling committees compiled by Charles Plott for allocations until 1985, FAA records for observation after 1985.
2. *Source: Moody's Transportation Manuals, 1969–91.*
3. 1979, 1980, and 1981 were included to control for the recession, 1986 was a very good year for the air transportation industry (see table 7.4).

$$Y_{it+1} = \alpha + \lambda Y_{it} + \beta X_{it} + u_{it+1}. \tag{7.2}$$

If estimated as is, assuming no autocorrelation (given the tests discussed above), least squares' procedures should yield consistent and asymptotically efficient estimators (Johnston, 1960: 304–7). OLS will yield biased estimates in small samples (and our sample is definitely small), but it is not clear from the literature that there are better alternatives (Johnston, 1960: 306–7). Results cited in the literature on the subject suggest that the presence of other exogenous variables on the RHS of the equation should help reduce the expected bias (Johnston, 1960: 311). Therefore, I ran the model using different specifications of (7.2). I obtained coefficients $\lambda \in (0.98, 1.05)$. In most cases these coefficients were statistically significantly different than one but, substantively, the difference $(1 - \lambda)$ was insignificant. Thus, I constrained $\lambda = 1$ to get (7.1), the estimates of which are reported in the text. It is unwise to leave the lagged dependent variable in the equation under these circumstances since it introduces too much multicollinearity to the model, which increases substantively the variance of the estimates of the coefficients. Note that I am not interested in predicting Y_{it+1}, *per se*, so that the effect of Y_{it} on Y_{it+1} is of no real interest here, and neither is R^2. If I included the lagged variable in the analysis I would obviously get a very high R^2, but very imprecise estimates for the regression coefficients.

The data set contains observations on fifteen carriers in two different airports for sixteen years. From a theoretical perspective, the important distinction is between the set of observations prior to the grant of private property rights, i.e. 1972–81 and the set of observations after the grant, i.e. 1985–8. The data between 1981–5 is mostly missing or unusable because of the air traffic controllers' strike.

According to the Grether *et al.* (1981) equilibrium argument, discussed above, we expect that under common ownership, size (x_1), would have had a negative effect on the marginal gains in slots. This is so because bigger carriers had stronger incentives to avoid FAA intervention. Since all carriers had to agree unanimously on any allocation, small carriers could "blackmail" big carriers and gradually accumulate slots.

The scheduling committees' mechanism disregarded carriers' economic performances. Thus, the effect of efficiency, (x_2), and profitability, (x_3), is expected to be small, if any. By contrast, after the grant of property rights, firms with low profit margins should lose operations to firms that realize benefits, and carriers that cannot fill their aircraft to profitable capacity should sell slots to carriers that sell more tickets on each flight and are, therefore, expected to expand operations. Actual load factors [ALF] are used as the operational measure of efficiency, x_2. Thus, we expect the coefficients of x_2 and x_3 to be positive and significant after the grant by the US government of private property rights. Table 7.3 summarizes the sign expectations for the regression equations before and after the creation of private property rights over the slots, and table 7.4 reports the results of the regression analysis, pooling together the data sets for Washington National and O'Hare airports.

Table 7.4 usually confirms my theoretical expectations. While size, (x_1), has the expected negative effect on the marginal gains in slots before the grant of private ownership, size still has a negative effect on the marginal gains in slots after the grant. While the latter is not significantly different than zero, it is important to note that the parameter after the grant of property rights is not significantly different from the parameter before the grant.

The variable "net operating income" (NOI, x_{31}) did not have the anticipated effect. It has an insignificant, positive, but unimportant effect before the grant of property rights and a significant negative effect after the grant. So, carriers with more net income obtained or purchased fewer slots under the new allocation mechanism. Any substantive interpretation of this result is difficult. Net operating income is a problematic measure of profitability of firms, because it compounds margins of profit with the size of the carrier and strategic reinvestment policies.[7]

---

[7] This unexpected result is probably due to major reorganizations of some of the carriers after the implementation of the new rule. an alternative explanation is the high correlation between x_{31} and x_{32} (Pearson $r = 0.79$ for the period after the grant of the

Table 7.3. *Expected signs of the main independent variables*

	Old "common pool" committees' mechanism	New buy/sell private ownership mechanism
Size	—	0
Efficiency	0	+
Margin of profits	0	+

In this respect x_{32}, NOI/TOC, is a much better indicator. The regression coefficients of x_{32} confirm my expectations, as stated in table 7.3. It was significantly *negative* before – and significantly *positive* – after the grant of property rights. Thus, before the grant, firms with *higher* margins of profits were *less likely* to obtain slots. After the grant, the more profitable firms were more likely to purchase slots. Thus, private ownership helped more profitable firms expand operations, and/or forced firms with lower margins of profit to sell slots.[8]

Yet, the most remarkable consequence of the grant of private property rights that this analysis reveals is its effect on efficiency. The direct indicator of this effect, by all standards, is the number of tickets sold on flights using this scarce resource, i.e. actual load factors (ALF, X_2). Prior to the grant of private property rights, load factors had no effect on slot allocations. The grant of private property rights changed this undesirable situation: after the grant, the more passengers a carrier transports on each plane, the more likely that carrier is to purchase slots. These results suggest that the efficiency of the use of air slots has improved considerably as a result of the institutional transition from common to private ownership, initiated and implemented by the US government.

Consumers' welfare: the benefits of reducing transaction costs

I now turn to the analysis of the consequences of the change in the structure of ownership on the welfare of consumers of air transportation. Before the grant of private property rights in slots, consumers' advocates

right, and $r = 0.65$ before the grant). To omit this variable would introduce bias in the estimates of the coefficient of the other variables. To be on the safe side, I ran a model that did not include NOI as an independent variable. The only important difference from the model reported in the text is that the regression coefficient of x_{32}, for the period after the grant drops, as expected, from 0.77 to 0.32. It is still significant at the 0.01 level of confidence. All the other coefficients remain very much the same.

[8] Checking individual carriers shows both patterns. Unsuccessful carriers sold their slots and went out of business, while successful carriers like American and United expanded their operations considerably.

Table 7.4. *Regression results*

Variables	Before the grant Parameter estimate (S. err.)	T for H_0 params = 0 (P values)	After the grant Parameter estimate (S. err.)	T for H_0 params = 0 (P values)	F tests H_0: parameter before = parameter after (P values)
Intercept	2.662 (3.744)	0.711 (0.477)	−25.917 (10.204)	−2.540 (0.011)	— —
1979	−3.224 (1.400)	−2.304 (0.022)			— —
1980	−2.685 (1.250)	−2.147 (0.032)			— —
1981	−3.115 (1.224)	−2.545 (0.011)			— —
1986			5.487 (1.567)	3.502 (0.0005)	— —
American	−2.467 (1.324)	−1.863 (0.063)	17.210 (3.526)	4.880 (0.0001)	27.288 (0.0001)
Continental	−2.127 (1.205)	−1.765 (0.078)	5.952 (1.816)	3.278 (0.001)	13.740 (0.0002)
Delta	0.511 (1.229)	0.416 (0.677)	4.602 (2.725)	1.688 (0.092)	1.871 (0.172)
US Air	0.227 (1.273)	0.179 (0.858)	−3.271 (2.55)	−1.279 (0.201)	1.500 (0.221)
United	−2.679 (1.392)	−1.924 (0.055)	17.37 (3.482)	4.988 (0.0001)	28.58 (0.0001)
$X_1 \equiv$ Size [ASM] (1,000 m)	−0.0125 (0.011)	−1.164 (0.245)	−0.027 (0.047)	−0.584 (0.559)	0.0967 (0.745)
$X_2 \equiv$ Efficiency [ALF] (%)	−0.015 (0.066)	−0.228 (0.819)	0.400 (0.170)	2.345 (0.019)	5.144 (0.023)
$X_{31} \equiv$ Profits [NOI] ($1,000)	0.008 (0.007)	1.257 (0.209)	−0.0234 (0.0069)	−3.410 (0.0007)	10.859 (0.001)
$X_{32} \equiv$ Margin of profit [NOI/TOC] (%)	−0.180 (0.108)	−1.661 (0.097)	0.7715 (0.1806)	4.272 (0.0001)	20.412 (0.0001)
n (DF)	592	(568)	F (P value)	6.23	(0.0001)
R (Adj. R)	0.21	(0.175)	Root MSE	7.33	

raised two main concerns: price hikes and the abandonment of small and medium-size cities. One would expect a competitive environment to keep prices relatively low, but cartel practices could result in carriers abusing their exclusive rights over air slots by way of excessive air fares. The other concern of consumers' advocates was that carriers would be encouraged to abandon communities that could not generate sufficient traffic to justify a service. They argued that, given the price of slots, after the grant of private ownership, carriers would only use slots to serve big cities that could generate enough traffic to maintain very high actual load factors (ALF). This section examines the evidence on these two dimensions of consumers' welfare.

Using data on four different airports, I constructed two "twin cities" natural experiments, comparing Washington, DC to Los Angeles in one natural experiment and Chicago's O'Hare airport to Atlanta's airport in the other. All four airports have congestion problems and work at full capacity. The airports at Washington, DC and Los Angeles serve mainly local residents. O'Hare and Atlanta are central hubs, examples of the new "hub-and-spoke" systems that developed after the deregulation of the industry in the early 1980s.[9] Carriers that serve O'Hare and National airports were granted private ownership of air slots. Los Angeles and Atlanta maintained the "first-come, first-served" system. Table 7.5 summarizes the patterns of price increases at O'Hare and Atlanta.[10] The difference is not significantly greater than zero,[11] but prices seem to have

---

[9] The hub-and-spoke system was developed by carriers to improve efficiency after deregulation. A crucial element in the profitability of carriers is the actual load factors (ALF), measured by the ratio of occupied and available seats on each flight. The hub-and-spoke system was designed to maximize ALF: at the spoke cities passengers board flights, regardless of their final destinations, to the hub cities, where they make connections to their final destinations. This allows more frequent flights and enables carriers to increase their average ALF.

[10] The increase in prices is remarkably higher than the price index for these years, but this does not imply that prices of flights, in general, have increased faster than the price index. To rule out, as much as possible, other factors that could have had an impact on prices, I included in the study only prices of direct flights. These flights were heavily subsidized until 1979 and, therefore, experienced the *steepest* price increases. Overall, average prices, since deregulation began in the early 1980s, have increased less than they would have under the standard industry fare level used by the regulators to determine prices in the 1970s (*New York Times*, January 2 1991: A1, C8).

[11] To test whether the difference is significantly greater than zero, I use standard ANOVA procedure, based on the following equation:

$$(\mu_{O'Hare} - \mu_{Atlanta}) = (\bar{X}_{O'Hare} - \bar{X}_{Atlanta}) \pm Z_t \cdot \sqrt{SE^2{}_{O'Hare} + SE^2{}_{Atlanta}} \qquad (7.3)$$

where Z_t is the critical point – e.g. $Z_{0.025}$ is the coefficient that solves this equation at the 0.05 significance level. Substituting my results and checking at a 0.1 significance level (i.e. $Z_{0.05}$) we get:

$$(\mu_{O'Hare} - \mu_{Atlanta}) = (0.052) \pm 1.66 \cdot \sqrt{0.0254^2 + 0.0163^2} = 0.052 \pm 0.0604. \qquad (7.4)$$

We see the difference is not significantly greater than zero.

Table 7.5. *Patterns of price increases at O'Hare and Atlanta*

		Average price increase between 1984 and 1988	SE $SE \cong \sqrt{\sigma^2/n}$	n
O'Hare	$\bar{X}_{O'Hare}$ $= 0.4685$		$SE_{O'Hare}$ $= 0.0254$	340
Atlanta	$\bar{X}_{Atlanta}$ $= 0.4165$		$SE_{Atlanta}$ $= 0.0163$	282
Difference	$\bar{X}_O - \bar{X}_A$ $= 0.0520$			

Table 7.6. *Patterns of price increases at Washington National and Los Angeles*

		Average price increase between 1984 and 1988	SE $SE \cong \sqrt{\sigma^2/n}$	n
National	$\bar{X}_{National}$ $= 0.5032$		$SE_{National}$ $= 0.0346$	288
Los Angeles	$\bar{X}_{Los\,Angeles}$ $= 0.7853$		$SE_{Los\,Angeles}$ $= 0.0594$	200
Difference	$\bar{X}_{Los} - \bar{X}_{Nat}$ $= 0.2821$			

risen at a higher rate at O'Hare when compared to Atlanta. Table 7.6 compares Washington National and Los Angeles airports. The difference is significantly greater than zero:[12] prices increased at a significantly higher rate at Los Angeles, where common ownership prevailed, compared to Washington DC where private ownership was granted in air slots.[13] Neo-classical economics promotes the expectation that privatization should bring about a reduction in consumers' prices, but the evidence summarized above is inconclusive in this regard.

It is hard to establish the exact effect that institutional changes in the structure of ownership may have on consumers' welfare through the study of price structures. Prices are affected by many variables in the economy, and it is almost impossible to separate the effect of the institutional change in ownership structures from the effects of other variables. The "twin cities" design was supposed to do exactly that, but the results of the comparison

[12] Using a significance test at the 0.01 significance level (i.e. $Z_{0.005}$) we get:

$$(\mu_{Los} - \mu_{Nat}) = (0.2821) \pm 2.66 \cdot \sqrt{0.0594^2 + 0.0346^2} = 0.2821 \pm 0.1829. \qquad (7.5)$$

The difference is significantly greater than zero.

[13] The price index for the two areas for the relevant period was almost identical: prices increased between 1983 and 1987 by 17.7% in Los Angeles and 16.4% in Washington, DC.

remain inconclusive. It is, therefore, of great interest to look at other aspects of consumers' welfare to establish how the change in the institutional structure of ownership has affected consumers' welfare.

As mentioned above, a second concern expressed by consumer advocates prior to the grant of private property rights in air slots was that carriers would be encouraged to abandon communities that could not generate sufficient traffic to justify a service. During the 1980s direct services to many small and medium-size cities were abandoned,[14] because subsidies for these routes were discontinued, and as a result of the evolution of the "hub-and-spoke" system. These trends were observable in almost every region of the USA during the 1980s. Here, I use the "twin cities" experimental design to check whether the grant of individual property rights made a significant difference in terms of the rate of abandonment of services to and from small and medium-size communities. Table 7.7 summarizes the patterns of service abandonment at O'Hare and Atlanta. This difference is significantly different from zero at the 0.01 significance level.[15] The same pattern is observed when we compare Washington's National and the Los Angeles airports, as shown in table 7.8. The difference is significantly different from zero at the 0.01 significance level.[16]

In both comparisons we find a significant difference in the opposite direction than opponents of the grant of private ownership suggested. One explanation of these findings is that the use of the routes to and from

Table 7.7. *General patterns of service abandonment at O'Hare and Atlanta*

	% of services abandoned between 1984 and 1988	SE $SE \cong \sqrt{\sigma^2/n}$	n
O'Hare	$\bar{X}_{O'Hare} = 0.440$	$SE_{O'Hare} = 0.0202$	340
Atlanta	$\bar{X}_{Atlanta} = 0.552$	$SE_{Atlanta} = 0.020$	606
Difference	$\bar{X}_A - \bar{X}_O = 0.112$		

[14] "Abandoned," here, is defined as discontinuation of direct service. Most "abandoned" communities, as defined, are served by an indirect service.

[15] Using a significance test at the 0.01 level of significance, we get:

$$(\mu_{Atlanta} - \mu_{O'Hare}) = (0.11) \pm 2.6 \cdot \sqrt{0.0202^2 + 0.02^2} = 0.11 \pm 0.0739. \qquad (7.6)$$

The difference is significantly greater than zero.

[16] Using a significance test at the 0.01 level of significance, we get:

$$(\mu_{Los} - \mu_{Nat}) = (0.14) \pm 2.6 \cdot \sqrt{0.0202^2 + 0.0193^2} = 0.14 \pm 0.0715. \qquad (7.7)$$

The difference is significantly greater than zero.

Table 7.8. *General patterns of service abandonment at Washington National and Los Angeles*

	% of services abandoned between 1984 and 1988	SE $SE \cong \sqrt{\sigma^2/n}$	n
National	$\bar{X}_{National} = 0.527$	$SE_{National} = 0.0202$	610
Los Angeles	$\bar{X}_{Los\,Angeles} = 0.667$	$SE_{Los\,Angeles} = 0.0193$	299
Difference	$\bar{X}_{Los} - \bar{X}_{Nat} = 0.140$		

airports where carriers were granted private property rights was more efficient, compared to the "first-come, first-served" mechanism used at Atlanta and Los Angeles. The latter induces uncertainties with respect to takeoff and landing schedules; well defined property rights reduce the uncertainty and, in consequence, the cost of each flight. This relative cost reduction apparently made it profitable for the carriers to serve routes in which they would not break even under the less efficient, alternative system. My results thus capture the precise way in which the grant of private ownership improved the efficiency of the use of air slots.

Neo-classical economics promotes the notion that private property rights reduce transaction costs. In our case, transaction costs resulted from uncertainty about when carriers expected to get permission to take off or land. Private ownership of slots must have reduced these transaction costs. Some of the efficiency gains were, apparently, transferred to the consumers by allowing carriers to continue direct service to communities that, otherwise, would have been suspended.

Economic organizations: quantitative evidence for uncertain expectations

What role in encouraging these institutional changes did organizational actors other than the central government play? I argued above that potential right-holders push for institutional change when they expect to benefit from such changes. At the same time, I mentioned that uncertainty about the number of carriers that supported the institutional change played an important role in delaying the final decision of the DOT.

This section provides quantitative evidence that seems to explain why some carriers were more active in promoting change, while others were more reluctant to endorse reforms in the structure of ownership. I assume that carriers knew what to expect of the allocations under the old and the new institutional structure of ownership. Using the regression results and data on carriers' performance in 1984 I compute the number of slots that carriers were to expect under the old and new ownership regimes. The results are summarized in table 7.9.[17]

Table 7.9 shows that after the grant of private property rights, American, Continental and United experienced expansion that they could not have hoped for under the old allocation mechanism. Table 7.9 also shows that Delta and US Air could have expected some growth in operations under the committee system and seem to have experienced a reduction in operations under the new rule. It is hard to establish whether the fact that some carriers reduced operations indicates that they were negatively affected by the grant of private property rights over slots. They may have wanted to reduce operations before the grant of private ownership by the government but, in the absence of a market, could not exchange them for anything valuable. We can assert with some confidence, however, that carriers that purchased considerable quantities of slots gained from the grant of private property rights, or else they would not have bought slots.

It is, therefore, of great interest to note that, according to government and Congressional records, American and Continental were the strongest supporters of the new rule.[18] According to the same records, US Air was the only carrier that consistently and forcefully opposed the rule. United consistently expressed an ambiguous position. Delta never expressed any support for the new rule, and on one occasion expressed opposition.[19]

Table 7.9 demonstrates the uncertainty involved in institutional reforms. It shows that different carriers should have expected to be affected differently by the grant of private property rights. Table 7.9 also provides a possible explanation for the ambiguous position of United Airlines with respect to the proposed change in the structure of property rights in slots. Comparing the expectations of United based on performance in 1983 and 1984 (last two rows in table 7.9) reveals another source of uncertainty in designing property rights' institutions: agents' performance, as well as their

---

[17] The right hand column of table 7.9 "Net expected gain/loss" is for one year only. After a while, we would expect the market to reach a new equilibrium and the number of transactions should diminish. The computation is straightforward. I take the value of each independent variable for each carrier in 1984 (or 1983) and use the regression results to predict the gains in slots the carrier would expect in the next allocation.

[18] The assessments concerning carriers' involvement in support or opposition to the new regime of ownership are based on documents from the Docket Room (no. 905) of the FAA in Washington, DC. The most relevant Dockets are no. 24110 and no. 24105. Some carriers expressed their views in public hearings as well (for a list of the relevant hearings' documents see the end of the References list, p. 198).

[19] In a verbal testimony and a written statement submitted during a public hearing (99-746) before the Subcommittee on Aviation, Committee on Commerce, Science and Transportation of the US Senate, February 6 1986: 81–8.

Table 7.9. *Expected number of slots that would be gained/lost by each carrier*

	Under old scheduling committees' mechanism	Under new property rights' mechanism	Net expected gain/loss
American	0.12	12.0	11.88
Continental	−1.56	10.06	11.64
Delta	2.56	−3.11	−5.67
US Air	1.40	−2.88	−4.28
United	0.95	8.16	7.21
United[a]	−1.075[a]	13.84[a]	14.91[a]

Note: [a]Computation based on performance of carrier in 1983.

environment, is volatile. United, for example, should have expected considerable gains from the institutional change in ownership structure, when the issue first came up in 1983. Yet, by 1984, when the issue was subject to US Congressional hearings, the management of United should have began to have their doubts. By my statistical analysis their expected benefit, in terms of expected number of gained slots, dropped by more than 50%.[20] This finding probably explains the consistently ambiguous position of United Airlines towards the proposed institutional change.

The more general lesson we learn from this section is how unrealistic it is to assume that property rights' institutions emerge in environments of complete and perfect information. Given the uncertainty that characterizes this type of environments, it should be hard for agents in the economy, as well as for government officials, to form precise expectations with respect to the exact effect that institutional changes in structures of ownership rights may have.

Concluding remarks

The most important point that this case study illustrates is the role that government officials have in shaping the structure of ownership rights in markets. By so doing, they can improve the efficiency of the exploitation of scarce resources, and extract some of the benefits for themselves. But efficiency of exploitation of scarce resources is not necessarily the main concern of government officials when they introduce

[20] United is not the only carrier that experienced such swings in financial performance. Most carriers did, and many firms in other industries experience such fluctuations. The case of United was cited because, in this case, I had the data to illustrate this point.

structural changes in the institutions that grant and maintain property rights.

In our case, government officials granted private ownership mainly because it helped them get rid of the gridlock in the high-density airports. It is harder to establish whether they hoped to get, or whether they received any credit, or increased tax revenues, from agents in society that benefited from the change in ownership structure. We could not even establish that consumers actually benefited from the expected price reduction due to privatization, and consumers' groups seem to have totally ignored the fact that the reduction in transaction costs due to privatization helped carriers maintain direct services to communities that would otherwise have been abandoned, let alone give any credit for this indirect effect to the relevant government officials.

Introducing government officials as crucial players in the process of the evolution of property rights enables us to provide an explanation for the tendency of governments to grant and protect such rights. To understand the emergence and the evolution of property rights in the polity, we must study carefully the actual incentives that lead governments to enforce one or another structure of individual rights in any particular case. This case is valuable as empirical evidence, since most of the actors involved were forthcoming with the information they possessed, providing first-hand testimony on the sequence of events, the motivations of the different actors involved, and the strategic maneuvers that resulted in the establishment of a particular structure of private property rights. The fact that the right could not be linked to any moral axioms made it much easier to distinguish positive explanations from normative rhetoric.

At this stage it is possible to relate this case study to the general theory of the emergence and evolution of institutions that protect private property rights, advanced in this book, through a few observations, derived from this case study, that are useful as illustrations of my theory and may apply more generally:

1. Special interests, neither morally nor politically justifiable, often hide behind justifications for competing structures of ownership. "Open skies" as a standard of justice assumes (normatively) that every carrier has a right to enter the queue. The scheduling committees modified that standard of justice, asserting that those who had a right to enter the queue in 1969 would have it thereafter. "Open skies" and the users' committees were based on the "standard of justice" that the right inheres in the investment, not in the service. A competing standard of justice in this case was "public service," which is closely related to efficiency standards. In general, simplistic standards of justice, as in this case, obscure the special interests of individual agents invested in

the market, regardless of how well or poorly the investment was made.

2. A second feature of ownership highlighted by this study is that different structures of ownership induce different incentives to use resources in different ways. Ownership is, of course, a way to assign someone to take care of a resource. When the owner is private, the resource is used to generate profits. When the ownership is common, the manager may have a variety of motives. In this case, common ownership meant, at times, FAA management, and at times scheduling committee management. The FAA has always preferred "open skies," a mechanism with a "fair" name, but an "unfair" and inefficient reality. I can only speculate that "open skies," served the FAA well in two ways: (a) it ensured its continued existence as an agency, and (b) it ensured that the agency kept a resource it could use to make allocations pleasing to particular Congressmen and other persons involved in supervising the agency. The general lesson is that analysts must always look carefully at the complex motives of owners and managers of scarce resources when they wish to study, or advise others about, different regimes of ownership or, more generally, different institutional designs.

3. Analysts should not expect private property rights to come into existence just because they increase efficiency. In this case, officials recognized the potential improvement in the efficiency of the exploitation of the scarce resource, but they also recognized that the expected improvement in efficiency did not necessarily mean that the change from common to private ownership was a Pareto improving move. Hence they had to act even though some of the main actors involved did not expect to benefit, and others expected to lose from the change from common to private ownership.

4. Furthermore, expectations of government officials and market organizations are expected to vary sharply over time. Add to that the strategic interests that agents have in the future structure of the market and ownership rights, and one finds another general lesson: government officials and economic organizations operate in environments characterized by incomplete and imperfect information. No one can rely completely on the testimony of prospective managers or private beneficiaries. Making policy decisions regarding the structure of ownership in the market is a complicated art. This lesson brings us back to the issue of institutional design. The main lesson here is that in designing institutions that grant and protect property rights, we cannot rely on general abstract justifications, and probably not even on general abstract theories. We must design institutions to fit the cases at hand, rather than our normative beliefs or abstract theories (cf. Ostrom, 1990).

Government officials, in this case, acted to bring about privatization with the confidence that it was the correct decision. Which leads me to my final observation: if officials always waited for changes in the structure of property rights to be unquestionably and unequivocally Pareto improving, then none would ever occur. Some interests inside and outside the government always benefit from such changes, while other are bound to lose. The officials immediately responsible for privatization were able to carry it through, despite all the obstacles cited, because it served the political program of the Reagan administration at the time. Changes in the structure of property rights reflect a complex mix of strategic incentives of powerful agents in the polity, but in the end they must serve a political program or a dominant ideology, and are probably impossible otherwise (cf. North, 1990: 85–6).

Conclusion: the political origin of human rights

In this book I derived from the basic premises of rationality a positive theory of the political origin of private property and related human rights. Such rights, I argue, are not derived from moral axioms or moral imperatives, and they are not more "natural" than any other creation of humans. Human rights result from a long political struggle of individuals to improve their well being. In the final analysis, both Adam Smith and Karl Marx were wrong. There has never been, and never will be, a class struggle that accounts for the institutional structure of society, nor could we blame the hidden hand, or "market forces" for the social institutions that protect our rights. The structures that induce law and order in society result from a long and complex political process, guided and determined by the desire of every man and woman to get the best out of his or her short life.

Civilization did not start with moral codes, as so many philosophers, old and new, try to convince us. It started with things like the famous stone of Hammuraby. The code of Hammuraby (eighteenth century BC), was not an essay on civil ethics. It was a code of laws specifying, in remarkable detail, the rights of Babylonian citizens and the procedures and penalties to be followed whenever these laws were broken. Why did Hammuraby ever bother to write this list of laws on a huge stone? We can only speculate that he did so to facilitate the management of the daily affairs of his prosperous empire. Three millennia later, William the Conqueror, wrote a similar list of property rights, *The Domesday Book* (1087), probably for the very same reason.

Why do powerful leaders, like Hammuraby and William the Conqueror bother to endow their subjects with property and other human rights? To answer this question, we must rethink the very concept of "human rights."

Most leaders, regardless of how powerful they are, depend on their subjects for their livelihood. The creation and enforcement of property and human rights enhances the productivity of their constituents which, in turn, allows the leading elites to live better, off this production. Greedy leaders "take the money and run," while smarter leaders invest and wait to collect the fruits of their investment. One way governments invest in the future of their polities is to spend time and money on the articulation and design of legal codes that endow their citizens with the necessary framework for a productive life.

When technology was scarce and natural resources abundant, the best strategy for the leader was to let the tribe gather and take his or her share, using threats and the pretension of magic powers. With the development of agricultural technology, it became more effective for leaders to force their subjects to work the fields, and then to collect taxes on the crop yield. But once those leaders became dependent on those crops, they had to guarantee the well being of the crops and the farmers. To do so, they had to endow farmers with basic rights such as property rights and physical protection.

As sophisticated technology evolved further, the role of central governments became progressively more complex, as it became necessary to secure more human and property rights that went beyond the simple physical safety of private individuals. The production of modern goods requires not just basic property rights and health, but also rights for decent education, safe traveling, copyrights, and many other property rights and human rights.

In chapter 1 I argued that authors of descriptive theories of human rights should be careful not to import, without careful scrutiny, ontological premises and ambiguous behavioral claims from the traditional, normative literature on this subject. Most theories of the evolution of rights suffer from carelessness in this regard. The tendency to confuse normative and positive theories of individual rights has led us to accept partial and defective theories concerning the very structure of our social life.

Chapter 2 emphasized the apparent damage resulting from the intentional absence of political entities in neo-classical theories of institutions. The abstraction of human interaction from any structure of authority, and the focus on price mechanisms, is easy to justify, as long as we confine ourselves to the study of interactions in the context of perfectly competitive, or any other *exogenously determined*, market structures. But when we study the origin of these structures, which is the essence and substance of the study of the evolution of property rights, we can no longer ignore the role of politics (Demsetz, 1982: 7).

In studying institutions that protect individual rights, I was disturbed by the fact that no clear standard existed in the literature as to what actually constituted an acceptable "explanation" of an institution. With all the recent discussion of "neo-institutionalism," I found the "hard core" of this new research program in disarray. Chapter 3 provided some guiding principles for the foundations of this new-born subfield of political science. I do not pretend to have found the golden standard for further research but, at the very least, the discussion in chapter 3 provides some basic guidelines that I followed in my study of the evolution of political structures that protect individual rights.

Chapters 4–6 are my own contribution to the study of the origin and evolution of individual rights. *The central argument is as follows*: individual rights are established only after a central force, that can grant and enforce individual rights, establishes its monopoly over the use of force. After establishing themselves, central agencies use their monopoly over the use of force to grant rights to individual members of society in order to further their egotistical interests. They do so to gain the political and economic support every leader needs to maintain control over society.

The central point of chapter 4 was that, in their quest to further their selfish interests, governments have an incentive to grant property and related individual rights to their constituents in order to improve production, thus enlarging the tax base from which they can draw taxes or, simply, in order to buy political support by granting rights to potential supporters.

But the model presented in chapter 4 also provided a positive explanation to the generally observed *maxim* of publishing a law prior to enforcement. We can now explain why Hammuraby and William the Conqueror were so eager to write down the law of their land. Public knowledge of the law, prior to enforcement, appears to be a necessary condition for any successful governmental enforcement of law and order. It turns out that the only way government officials can make their "threat" to enforce the law *credible*, is to commit themselves to enforce the law by publicly publishing it. By making the law public knowledge, governments commit themselves to enforcing the rights they have promised to enforce. This pre-commitment results in the general obedience of the subjects that makes this commitment credible.

The analysis in chapter 4 assumed that governments have complete information about expectations and preferences of individual agents regarding such legal actions. In chapter 5, I relaxed this unrealistic assumption. The central point of chapter 5 was that government officials operate under conditions of incomplete information regarding the interests of their constituents. Consequently, they often grant rights they would be better off not granting, or fail to grant individual rights they could be made better off by granting. The main argument of chapter 5 was that the role of political activism and protest is to send messages to central authorities that amending existing institutional structures of rights could make some citizens and, eventually, the government itself, better off.

At the same time, the analysis in chapter 5 showed that both governments and individual agents generally benefit from playing the game of petition-ing for and granting property rights. This result provides an elegant explanation for the emergence of individual rights at two different levels. It explains the process by which property rights are created, and how they evolve. But it also explains some of the most fundamental human rights enjoyed by most citizens in modern western democracies: namely, the right to freedom of speech, organized protest, and other types of free expression of personal preferences.

We no longer have to rely on the assumption that we have the right to freedom of speech *qua* human beings. Nor do we need to rely on other, dubious, moral justifications for such basic rights. The fundamental right of freedom of speech has a simple positive justification: *ex ante*, it makes governments and individual agents – i.e., every agent in society – better off.

In the course of the argument I have established two important points. First, I have proved mathematically that, *ex ante*, governments are expected to benefit from permitting freedom of speech and other forms of political protest, because these forms of expression help governments collect essential information concerning the way they should construct the institutional structure of individual rights in the polity. Second, the problem of collective action and the possibility that the government may under- or overestimate the signals sent by the public, leaves much room for error in the process by which governments evaluate and decide whether or not to grant any particular right.

In chapter 6 I explained the role of political entrepreneurs in the evolution of human rights and property rights. Political entrepreneurs serve as a link between special interests and governments. They help groups of individuals to form and elaborate their interests. They help group members understand how these interests may be advanced or damaged by different institutional structures. They also help individuals mobilize in support of a cause or a public figure that may help alter the legal structure of individual rights in their favor. Just as important, political entrepreneurs help members of their groups focus on one or another mode of action by sending signals to members concerning the chances of success and their evaluation of what other members in the group are most likely to do.

On the government side, political entrepreneurs transmit crucial infor-mation to government officials regarding the number of interested individuals they represent, and the ability of these groups to provide government officials with electoral or economic support. Again, this information is revealed not because of some genuine "truthfulness" of political entrepreneurs, but because the selfish interests of the political entrepreneur is "transparent." This transparency enables group members and government officials alike to extract from the actions of the entrepre-neur the private information he or she possesses. After gathering this information, government officials use their updated beliefs to assign weights to the signals sent by the different political entrepreneurs and construct institutional structures of individual rights for the polity so as to maximize the political and economic support they can get from members of the polity.

I concluded my argument with a study of one instance in which the emergence of property rights of some consequence evolved very much along the lines of the model promoted by this book. All too often, in this rapidly developing approach to the study of political science, empirical evidence is overlooked in favor of mathematical elegance. I tried to strike a more balanced accord in this respect.

This book points at a very different mode of aggregating individual preferences into social choices than is usually presumed by the literature on social choice. The bulk of this literature assumes a very sparse institutional environment in which individual preferences are aggregated into social choices through mechanisms that satisfy some basic normative requirements (Schofield, 1986), but bear little, if any, resemblance to real world institutions. This literature led us to decisive conclusions regarding the normative merits of such mechanisms (Arrow, 1951; Riker, 1982), but told us little about how preferences are actually aggregated into social choices in the real world.

Scholars who study how *institutions operate in the real world* usually focus their attention on different legislative bodies, that use different versions of the majority rule to make decisions (Krehbiel, 1992; Laver and Schofield, 1990; Laver and Shepsle, 1996). Such legislative bodies rely on general elections as their main source of legitimacy. A central issue in this literature is the extent to which these legislative bodies actually represent the "will" of the people who elect their members in any meaningful way.

The process of granting and petitioning for private property and related individual rights, as described in this book is, in and by itself, a mechanism of aggregating individual preferences into social choices. Instead of working through the legislative process and variations on the majority rule, this process works through political activism and protest, that sometimes operate within legislative bodies, but is often external, or parallel, to the legislative process.

My neo-liberal theory of the state finds the origins of property and other human rights in a social contract. It does not assume or rely on any particular set of initial rules. I argue that the social contract is constantly written and rewritten by powerful officials who provide different structures of law and order in return for economic and political support. Whether in western societies, who rely on elections and majority rule, or in other institutional setups, powerful politicians depend on the support of their constituents. They must, therefore, satisfy the unalienable preferences of their constituents that are revealed through petition and protest but also by the extent to which each agent is willing, and able, to be a productive member of society. This is why government officials constantly search for new ways to modify the social contract, committing themselves to grant and protect the property and human rights of their constituents.

So, in this way, by this constant process of bargaining between powerful government officials and the different agents in society, a "social contract" emerges that reflects the "will of the people" in a very different way than we are used to thinking about this term. This social contract does not reflect our opinions or preferences on the political issues of the day, as legislative bodies do. But it does reflect very deep preferences concerning our basic rights, and our preferences with respect to the way society should organize the provision of law and order.

Years of systematic research have considerably advanced our understanding of legislative institutions. The theory advanced here suggests that it is time to look at other institutions that constrain and determine our daily life. There are no axioms of social order, and there is no simple solution to the question of institutional design of legal, property, and human rights. Yet, the legal systems that protect our day-to-day life may be of much greater consequence, to each and every one of us, than the politics of legislative bodies.

If we accept the premise that our most basic property and human rights are the result of a political process, maybe it is time to reconsider the institutional designs that protect these rights, and spend more time studying them. Because this structure evolves in a world with high transaction costs, conflicting interests and asymmetric powers, we must realize that we cannot assume that "market forces" have resolved, or will ever resolve, this complexity for the better. If we realize that it was not nature, or high moral axioms, but human beings that determined the structure of our most cherished individual rights, and if we are, finally, willing to admit that the world of politics is unlikely to lead to any kind of efficient outcomes, maybe it is time to start a systematic study of the institutional designs that protect, or fail to protect, our human rights.

There are at least three different interesting avenues of research that these insights open up. First, we have learned a great deal about legislative bodies in the last three decades. Yet, when it comes to the most profound structures of social order, we are still accustomed to believing in ambiguous normative theories, unwarranted ontological premises, and simplistic models of human behavior. It is time to begin unraveling the origin of social order using more rigorous positive theories. Second, we take too many institutions that protect our basic rights to be self-evident. I hope this book has shown that they are not. So, it will be interesting to begin a systematic, comparative study of the merits and flaws of different institutional structures that protect different sets of rights. Finally, with all the new advances in the study of institutional designs, maybe we can hope that some of the institutions that protect our property and other human rights can be better designed. After all, we know by now that these institutions are the result of human actions within a complex, political, bargaining process, taking place in a world of incomplete and imperfect information with high transactions costs, asymmetrically powerful agents, and limited insight. With all we have learned about institutions and institutional design in recent years, we can probably hope to redesign at least some of these institutions to be better.

References

Books and articles

Abreu, Dilip and Ariel Rubinstein, 1988. "The Structure of Nash Equilibria in Repeated Games with Finite Automata," *Econometrica*, 56: 1259–82

Ainsworth, Scott, 1993. "Regulating Lobbyists and Interest Group Influence," *Journal of Politics*, 155: 41–56

Ainsworth, Scott and Itai Sened, 1993. "The Role of Lobbyists: Entrepreneurs with Two Audiences," *American Journal of Political Science*, 37(4): 834–66

Aivazian, A. Varouj and Jeffrey L. Callen, 1981. "The Coase Theorem and the Empty Core," *Journal of Law and Economics*, 24: 175–181

Aivazian, A. Varouj, Jeffrey L. Callen and Irwin Lipnowski, 1986: "The Coase Theorem and Coalition Stability," *Economica*, 54: 517–20

Aldrich, John H., Gary J. Miller, Charles W. Ostrom, Jr. and David W. Rohde, 1986. *American Government*, Boston: Houghton Mifflin

Anderson, T. L. and J. P. Hill, 1975. "The Evolution of Property Rights: A Study of the American West," *Journal of Law and Economics*, 18(1): 163–179

Arrow, Kenneth, 1951. *Social Choice and Individual Values*, New Haven: Yale University Press

Åslund, Anders, 1995. *How Russia Became a Market Economy*, Washington DC: The Brookings Institution

Austen-Smith, David, 1983. "The Spatial Theory of Electoral Competition: Instability, Institutions, and Information," *Environment and Planning*, 1: 439–59

　　1984. "The Pure Theory of Large Two-Candidate Elections: A Comment on the Ledyard Paper," *Public Choice*, 44: 43–7

Austen-Smith, David and Jeffery S. Banks, 1988. "Elections, Coalitions and Legislative Outcomes," *American Political Science Review*, 82: 405–22

Austen-Smith, David and William H. Riker, 1987. "Asymmetric Information and the Coherence of Legislation," *American Political Science Review*, 81: 897–918

Austen-Smith, David and John R. Wright, 1992. "Competitive Lobbying for a Legislator's Vote," *Social Choice and Welfare*, 19: 229–57

Axelrod, Robert, 1980a. "Effective Choice in the Prisoners' Dilemma," *Journal of Conflict Resolution*, 24: 3–25

1980b. "More Effective Choice in the Prisoners' Dilemma," *Journal of Conflict Resolution*, 24: 379–403

1981. "The Emergence of Cooperation Among Egoists," *American Political Science Review*, 75: 306–18

1984. *The Evolution of Cooperation*, New York: Basic Books

1986. "An Evolutionary Approach to Norms," *American Political Science Review*, 80: 1095–1112

Bailey, E. Elizabeth, 1986. "Economic Models and Policy Reality: Lessons from Airport Access," in M. E. Peston and E. R. Quant (eds.), *Price Competition and Equilibrium*, Oxford: Oxford University Press

Banks, Jeffrey S., 1985. "Sophisticated Voting Outcomes and Agenda Control," *Social Choice and Welfare*, 1: 295–306

1991. *Signaling Games in Political Science*, Chur: Harwood Academic Publishers

Banks, Jeffery S. and Randall L. Calvert, 1992. "A Battle-of-the-Sexes Game with Incomplete Information," *Games and Economic Behavior*, 4: 347–72

Banks, Jeffrey S. and Joel Sobel, 1987. "Equilibrium Selection in Signaling Games," *Econometrica*, 55: 647–61

Banks, Jeffrey S. and Rangarajan K. Sundaram, 1990. "Repeated Games, Finite Automata, and Complexity," *Games and Economic Behavior*, 2: 97–117

Baron, David P. and John A. Ferejohn, 1989. "Bargaining in Legislatures," *American Political Science Review*, 83: 1181–206.

Barzel, Yoram, 1989. *Economic Analysis of Property Rights*, Cambridge: Cambridge University Press

Bates, Robert H., 1987. *Essays on the Political Economy of Rural Africa*, paperback edn, Berkeley: University of California Press (first published by Cambridge University Press, 1983)

Bauer, Raymond A., Ithiel de Sola Pool and Lewis A. Dexter, 1968. *American Business and Public Policy*, New York: Atherton

Bentham, Jeremy, 1952–4. *Jeremy Bentham's Economic Writings*, W. Stark (ed.), London: George Allen & Unwin

Berlin, Isaiah, 1958. *Two Concepts of Liberty*, Oxford: Clarendon Press

Berry, William D. and Stanley Feldman, 1985. *Multiple Regression in Practice*, Beverly Hills: Sage University Publications

Bianco, William T., 1988. "The Limits of Cooperation: Sanctioning Problems in Dilemma Games," *Political Economy Working Paper*, Duke University

Bianco, William T. and Robert H. Bates, 1990. "Cooperation by Design: Leadership, Structure and Collective Dilemmas," *American Political Science Review*, 84, 133–49

Binmore, Ken and Partha Dasgupta (eds.), 1987. *The Economics of Bargaining*, New York: Basil Blackwell

Black, Duncan, 1958. *The Theory of Committees and Elections*. Cambridge: Cambridge University Press

Blau, J. H., 1972. "A Direct Proof of Arrow's Theorem," *Econometrica*, 40(1): 61–7

Bliss, Christopher and Barry Nalebuff, 1984. "Dragon-slaying and Ballroom Dancing: The Private Supply of a Public Good," *Journal of Public Economics*, 25: 1–12

Bluhm, William T., 1984. *Force or Freedom?*, New Haven: Yale University Press.

Bogdanich, Walt, 1991. *The Great White Lie*, New York: Simon Schuster

Boycko, Maxim, Andrei Shleifer and Robert Vishny, 1995. *Privatizing Russia*, Cambridge, MA: MIT Press

Buchanan, James M., 1975. *The Limits of Liberty*, Chicago: The University of Chicago Press

    1986. *Liberty, Markets and State*, New York: New York University Press

    1988. "The Economic Theory of Politics Reborn," *Challenge*, (March–April)

Buchanan, James M. and Gordon Tullock, 1962. *The Calculus of Consent*, Ann Arbor: The University of Michigan Press

Calvert, Randall L., 1986. *Models of Incomplete Information in Politics*, New York: Harwood Academic Publishers

    1987. "Reputation and Legislative Leadership," *Public Choice*, 55: 81–119

    1989. "Reciprocity among Self-Interested Actors: Uncertainty, Asymmetry, and Distribution," in P. C. Ordeshook (ed.), *Models of Strategic Choice in Politics*, Ann Arbor: The University of Michigan Press

    1995. "Rational Actors, Equilibrium and Social Institutions," in J. Knight and I. Sened (eds.), *Explaining Social Institutions*, Ann Arbor: The University of Michigan Press

Calvert, Randall L. and Robert B. Wilson, 1984. "Comment," *American Political Science Review*, 78: 496–7

Cho, In-Koo, 1987. "A Refinement of Sequential Equilibrium," *Econometrica*, 55: 1367–89

Cho, In-Koo and David Kreps, 1987. "Signaling Games and Stable Equilibria," *Quarterly Journal of Economics*, 102: 179–221

Coase, Ronald H., 1960. "The Problem of Social Cost," *Journal of Law and Economics*, 3: 1–44

    1981. "The Coase Theorem and the Empty Core: A Comment," *Journal of Law and Economics*, 24: 183–7

Cohen, Linda, 1979. "Cyclic Sets in Multidimensional Voting Models," *Journal of Economic Theory*, 20: 1–12

Cohen, Linda and Stephen Matthew, 1980. "Constrained Plott Equilibria,

Directional Equilibria and Global Cycling Sets," *Review of Economic Studies*, 74: 975–86

Cranston, Maurice William, 1954. *Freedom*, London: Longmans & Green

Crawford, Sue E. S. and Elinor Ostrom, 1995. "A Grammar of Institutions" *American Political Science Review*, 89(3): 582–600

Crawford, Vincent P. and H. Haller, 1989. "Learning how to Cooperate: Optimal Play in Repeated Coordination Games," University of California, San Diego, mimeo

Dasgupta, Partha, 1974. "On Some Problems Arising from Professor Rawls' Conception of Distributive Justice," *Theory and Decision*, 4: 325–44

Demsetz, Harold, 1964. "The Exchange and Enforcement of Property Rights," *Journal of Law and Economics*, 7: 11–26

1967. "Toward a Theory of Property Rights," *American Economic Review*, 57: 374–59

1969. "Information and Efficiency: Another Viewpoint," *Journal of Law and Economics*, 12: 1–22

1982. *Economic, Legal, and Political Dimensions of Competition*, Amsterdam: North-Holland

De Tocqueville, Alexis, [1834] 1951. *Democracy in America*, New York: Knopf

Dewey, John, 1962. *Individualism, Old and New*, New York: Capricorn Books

The Documentary History of the Ratification of the Constitution, Merrill Teusensen (ed.) (1976–8), Madison: State Historical Society of Wisconsin

Doron, Gideon and Martin Sherman, 1995. "A Comprehensive Decision-Making Exposition of Coalition Politics: The Framer's Perspective of Size," *Journal of Theoretical Politics*, 7(3): 317–33

Downs, Anthony, 1957. *An Economic Theory of Democracy*, New York: Harper & Row

Eggertsson, Thrainn, 1990. *Economic Behavior and Institutions*, Cambridge: Cambridge University Press

Ensminger, Jean and Andrew Rutten, 1990. "The Political Economy of Changing Property Rights: Dismantling a Kenyan Commons," *Political Economy Working Paper*, 146, CPE, Washington University, St. Louis

Epstein, Richard, A., 1985. *Takings*, Cambridge, MA: Harvard University Press

Farrell, J, 1987. "Cheap Talk, Coordination, and Entry," *Rand Journal of Economics*, 18: 34–9

Farquharson, Robin, 1969. *Theory of Voting*, New Haven: Yale University Press

Feddersen, Timothy J., Itai Sened and Stephen G. Wright, 1990. "Sophisticated Voting and Candidate Entry Under Plurality Rule," *American Journal of Political Science*, 34: 1005–16

The Federalist Papers, New York: Bantam Books

Ferejohn, John and James Kuklinski (eds.), 1990. *Information and Democratic Process*, Urbana: The University of Illinois Press

Fink, Carol Evelyn, 1987. *Political Argument and Strategic Choice in the Ratification Conventions on the US Constitution*, University of Rochester, unpublished doctoral dissertation

Friedman, James W., 1986: *Game Theory with Applications to Economics*, Oxford: Oxford University Press

Frohlich, Norman and Joe A. Oppenheimer, 1974. "The Carrot and the Stick," *Public Choice*, 19: 43–61

Frohlich, Norman, Joe A. Oppenheimer and Cheryl L. Eavey, 1987a. "Choices of Principles of Distributive Justice in Experimental Groups," *American Journal of Political Science*, 31: 606–36

1987b. "Laboratory Results on Rawls' Distributive Justice," *British Journal of Political Science*, 17: 1–21

Frohlich, Norman, Joe A. Oppenheimer and Oran R. Young, 1971. *Political Leadership and Collective Goods*. Princeton: Princeton University Press

Fudenberg, Drew and Erik Maskin, 1986. "The Folk Theorem in Repeated Games with Discounting or with Incomplete Information," *Econometrica*, 54: 533–54

Furubotn, Eirik and Svetozar Pejovich, 1972. "Property Rights and Economic Theory: A Survey of Recent Literature," *Journal of Economic Literature*, 110(4): 1137–62

Gardner, R. and E. Ostrom, 1991. "Rules and Games," *Public Choice*, 70(2): 121–50

Grether, D. M., R. M. Isaac and Charles R. Plott, 1981. *The Allocation of Scarce Resources: Environmental Economics and the Problem of Allocation of Airport Slots*, San Diego: Westview

Grofman, Bernard (ed.), 1993. *Information, Participation and Choice*, Ann Arbor: The University of Michigan Press

Hahn, Robert W. and Gordon L. Hester, 1989. "Marketable Permits: Lessons for Theory and Practice," *Ecology Law Quarterly*, 16

Hammond, Thomas H. and Gary J. Miller, 1987. "The Core of the Constitution," *American Political Science Review*, 81: 1156–74

Hardin, Garrett, 1968. "The Tragedy of the Commons," *Science*, 162: 1243–8

Hardin, Russell, 1971. "Collective Action as an Agreeable *n*-Persons' Dilemma," *Behavioral Science*, 16: 472–81

1982. *Collective Action*, Baltimore: Johns Hopkins University Press

Harriss, G. L., 1975. *King, Parliament, and Public Finance in Medieval England to 1369*, Oxford: Clarendon Press

Harsanyi, John, 1967–8. "Games with Incomplete Information Played by Bayesian Players," *Management Science*, 14: 159–82, 320–34, 486–502

Hart, H. L. A., 1979. "Between Rights and Utility," in A. Ryan (ed.), *The Idea of Freedom*, Oxford: Clarendon Press

Hayek, Friedrich A., 1945. "The Use of Knowledge in Society," *American Economic Review*, 135: 519–30

1967. "Notes on the Evolution of Systems of Rules of Conduct," in F. A. Hayek, *Studies in Philosophy, Politics, and Economics*, Chicago: The University of Chicago Press

Hegel, George Wilhelm Friedrich, [1821] 1942. *Hegel's Philosophy of Right*, T. M. Knox (trans.), New York: Oxford University Press

Hinich, Melvin J., John O. Ledyard and Peter C. Ordeshook, 1972. "Nonvoting and the Existence of Equilibrium Under Majority Rule," *Journal of Economic Theory*, 4: 144–53

Hobbes, Thomas, [1651] 1968. *Leviathan*, New York: Penguin Classics

Hohfeld, Wesley Newcomb, 1919. *Fundamental Legal Conceptions*, New Haven: Yale University Press

Hollingsworth, Jerald Hage and Robert A. Hanneman, 1990. *State Intervention in Medical Care, Ithaca: Cornell University Press.*

Holt, J. C., 1985. *Magna Carta and Medieval Government*, London: The Hambeldon Press.

1992. *Magna Carta*, Cambridge: Cambridge University Press

Homans, George, 1950. *The Human Group*, New York: Harcourt Brace & World

Hotelling, Harold, 1929. "Stability in Competition," *Economic Journal*, 39: 41–57

Hume, David, 1752. *Essays Moral, Political and Literary, Part II*, London: Cadell

1888. *A Treatise of Human Nature*, L. A. Sely-Bigge (ed.), Oxford: Clarendon Press

James, William George (ed.), 1982. *Airline Economics*, New York: Lexington Books

Jenkins, Vlad, A. Gomez-Ibanez and John Meyer, 1987. "The Department of Transportation and Airport Landing Slots," Case-Study, C16-87-7800.0, Case Program of the Kennedy School of Government at Harvard University

Johnston, J., 1960. *Econometric Methods*, 2nd edn., New York: McGraw-Hill

Joskow, Paul, 1974. "Inflation and Environmental Concern: Structural Change in the Process of Public Utility Regulation," *Journal of Law and Economics*, 17: 291–327

Kalai, E. and A. Neme, 1989. "The Strength of a little Perfection," Northwestern University, unpublished mimeo

Kant, Imannuel, [1785] 1981. *Grounding for the Metaphysics of Morals*, Indianapolis: Hackett

[1794] 1983. *Perpetual Peace and Other Essays*, Indianapolis: Hackett

Kiser, Larry L. and Elinor Ostrom, 1982. "The Three Worlds of Action: A Metatheoretical Synthesis of Institutional Approaches," in E. Ostrom (ed.), *Strategies of Political Inquiry*, Beverley Hills: Sage.

Knight, Jack, 1992. *Institutions and Social Conflict*, Cambridge: Cambridge University Press

Knight, Jack and Itai Sened (eds.), 1995. *Explaining Social Institutions*, Ann Arbor: The University of Michigan Press

Krehbiel, Keith, 1992. *Information and Legislative Organization*, Ann Arbor: The University of Michigan Press

Kreps, M. David and Gary Ramey, 1987. "Structural Consistency, Consistency, and Sequential Rationality," *Econometrica*, 55: 1331–48

Kreps, M. David and Robert Wilson, 1982. "Sequential Equilibria," *Econometrica*, 50: 1003–37

Kuhn, Thomas, S., 1970. *The Structure of Scientific Revolutions*, Chicago: The University of Chicago Press

Lakatos, Imre, 1986. *The Methodology of Scientific Research Programmes*, London: Cambridge University Press

Laver, Michael and Norman Scofield, 1990. *Multi-Party Governments*, Oxford: Oxford University Press

Laver, Michael and Kenneth S. Shepsle, 1996. *Making and Breaking Governments*, Cambridge: Cambridge University Press

Ledyard, John O., 1978. "The Paradox of Voting and Candidate Competition: A General Equilibrium Analysis," California Institute of Technology, mimeo

1984. "The Pure Theory of Large Two-Candidate Elections," *Public Choice*, 44: 43–7

Levi, Margaret, 1988. *Of Rule and Revenue*, Berkeley: The University of California Press

Lewis, David, 1969. *Convention: A Philosophical Study*, Cambridge, MA: Harvard University Press

Libecap, Gary D. 1989. *Contracting for Property Rights*, New York: Cambridge University Press

Locke, John, [1690] 1980. *Second Treatis on Government*, Indianapolis: Hackett

Lohmann, Susanne, 1993a. "A Welfare Analysis of Political Action," in W. Barnett, N. Schofield and M. J. Hinich (eds.), *Political Economy: Institutions, Competition and Representation*, Cambridge: Cambridge University Press

1993b. "A Signaling Model of Informative and Manipulative Political Action," *American Political Science Review*, 87: 319–33

Luce, R. Duncan and Howard Raiffa, 1957. *Games and Decisions: Introduction and Critical Survey*, New York: Wiley

Manion, Melanie, 1990. "Reluctant Duelists: The Logic of the 1989 Protests and Massacre," in M. Oksenberg, L. R. Sullivan and M. Lambert (eds.), *Beijing Spring, 1989*, Armonk: M. E. Sharpe

McDonald, John and G. D. Snooks, 1986. *Domesday Economy*, Oxford: Clarendon Press

McKelvey, Richard D, 1976. "Intransitivities in Multidimensional Voting Models and Some Implications for Agenda Control," *Journal of Economic Theory*, 12: 472–82

1979. "General Conditions for Global Intransitivities in Formal Voting Models," *Econometrica*, 47: 1085–112

1986. "Covering, Dominance and Institution Free Properties of Social Choice," *American Journal of Political Science*, 30: 283–314

McKelvey, Richard D. and Norman Schofield, 1987. "Generalized Symmetry Conditions at a Core," *Econometrica*, 55: 923–33

McKelvey, Richard D. and Richard E. Wendell, 1976. "Voting Equilibria in Multidimensional Choice Spaces," *Mathematics of Operations Research*, 1: 144–58

Milbarth, Lester W., 1963. *The Washington Lobbyists*, Chicago: Rand McNally

Mill, John Stuart, [1859] 1978. *Utilitarianism*, Indianapolis: Hackett
[1861] 1979. *On Liberty*, Indianapolis: Hackett

Mitchell, William C. and Michael C. Munger, 1991. "Economic Models of Interest Groups," *American Journal of Political Science*, 135: 512–46

Moe, T. M., 1980. *The Organization of Interests*, Chicago: The University of Chicago Press

Montesquieu, Charles Louis de Secondant, [1848] 1949. *The Spirit of Law*, Thomas Nugent (trans.), New York: Hafner Publishing Co.

Moody's Transportation Manuals, 1969–89. New York: Moody's Investor Service, Inc.

Myerson, Roger, 1978. "Refinements of the Nash Equilibrium Concept," *International Journal of Game Theory*, 7: 73–80

Nash, John, 1950a. "The Bargaining Problem," *Econometrica*, 18(2): 155–62
1950b. "Equilibrium Points in *n*-Person Games," *Proceedings of the National Academy of Science*, USA, 36(1): 48–9
1951. "Non-Cooperative Games," *Annals of Mathematics*, 54(2): 286–95
1953. "Two Persons Cooperative Games," *Econometrica*, 21: 128–40

von Neumann, John and Oskar Morgenstern, 1944. *The Theory of Games and Economic Behavior*, New York: Wiley

Niebanck, Paul L. (ed.), 1985. *The Rent Control Debate*, Chapel Hill: The University of North Carolina Press

Noll, Roger, 1985. "Government Regulatory Behavior: A Multidiciplinary Survey and Synthesis," in R. Noll (ed.), *Regulatory Policy and the Social Sciences*, Berkeley: The University of California Press

North, Douglass C., 1981. *Structure and Change in Economic History*, New York: Norton
1984. "Government and the Cost of Exchange in History," *Journal of Economic History*, 44(2): 255–64
1987. "Institutions, Transaction Costs and Economic Growth," *Economic Inquiry*, 125(3): 419–28
1990. *Institutions, Institutional Change and Economic Performance*, Cambridge: Cambridge University Press
1993. "Economic Performance Through Time," presented as the Prize Lecture in Economic Science in Memory of Alfred Nobel

North, Douglass C. and Andrew R. Rutten, 1987. "The Northwest Ordinance in Historical Perspective," in David C. Klingaman and Richard K. Vedder (eds.), *Essays on the Economy of the old Northwest*, Athens: The University of Ohio Press

North, Douglass C, and R. P. Thomas, 1973. *The Rise of the Western World: A New Economic History*, Cambridge: Cambridge University Press

North, Douglass C. and Barry W. Weingast, 1989. "The Evolution of Institutions, Governing Public Choice in 17th Century England," *Journal of Economic History*, 49: 803–32

Nozick, Robert, 1975. *Anarchy, State and Utopia*, New York: Basic Books

Olson, Mancur, Jr., 1965. *The Logic of Collective Action*, Cambridge, MA: Harvard University Press (2nd edn. 1971)

 1993. "Dictatorship, Democracy, and Development," *American Political Science Review*, 83(3): 567–76

Olson, Mary, 1995. "Regulatory Agency Discretion among Competing Industries: Inside the FDA," *The Journal of Law, Economics and Organization*, 11(2): 379–405

Onuf, Peter S., 1987. *Statehood and Union*, Bloomington: University of Indiana Press

Ordeshook, Peter C., 1980. "Political Disequilibrium and Scientific Inquiry: A Comment on W. H Riker's 'Implications from the Disequilibrium of Majority Rule for the Study of Institutions,'" *American Political Science Review*, 74: 447–50

 1986. *Game Theory and Political Theory*, Cambridge: Cambridge University Press

Ordeshook, Peter C. and Thomas Schwartz, 1987. "Agenda and the Control of Political Outcomes," *American Political Science Review*, 81: 179–99

Ostrom, Elinor, 1986. "An Agenda for the Study of Institutions," *Public Choice*, 148: 3–25

 1990. *Governing the Commons*, Cambridge: Cambridge University Press

Ostrom, Vincent, 1971. *The Political Theory of a Compound Republic: A Reconstruction of the Logic Foundations of Democracy as Presented in The Federalist*, Blacksburg, VPI Center for Study of Public Choice

Ostrom, W. Charles, Jr., 1990. *Time Series Analysis*, Beverly Hills: Sage University Publications

Palfrey, R. Thomas and Howard Rosenthal, 1984. "Participation and the Provision of Discrete Public Goods: A Strategic Analysis," *Journal of Public Economics*, 24: 171–93

 1985. "Voter Participation and Strategic Uncertainty," *American Political Science Review*, 79: 62–78

 1988. "Private Incentives in Social Dilemma: The Effects of Incomplete Information and Altruism," *Journal of Public Economics*, 28: 171–93

Peled, Yoav, 1980. "Rousseau's Inhibited Radicalism: An Analysis of his Political Thought in light of his Economic Ideas," *American Political Science Review*, 74(4): 1034–45

Peltzman, Sam, 1976. "Towards a More General Theory of Regulation," *Journal of Law and Economics*, 35: 133–48

Petit, Philip, 1974. "A Theory of Justice?," *Theory and Decision*, 4: 311–24

Phelps, Charles. E., 1992. *Health Economics*, New York: Harper Collins

Pindyck, Robert S. and Daniel L. Rubinfeld, 1976. *Econometric Models and Economic Forecasts*, New York: McGraw-Hill

Plato, 1955 (≈ 375 BC). *The Republic*, Desmond Lee (trans.), New York: Penguin Classics

Plott, Charles R., 1967. "A Notion of Equilibrium and its Possibility Under Majority Rule," *American Economic Review*, 57: 787–806

1976. "Axiomatic Social Choice: An Introduction and Overview," *American Journal of Political Science*, 20: 511–96

Poole, Keith and Howard Rosenthal, 1991. "Patterns of Congressional Voting," *American Journal of Political Science*, 35: 228–43

Rapoport, Elizabeth, 1978. "Editor's Introduction" to John Stuart Mill ([1859] 1978), *On Liberty*, Indianapolis: Hackett

Rapoport, Anatol and Melvin Guyer, 1966. "A Taxonomy of 2 × 2 Games," *General Systems*, 11: 203–14

Rasmusen, Eric, 1989. *Games and Information*, Oxford: Basil Blackwell

Rawls, John, 1971. *A Theory of Justice*, Cambridge, MA: Harvard University Press

1993. *Political Liberalism*, New York: Columbia University Press

The Records of the Federal Convention (1787), 2 vols.

Riker, William H., 1957. "Events and Situations," *Journal of Philosophy*, 54, 57–70

1962. *The Theory of Political Coalitions*, New Haven: Yale University Press

1964. *Federalism: Origin, Operation, Significance*, Boston: Little Brown & Co

1971. "Public Safety as a Public Good," in E. Rostow (ed.), *Is Law Dead?*, New York: Simon & Schuster

1976. "Comments on Vincent Ostrom's Paper," *Public Choice*, 27: 13–15

1980. "Implications from the Disequilibrium of Majority Rule for the Study of Institutions," *American Political Science Review*, 74: 432–46

1982. *Liberalism Against Populism*, San Francisco: Freeman

1986. *The Art of Political Manipulation*, New Haven: Yale University Press

1988. "The Place of Political Science in Public Choice," *Public Choice*, 57: 247–57

1990. "Civil Rights and Property Rights," in E. F. Paul and H. Dickman (eds.), *Liberty, Property, and the Future of Constitutional Development*, Albany: SUNY Press

1995. "The Experience of Creating Institutions: The Framing of the United States Constitution," in J. Knight and I. Sened (eds.), *Explaining Social Institutions*, Ann Arbor: The University of Michigan Press

1996. *Strategic Rhetoric*, New Haven: Yale University Press

Riker, William H. and Peter C. Ordeshook, 1973. *An Introduction to Positive Political Theory*, Englewood Cliffs: Prentice-Hall

Riker, William H. and Itai Sened, 1991. "A Political Theory of the Origin of Property Rights: Airport Slots," *American Journal of Political Science*, 35: 951–69

Roth E. A., 1979. *Axiomatic Models of Bargaining*, New York: Springer-Verlag

Rousseau, Jean-Jacques, 1966. *Essay on the Origin of Languages*, in J. H. Moran and A. Gode (trans.), *On the Origin of Language*, New York: Frederick Unger

1981a. *The Basic Political Writings*, Indianapolis: Hackett

[1754] 1981b. *Discourse on the Origin and Foundation of Inequality Among Men*, in J.-J. Rousseau, *The Basic Political Writings*, Indianapolis: Hackett

[1757] 1987. *The Social Contract*, Indianapolis: Hackett

Rubinstein, Ariel, 1982. "Perfect Equilibrium in a Bargaining Problem," *Econometrica*, 50(1): 97–109

1985. "A Bargaining Model with Incomplete Information about Time Preferences," *Econometrica*, 53(5): 1151–72

1986. "Finite Automata Play in Repeated Prisoner's Dilemma," *Journal of Economic Theory*, 3: 83–96

Salisbury, Robert H., 1969. "An Exchange Theory of Interest Groups," *Midwest Journal of Political Science*, 13: 1–32

Samuelson, Paul, 1947. *Foundation of Economic Analysis*, Cambridge, MA: Harvard University Press

1954. "The Pure Theory of Public Expenditure," *Review of Economics and Statistics*, 36: 387–90

1955. "Diagrammatic Exposition of the Theory of Public Expenditure," *Review of Economics and Statistics*, 37: 350–6

1958. "Aspects of Public Expenditure," *Review of Economics and Statistics*, 40: 332–8

Sayrs, Lois W., 1989. *Pooled Time Series Analysis*, Newbury Park: Sage

Schelling, Thomas C., 1984. *Choice and Consequences: Perspective of an Errant Economist*, Cambridge, MA: Harvard University Press

Schofield, Norman, 1978. "Instability of Simple Dynamic Games," *Review of Economic Studies*, 45: 575–94

1983. "Generic Instability of Majority Rule," *Review of Economic Studies*, 50: 695–705

1984a. "Social Equilibrium and Cycles on Compact Sets," *Journal of Economic Theory*, 33(1): 59–71

1984b. "Classification Theorem for Smooth Social Choice on a Manifold," *Social Choice and Welfare*, 1: 187–210

1984c. "Generic Properties of Simple Bergson–Samuelson Welfare Functions," *Journal of Mathematical Economics*, 7: 175–92

1985. "Anarchy, Altruism and Cooperation," *Social Choice and Welfare*, 2: 207–19

1986. *Social Choice and Democracy*, Berlin: Springer-Verlag

Schotter, Andrew, 1981. *The Economic Theory of Social Institutions*, Cambridge: Cambridge University Press

Schwartz, Thomas, 1970. "On the Possibility of Rational Policy Evaluation," *Theory and Decision*, 1: 89–106

Scitovsky, Tibor, 1951. "The State of Welfare Economics," *American Economic Review*, 41: 303–15

Selten, Reinhard, 1975. "Reexamination of the Perfectness Concept for Equilibrium Points in Extensive Games," *International Journal of Game Theory*, 4: 25–55

Sen, Amartya K., 1970. "The Impossibility of a Paretian Liberal," *Journal of Political Economy*, 78(1): 152–7

    1974. "Rawls Versus Bentham," *Theory and Decision*, 4: 301–10

    1982. *Choice, Welfare and Measurement*, Cambridge, MA: MIT Press

    1986. *On Ethics and Economics*, New York: Basil Blackwell

Sened, Itai, 1990. *A Political Theory of Rights*, Ph.D. dissertation, University of Rochester Library

    1991. "Contemporary Theory of Institutions in Perspective," *Journal of Theoretical Politics*, 3(4): 379–402

    1995. "A Political Theory of the Evolution of Rights," in J. Knight and I. Sened (eds.), *Explaining Social Institutions*, Ann Arbor: The University of Michigan Press

    1996: "A Model of Coalition Formation: Theory and Evidence," *The Journal of Politics*, 58(2)

Sened, Itai and William H. Riker, 1996. "Common Property and Private Property: The Case of Air Slots," *Journal of Theoretical Politics*, 8(4): 527–47

Shepsle, Kenneth A., 1979. "Institutional Arrangements and Equilibrium in Multidimensional Voting Models," *American Journal of Political Science*, 23: 27–59

    1986. "Institutional Equilibrium and Equilibrium Institutions," in H. F. Weisberg (ed.), *Political Science: The Science of Politics*, New York: Agathon Press

    1990. *Models of Multiparty Competition*. Chur: Harwood Academic Press

Shepsle, Kenneth A. and Barry R. Weingast, 1981. "Structure-Induced Equilibrium and Legislative Choice," *Public Choice*, 37: 503–519

    1984a. "Uncovered Sets and Sophisticated Voting Outcomes with Implications for Agenda Institution," *American Journal of Political Science*, 28: 49–74

    1984b. "Legislative Political and Budget Outcomes," in G. B. Mills and J. L. Palmer (eds.), *Federal Budget Policy in the 1980's*, Washington, DC: The Urban Institute

Sher, George, 1979. Introduction to J. S. Mill, [1859] 1978, *Utilitarianism*, Indianapolis: Hackett

Simpson, A. W. B., [1962] 1986. *A History of the Land Law*, Oxford: Oxford University Press

Slutsky, Steven, 1975. "Abstention and Majority Equilibrium," *Journal of Economic Theory*, 11: 292–304

Smith, Steven B., 1989, "What is 'Right' in Hegel's Philosophy of Right?," *American Political Science Review*, 83: 3–18

Specter, Michael, 1986a. "Soft Landing," *The New Republic*, April: 10–11
  1986b. "Rule Allowing Sale of Landing Slots of Airports Attacked," *Washington Post*, March 31: 83, col. 1

Stigler, George J., 1942. *The Theory of Competitive Price*, New York: Macmillan
  1971. "The Economic Theory of Regulations," *Bell Journal of Economics and Management Science*, 2(3): 3–21

Sugden, Robert, 1986. *The Economics of Rights, Co-operation and Welfare*, Oxford: Basil Blackwell

Sumner, L. W., 1987. *The Moral Foundations of Rights*, Oxford: Oxford University Press

Talmon, Ya'acov, 1955. *The Origins of Totalitarian Democracy*, New York: Praeger

Taylor, Michael, 1987. *The Possibility of Cooperation*, New York: Cambridge University Press

Thomson, William, 1989. *Axiomatic Theory of Bargaining with a Variable Number of Agents*, Cambridge: Cambridge University Press

Thoreau, Henry David, 1849. *Civil Disobedience*, Boston: Houghton Mifflin

Tullock, George, 1967. "The General Irrelevance of the General Impossibility Theorem," in G. Tullock (ed.), *Towards a Mathematics of Politics*, Ann Arbor: The University of Michigan Press

Ullmann-Margalit, Edna, 1979. *The Emergence of Norms*, Oxford: Clarendon Press

Umbeck, John R., 1981. *A Theory of Property Rights*, Ames: Iowa State University Press

Varian, Hal R., 1984. *Microeconomic Analysis*, New York: Norton & Co

Waldron, Jeremy, 1992. *Liberal Rights*, Cambridge: Cambridge University Press

Weber, Max, 1958. "Politics as a Vocation," in H. H. Gareth and W. C. Mills (eds.), *From Max Weber*, New York: Oxford University Press

Weimer, David L. and Aidan R. Vining, 1989. *Policy Analysis: Concepts and Practice*, Englewood Cliffs: Prentice-Hall

Weingast, Barry, R., 1995: "The Economic Role of Political Institutions: Market-Preserving Federalism and Economic Development," *Journal of Law, Economics and Organization*, 11(1): 1–31

Williamson, Oliver, 1986. "The Economics of Governance: Framework and Implications," in R. N. Langois (ed.), *Economics as a Process: Essays in the New Institutional Economics*, Cambridge: Cambridge University Press

Wittman, Donald, 1989. "Why Democracies Produce Efficient Results," *Journal of Political Economy*, 97(6): 1395–1424
  1995. *The Myth of Democratic Failure*, Chicago: The University of Chicago Press.

Government Documents

Hearing 98-63, 1983. "Report of the Airport Access Task Force." Before the
    Subcommittee of Investigation and Oversight, Committee on Public
    Works and Transportation, the House of Representatives, May 17

Hearing 99-33, 1985. "Government Policies on the Transfer Operating Rights."
    Before the Subcommittee on Aviation; Committee on Public Works and
    Transportation, the House of Representatives, September 10, 19; October
    22

Hearing 99-746, 1986. "Buying and Selling Airport Operating Rights." Before
    the Subcommittee on Aviation; Committee on Commerce, Science and
    Transportation, US Senate, February 6

Hearing 99-59, 1986. "Government Policies on the Transfer Operating Rights."
    Before the Subcommittee on Aviation; Committee on Public Works and
    Transportation, the House of Representatives, June 12

Report 99-299, 1986. "Operating Rights at Congested Domestic Airports."
    Submitted by Senator Danforth, Committee on Commerce, Science and
    Transportation, US Senate, May 14

Index